inspiration
divine

iD

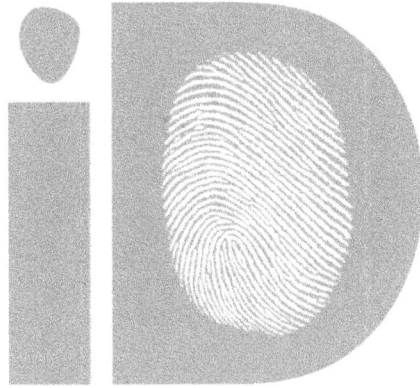

inspiration
divine

Your Purpose and Path to

Health, Happiness and Enlightenment

Darwin Stephenson

Published in the United States by Theopneusty Media, San Francisco

ISBN: 0-9799721-0-8

Library of Congress Control Number: 2009929820

Stephenson, Darwin.

Inspiration Divine: *Your Purpose and Path to Health, Happiness and Enlightenment*

Includes bibliographical references, index

ISBN-13: 978-0-9799721-0-2

1. Spirituality 2. Mind and Body 3. Self-Help Techniques
I. Stephenson, Darwin. II. Title
First Edition

For more information:

Website: http:// www . inspirationdivine . com

Facebook: http:// fb . inspirationdivine . com

Book cover design by Joy Hart (www.heyjoy.com)

Photography by Laurie Gallagher (barefootbhakti.wordpress.com)

For our Children, as they remind us how far we have to go.

For our Mother, as she gave us the courage to listen.

For our Father, as without Him we would not be.

Inspiration Divine is dedicated to my wife.

Contents

Preface ix

   Spiritual Evolution.. xi

   Understanding Inspiration Divine xv

   Your Path xix

Walkers of the Path xxi

The Great Mediator 1

   A Lesson for Humanity 2

   Your Reality, My Reality, Our Reality 4

A Purposeful Life 11

   Happiness Through Purpose.. 15

Meet Yourself... 19

   Body, Spirit and Mind 22

   11 Dimensions?..38

Energy 51

   Einstein's Blunder...54

   The Domain of the Spirit...61

   The Language of Connecting Bonds 64

   The Interpretation of the Mind 72

   To Which an Entity Communicates It Also Governs 73

   Lessening the Grip of the Mind..81

Nirvana 91

    The Golden Ratio 100

    Enlightenment 107

Harmony 115

    Spiritual Transformation 122

    Breaking the Evolutionary Code 128

The Universe 137

    Humanity's Purpose 141

    Expanding Universe 145

Collective Consciousness 153

    Sharing Original Ideas 157

    Absorbing Collective Consciousness 163

    The Cosmic Joke and Beautiful Punch line 167

Conflict 175

Judgment 183

    A Life Devoid of Judgment 188

    Listen to Yourself 190

Cycles 199

    Roles in Relationships 202

    Platonic Correlations 205

Listening 213

    Full Time Listening 216

Happiness 223

Love 231

Healing 243

Channeling Energy.. 244

Healing Others 258

The Healer's Predicament....................................... 260

Maintaining Health.. 262

Non-Judgmental Healing.. 264

    Awareness of Healing.. 265

Moving Energy.. 269

    Riding the Efficient Frontier................................ 274

        Optimizing Energy within the Body..................... 277

        Optimizing Energy within the Spirit.................... 281

        Optimizing Energy within the Mind..................... 289

    A Path to Integrity... 296

Spiritual Evolution... 301

    God's Intent... 303

    Why Does God Want an iPhone? 309

    Spiritual Evolution... 310

Your Purpose 315

    Sri Aurobindo 317

    Be in Communication... 319

    Communication Channels 323

    Evolution of Humanity 325

    Your Purpose.. 329

    Begin Anew.. 332

    Closing Thoughts.. 334

    The Dream Twilight of the Earthly Real............... 339

Inspiration Practice.. 341

30 Day Inspiration Practice 343

Beginning the Inspiration Practice 347

Inspiration Practice Materials 347

Inspiration Practice Components 349

    Sensual Dimensions 349

    Emotive Dimensions 350

    Mental Dimensions 350

Yoga Postures 351

Inspiration Practice Schedule 353

    Nine Day Orientation 355

Finding Your Purpose 357

Bibliography 359

Inspiration Workshops 367

Additional Copies of Inspiration Divine 367

Downloadable Workbooks & Book Club Guides........... 367

Connecting 367

Your Message 368

PREFACE

The book you are about to read is God revealed and will change your life forever. Inspiration Divine foretells a journey you and mankind will take together. Unlike other books that seek to enlighten you with a new perspective, Inspiration Divine seeks to guide you down the path of your own enlightenment so that you may unlock the keys to your full human potential. In short, this book will reveal your purpose and through this purpose, you will find enlightenment.

A lot of people talk about enlightenment as if it were a state of mind that only a privileged few are capable of attaining. Similarly other people play down enlightenment as if it were nothing more than a heightened state of awareness. Neither statement is true, nor would anyone who is truly enlightened describe enlightenment in these ways. For enlightenment is a connection to God that reveals not only a complete understanding of everything you desire to know, but also provides a path to understanding everything you don't desire to know. That's a whole lot of information to know and thus enlightenment isn't as much about knowing as it is about knowing how to understand. And this ability to understand is available to each and every one of us including you.

Similarly, enlightenment doesn't have anything to do with religion. This isn't to say that the understanding one can attain through enlightenment will be in conflict with one's religion, but so too, it doesn't mean that it won't be in conflict either. In spirit and intent, enlightenment is above religion as it embodies a direct and communal relationship with God directly rather than through what others have written about God (no matter how divinely inspired their message was or not).

Simply put, enlightenment is a connection to truth. No matter what we believe about the Universe, God or Humanity, the truth is the truth. Our opinions about what is true or what is not true is irrelevant and we have a better than average chance that our current set of beliefs aren't entirely true. One thing is for certain: enlightenment will be a humbling experience.

When we embrace the grace of the divine and the truth as being beyond reproach, we open up our hearts and minds beyond our current mode of operating in the world. And this is great news, for both the faithful and the atheist desire the truth. They may have contradictory points of view on what they believe the truth to be, but they both truly seek the truth. And in enlightenment they will both find the truth (one of them is going to be greatly disappointed).

Even staunch atheists like Christopher Hitchens, author of *God is Not Great*, are calling for a new revelation of the truth:

> Above all, we are in need of a renewed Enlightenment, which will base itself on the proposition that the proper study of mankind is man, and woman. This Enlightenment will not need to depend, like its predecessors, on the heroic breakthroughs of a few gifted and exceptionally courageous people. It is within the compass of the average person. (Hitchens 2007)

What Hitchens is alluding to is the capability of enlightenment to be possible in every human being rather than a handful of prophets. And while it would be an odd world where God selectively picked who should be enlightened, our religious history certainly depicts Divine communication being highly selective. And with enlightenment not being a regularly occurring experience in our lives and the ancient texts demonstrating it only being blessed upon a select few, we've wrongly assumed that enlightenment isn't possible for us. And so we don't even consider it something worth pursuing.

Consider for a moment, if enlightenment was possible for you and the rest of mankind. What if we've been missing the messages from God that are all around us? What if our enlightenment was not only possible, but also part of our human evolution? Consider the possibility that the keys to enlightenment are in our hands and we only need to learn how to insert the key and turn the lock.

Spiritual Evolution

The message documented in Inspiration Divine is not a self-help prescription nor does it contain mystical secrets that have eluded mankind. The lessons that you will learn by reading these pages are drawn from the messages that have been broadcast to mankind since the dawn of time. Only now are we awakening to these lessons and tuning in to listen like never before. These messages have existed since the beginning and are actually interwoven into our cultures, religions and fundamental assumptions. Beyond the wisdom conveyed by those that have previously discovered these lessons, you too will find that you have heard these messages deep within the essence of your soul. However, there is much more available to you.

Inherent in life are the keys to understanding everything. However, through the ages we have lost the ability to listen and thus we seek that which is actually already within our possession. From the very beginning, mankind has wrestled with elementary questions that we still desire to be answered:

> Why am I here?
> What is my purpose?
> Who is God?

From there, our questions branch into many directions, but the underlying answers continue to elude mankind. Trying to make sense of it all seems to be impossible and thus most of Humanity leaves this task to those that study philosophy, psychology and theology. But even though we tell ourselves that the answers are beyond our grasp, we still desire to understand the Universe, God and Humanity.

The path to this understanding is inherently part of living and surprisingly simple. In fact, the path is so elemental that your Mind may reject it for not being complex enough. Our Minds are advanced thinking machines that crave complexity despite our attempt to simplify our lives. So too, we have established a partial understanding of life through our cultures, religions and personal experiences. In combination, our Minds tell us that the truth must be complex and in line with what we already believe to be true. And so we continue through life with the answers to these questions all around us, without an awareness of how close we are to the truth.

The world in which we live is advancing to an inflection point of enlightenment as is evident by the exponential change that is occurring around the world. Each and every day we create more information, knowledge and wisdom than we did the previous day. In Karl Fisch's *Did You Know* presentation [Fisch 2007], he chronicled many of the amazing statistics that describe the exponential times we're living in:

- The first commercial text message was sent in December 2002; the number of text messages sent today exceeds the population of the planet.

- There are more than 8 billion searches performed on Internet Search Engines every month (4.1 billion on Google alone).

- There are more than 540,000 words in the English language; about 5 times as many as during Shakespeare's time.

- The amount of technical information being produced is doubling every two years and is estimated to soon double every day.

As we expand this collective knowledge, we gain insight, perspective and a bit more of the truth. Whereas previous generations could passively pursue the truth, our generation is called to an active participation in living the truth. In short, we are being called to understand.

Inspiration Divine foretells the evolution of mankind from a physical existence to a Spiritual existence. When most of us think of evolution, we envision Charles Darwin shocking the world with his evolutionary description of our lineage to our primate cousins. And while Darwin's focus was largely biological, even he was aware of the future that awaits Humanity:

> As man advances in civilization and small tribes are united into larger communities, the simplest reason would tell each individual that he ought to extend his social instincts and sympathies to all the members of the same nation though personally unknown to him. This point being once reached, there is only an artificial barrier to prevent his sympathies extending to the men of all nations and races. If indeed such men are separated from him by great differences in appearance or habits, experience unfortunately shows us how long it is before we look at them as our fellow creatures. (Darwin 1871)

As Darwin warned, the solidarity of mankind is a future state that we have yet to reach. The physical lives we live today fail to provide us with a path to solidarity or any glimpse that this path is in our near future. Clearly our physical evolution has brought us quite far, but the rest of the journey will require us moving to the next phase in our evolution: a Spiritual existence.

As you have gone through life, you have no doubt experienced amazing coincidences, ironic threads between two or more people in your life and chance encounters that could not be logically explained. We have all had "ah-ha" moments in which an idea leaps into our head or the answer to a seemingly unsolvable problem suddenly reveals itself to us. Moreover, even if these moments are rare, they provide us with a glimpse into the potential of a Spiritual existence. Inspiration Divine reveals how these connections operate in the Universe and how we can tap into God's wisdom in order to achieve our hopes and dreams.

Understanding Inspiration Divine

Inspiration generally refers to an unconscious burst of creativity, but in the context of divine inspiration we're invoking its original Roman relation to the term afflatus:

> Cicero, in the oration for Archias, speaks of the poet as one who was breathed upon or *into* by some divine spirit, - *poetam quasi divino spiritu inflari*. Plato held the same view with regard to poetry. He believed that the poet was often so inspired that he said things that he did not himself fully understand.
>
> "Himself From God he could not free;
>
> He builded better than he know."
>
> Josephus, who was a cotemporary of Paul, in his first book against Apion, speaks of the *twenty-two* sacred books of the Jews as having been written by an inspiration which came from God, or according to a breathing upon them of God. (Evans 2004)

Similarly the term *Divine*, which has many meanings, refers to the concept that human beings are "God revealed" -- living representations of God on Earth as they live in accordance with God's intent. In combination, Inspiration Divine is about expanding our consciousness to tap into personal prophecy (the disclosing of information that is not known to the prophet by any ordinary means). (Davison 2005) Rabbinic scholar Maimonides, suggested that "prophecy is, in truth and reality, an emanation sent forth by the Divine Being through the medium of the Active Intellect, in the first instance to man's rational faculty, and then to his imaginative faculty." (Sunwall 1996)

Thus the title Inspiration Divine describes Humanity's path to enlightenment as conveyed by the Divine Being (God). Most readers will immediately become skeptical of any proclamation of Divine communication, as our society has given up on direct communication with God. In our modern understanding of life, we've come up with lots of reasons why God doesn't talk to us anymore, but for some reason, most of these theories leave out the simple fact that we're not listening.

We assume that because God can communicate with us via any method of His[1] choosing, that He will appear to us in a form that we will understand. We picture ourselves as Charlton Heston climbing to the summit of Mount Sinai in pursuit of the burning bush and hearing the voice of God. With a deep, raspy voice God will call our name and command us to listen.

And if God called out to us in this way, why wouldn't we listen? This isn't to say that God wouldn't call to us in this manner. However, this sensational version of Divine communication is more appropriate for a single conversation rather than one with all of Humanity. Possibly God reserves the attention grabbing, burning bush communication styles for one on one conversations.

Inspiration Divine documents God's message of love, acceptance and understanding for all of mankind. The message that is being broadcast is intended for everyone, rather than a chosen few. We are all called to listen and Inspiration Divine contains lessons on how to listen, how to communicate with God and, most importantly, how to evolve into a Spiritual existence that embodies the beauty of sustained enlightenment.

---

[1] Throughout Inspiration Divine I refer to God as He and Him but do not mean to imply that God has gender.

Whereas other books extol the benefits of enlightenment, Inspiration Divine brings enlightenment into your daily life with practical and accessible methods for achieving harmony with the Universe, connecting with your Spirit and maintaining balance in your life. However, beyond what Inspiration Divine can do for you, the lessons contained in this book are for Humanity as a whole and your role in bringing about the Spiritual enlightenment of Humanity is embedded in the message itself. In short, you have an unshakable responsibility to personally bring forth the next phase in the evolution of mankind.

In attempting to understand Inspiration Divine, you have already begun to experience the logical battle that will take place within your Mind. As human beings, we interpret and understand the world around us through our sensations, emotions and thoughts. When things *make sense* we accept them and when they *don't make sense* we tend to refute them. There is no other way for human beings, for everything must ultimately be interpreted, analyzed and accepted by our Minds. However, in putting the essence of understanding entirely within the domain of the Mind, we also ignore both the Body and the Spirit.

In modern metaphysical circles there is quite a bit of discussion about the Body, Spirit and Mind. Our society readily accepts these three ways of describing being human but we rarely stop to understand the deep, meaningful consciousness that is present in these simple distinctions. They are so elemental a part of being human that we tend to accept them without fully considering the insightful role they play in our lives. But as soon as we start to encounter concepts that *don't make sense*, we instantly become aware of just how entirely caught up in our Minds we really are.

By ignoring the Spirit and the Body in figuring out what is true, we ignore God and make our way through life embracing most situations based entirely on logical thinking. The problem with this approach is that with a mental existence we risk missing out on any relationship with God that doesn't fall into the logical patterns that our Minds demand. Surely the burning bush and booming voice from the Heavens didn't make sense to Moses either, but in trusting his Spiritual side, he was able to accept, understand and believe in the voice of God.

In bringing you Inspiration Divine, I'm not asking you to accept these words as the voice of God. I believe Inspiration Divine to be a message from God, for all of Humanity, which is intended to teach mankind how to attain enlightenment, how to serve God and how to be in communication with God. To your Mind, these words will represent a paradigm shift that will cause you to rethink your current understanding of the Universe, God and Humanity.

What I would ask you to do is consider the message contained in Inspiration Divine with more than the logical analysis of your Mind. As you read each chapter, your Mind may refute concepts that are presented and I encourage you to not fight or judge your Mind for being so quick to separate truths from un-truths. Instead let your Mind's thoughts be nothing more than thoughts and instead let your Spirit engage in the conversation. In collaboration, the Body, Spirit and Mind will guide you down the path of determining what is right for you. By engaging all three in the conversation, you will find more wisdom and insight than could ever be provided to you by another.

Your Path

It is no accident that you are reading this book at this time in your life. No matter if you are reading this in a library or someone gifted this book to you, the motion of the Universe is unmistakable and there is a reason you were brought to these words. No two people have the same role to play, despite us all sharing a common purpose in life. And with this comes your awakening to a purpose that can only be revealed by a connection to your own Spirit. The words contained in this book will not dictate your purpose, for that message can only come from your Spirit. However, this book will show you how to connect to your Spirit and keep that relationship strong for eternity. In this, your path to enlightenment will be revealed through your discovery of purpose.

The final note I will add to this introduction speaks to the energy contained in this book. Your bookshelf is full of books that you find amusing, insightful, and inspiring. I truly hope that you find this book to be worthy of your bookshelf but ask that you do not park it there. Instead, learn what you can from this book and gift it to another. Take the teachings of this book and then give this book to someone else. If you cannot think of whom to give it to then pick someone at random, but make sure that it gets into the hands of someone that can benefit from its message of love, harmony and universal possibilities.

If you are one of the people that was handed this book, count yourself as both deserving and the most valuable person in the world. You have provided someone else the opportunity to practice sharing, to try giving and to experience what it feels like to take a chance on someone else. By receiving this book, you know that there is beauty in the Universe and that you are part of the evolution of Humanity towards a new, Spiritual existence. For you, the path is similarly simple: learn the lessons contained herein and gift this book to another. One by one, the human race will move forward to truly understand a new relationship with the Universe, God, and Humanity.

As we investigate the countless models seeking to explain the Universe, God and Humanity we should be inherently skeptical of complexity. A simple and rich river runs through us despite our propensity to focus on the wider ocean. When we find an understanding of the ocean that also explains the river, we will have found the truth. In short, any explanation of life that is complex may be interesting, but it certainly isn't enlightening.

Without a grasp of the path to enlightenment, our Minds are helplessly drawn to complexity. Followers of that path will certainly obtain knowledge, but they will be no closer to a union with the Divine than before they began.

In walking the path we seek the truth. Be the truth beautiful or be it ugly, we seek the truth in its purest form. We care not for what is appealing to our senses nor what calms the masses, but instead desire to know what we are, why we're here and what is our purpose.

Already God is near, the Truth is close…

Walkers of the Path

Inspiration Divine is a handbook for Humanity designed to bring about enlightenment one person at a time. You are but one person in this chain, but the chain reaction cannot continue without you. For this reason, the journey you are about to take is both a personal one and an enabling key to another's journey. Upon reading these pages, you will understand the beauty, peace and love contained in the message. Sharing this message with others will not only bring about the Spiritual evolution of mankind, but will also propel you on this path. Record your name below before beginning this journey. In time, you will know who should appear next on this list. Your time is now and by inking your name below you begin your journey:

1. _____

2. _____

3. _____

4. _____

5. _____

6. _____

7. _____

8. _____

9. _____

10. _____

11. _____

The ordinary life is that of the average human consciousness separated from its own true self and from the Divine and led by the common habits of the mind, life and body which are the laws of the Ignorance...

The spiritual life, on the contrary, proceeds directly by a change of consciousness, a change from the ordinary consciousness, ignorant and separated from its true self and from God, to a greater consciousness in which one finds one's true being and comes first into direct and living contact and then into union with the Divine.

For the spiritual seeker this change of consciousness is the one thing he seeks and nothing else matters.(Aurobindo, Letters on Yoga 1970)

1

THE GREAT MEDIATOR

To grow into the fullness of the divine is the true law of human life and to shape his earthly existence into its image is the meaning of his evolution. – Sri Aurobindo

In your first breath, you opened up to the magnificent world around you.

Through your eyes, the Mind received its first input from the outside world representing the three dimensions of length, width, and depth. Your Body, suddenly exposed to a new and vibrant environment, came alive via an abundance of sounds and smells. Your Spirit cried out in pain as the warmth and comfort of your Mother's womb was replaced with the sudden, cold expanse of your new world. However this soon passed, as your Mother put you to her breast for your first taste of her nurturing milk.

Even though you were not aware, in the first minute of your young life, you experienced the dimensions of being human and your life began. You were born in a state of potential harmony and, through the dimensions of being human, you will now achieve harmony, accomplish your hopes and dreams, and experience ultimate happiness.

A Lesson for Humanity

We are at the brink of a new phase in the evolution of mankind. However, this next step will not be a physical leap but rather a Spiritual elevation from our current mode of operating in the Universe. Why we have not made this change earlier in history is anyone's guess, but why we are transforming now is simply because we, as a whole, are ready. One could surmise that we previously were not ready and no doubt the history of mankind documents just how unready we have been until now.

The progression of this evolutionary leap will begin with those that are Spiritually grounded and free from the attachments of this life. In sharp contrast to the definition of religion, this leap will occur in the most unlikely of souls and unfold from the inside with no visible signs of change to the outside world. In fact, many around us have already evolved and are waiting, rather than proselytizing, for the rest of Humanity to join them. Unlike status, this Spiritual transformation brings with it an inner peace that one wants to share with others but cannot be bestowed upon another.

The fact that you are even reading this book demonstrates that the evolutionary process has already begun within you. There is no single book, video, guru or charismatic speaker that can light the spark inside that started you down this path, but now that you have begun, there are many that can help you through this wonderful transformation. No doubt, this is not the first book you have read on Spirituality, nor will it be your last, as your thirst for insight deepens within you. Your journey will be as unique as your fingerprints and will be filled with new experiences that you will find remarkable, striking, and often coincidental.

The path you are traveling is not a religion nor does it conflict with the faith you have developed over many years. In fact, along the way you will find connections to your faith and religion that ring true in your heart. However, this evolutionary transformation is for all of Humanity and each human being that travels the path will have this same experience despite their striking differences. In this, you will wrestle with your most basic constructs of yourself, the Universe, God and Humanity.

What you will find at the end of this journey is a fresh beginning. Too often in this world, we strive to accomplish and ignore the blessings that are infused in the journey itself. And why wouldn't we? The world we have known since birth is a continual cycle of birth and death of everything from the flowers in our garden to the people in our lives. Survival of the fittest necessitates accomplishment in order to provide for ourselves, our families, and the rest of our clan. However, these are the ways of your ancestors. In our hearts, we know there is more but we have thus far been unable to sustain this harmonious beauty longer than for the moment. And that is all about to change.

A Spiritual existence is one that blends the ways of the old and the ways of the new. When we emerge from the other end, we will look no different but in our hearts, we will be blessed with a connection to God that is unmistakable. Rather than learning about God through the written word, you will come to know God in an intimate, personable, and honorable way. In addition, while knowing God rather than learning about Him has not been the way of mankind thus far, you will find that this relationship is core to being human.

In this book, you will find no declarative statements for you to follow, no absolute truths, nor quotable sound bites. So too you will not find feel good speak about beauty without regard for the tools that one uses to find beauty. Here you will find a manual for conscious evolution and lessons that will guide you through your own personal journey. As your journey has clearly already begun, this book should be viewed as a collection of signposts laid down by the travelers that have embarked on this journey before you. Their tips, lessons, questions, and answers are available to you in these pages as well as within your own conscious experience. Through this journey, you too will develop a keen ability to listen, distinguish, and contribute to this same collective consciousness.

Your Reality, My Reality, Our Reality

Our elders taught us the four dimensions of height, width, depth, and time through guidance and shared experience. Through three-dimensional space, we navigate through the world around us with grace and balance. Our first toddler steps were wobbly but through practice, we developed an ability to put one foot in front of another without crashing to the ground. However, there were quite a few stumbles before we could eloquently walk across the room. No wonder we watch babies take their first steps with a sense of awe and wonder.

That same sense of awe and wonder awaits our next evolutionary leap to a Spiritual existence. You may be asking yourself, "Just what is this Spiritual existence that awaits me?" An explanation that properly describes it for everyone is beyond language for it brings together much that cannot be described with words. Much like musical notes convey meaning to those that can read them, a Spiritual existence can only partially be reduced to language. Life is experiential, meaning that life is something that you know through personal experience rather than something that can be described to another.

In short, a Spiritual existence is a life in harmony. The very essence of your soul emerges to connect with everything that is beautiful, glorious and wonderful. And this is precisely where words defy explanation for the Spiritual existence is embodied in a life devoid of judgment. Your definitions of beauty, glory, joy and happiness no longer apply for you will no longer give ugliness, sadness, anger and pain the same power you do today. Without judgment governing your life, your true self will emerge to live a life that is both fulfilling and charitable. But to get there, you will first need to re-learn many fundamentals that you've probably never questioned.

String theory physicists mathematically describe our Universe necessitating between ten to eleven dimensions. Not only are these previously unrecognized dimensions present in the Universe in which we live but they have been there since the birth of our Universe. In fact, the very dimensions of our Universe have been part of your reality since the second you were conceived. In addition, just like the four dimensions that you mastered in order to walk, the remaining seven dimensions represent the reality that you will master in order to live a Spiritual existence.

Somewhere between four and eleven dimensions exists a complete understanding of the Universe, God, and Humanity. You, as rightful member of the human race, have both the opportunity and obligation to embrace and understand how to reach your potential in an eleven dimensional Universe.

Eleven dimensions are a lot to contemplate when you have lived your whole life understanding only four. Immediately our Minds push the remaining seven dimensions into the category of *impossible*. Advanced physicists have acted accordingly by describing these previously unclassified dimensions as beyond our comprehension. However, with our Spiritual existence comes an understanding of our Universe that is beyond our current comprehension and thus the adoption of these remaining dimensions into our awareness is not impossible. Quite the opposite, as with *discovering* comes new frontiers that previous explorers have yet to cross.

For a moment, try to accept that your understanding of the world around you comes largely from what you have been taught. Earlier in history there was a very different understanding of how things work and, with that difference in understanding, we have consequently both gained and lost truth. One look at our busy lives compared to our forefathers shows that despite our advancement, we have also lost balance in our lives. No wonder we flock to religious services, take yoga classes after work and seek meditation retreats to return ourselves to a place of balance.

In this modern world of ours, we maintain a somewhat common understanding of the Universe, God, Humanity and human beings. Sure there are differences amongst us, but at the core we share a fairly common understanding that our principles and beliefs are built upon. The concept of God is consistent amongst different cultures despite our arguments about which God is the true God, how many Gods there are and what God wants from us. For example, underlying these differences is a common belief that God is superior to human beings. From there we weave in cultural definitions of God based on our religions, which unfortunately often results in the ugliest behavior in human beings as evidenced by world wars, genocide and most episodes of the evening news.

Occasionally we will see a T.V. show or read a book, which will expand the horizons of these concise buckets of knowledge. However, for the most part, we have everything organized into discrete and comfortable chunks of commonly accepted theories on how things work. As time progresses, we forget that past generations did not always see things the same way we do and thus we mistakenly assume that our understanding is universal. Therefore, we conclude that those that disagree with us are obviously ignorant, unaware, or just plain stupid. In our perception of commonly accepted knowledge, we leave little room for differences. However, our view of the *how* and *why* things work the way they do has not always been this way.

For example, the great philosopher Plato clearly distinguished between aestheta (that which is perceived through the Body's senses) and noeta (that which is known to the Mind). [Browne 1991] However, with today's understanding of the human brain, sensations are believed to be perceived, appreciated, and even controlled by the brain rather than within the Body itself. Thus it was not all that long ago that our basic understanding (of how sensation flows within us) was quite different from our current understanding. However, in order to understand our role to play in life, we need to rethink some of these most basic understandings.

More recently ethnographer John Forrest eloquently wrote, "What could be more potent than a form that bridges the world of the senses, links spatio-temporal dimensions, and joins the two; a form that acts as mediator between felt experience and cognitive appreciation - and what could be more human?" [Forrest 1988]

What Forrest is referring to is the convergence of two dimensional planes that define the human experience. You may not think of mediating between felt experience and cognitive processing as anything special, but this is only because you're experiencing this convergence passively. With a passive experience, sensation happens to you and has no meaning beyond the determination of cause and effect. In this, you feel pain and deductively figure out what caused the pain.

However, hidden in this is a myriad of communications that occur between the Body, Spirit and Mind. When we slow down our perception and enhance our awareness, we awaken to the symphony that is occurring within us. Basic sensations become much more meaningful because we are able to understand beyond the simple stimulus which brought the sensation to our awareness. By moving to an active participation, you become the mediator and in the role of mediator you are able to govern, influence, and channel sensation rather than letting sensation be something that you merely experience. This subtle difference in participation is one of many differences between a physical and Spiritual existence.

You are that great mediator that joins and binds the eleven dimensions into a being that is uniquely human. Through this mediation, you can achieve greatness, discover the power of healing, and understand your role to play in life. To do so, you must first understand what you are, how you were designed to fulfill your purpose, and why God loves you.

Let us begin.

2

A PURPOSEFUL LIFE

Around the world, there is an emergence of a Spiritual awakening. The usual declining attendance in religious services is instead growing and new houses of worship open their doors everyday. Beyond traditional religions, an awakening is also occurring around the world in the homes of everyday people just like you and me. People are realizing that there is more to life than they believed and they are seeking answers like never before.

And then there is you. You have wondered how to be happy, avoid sorrow, be healthy, avoid sickness, be gracious, and avoid anger... the list goes on and on. You may have found answers in the past and, in seeking more, you are not rejecting those answers but instead looking to better understand. What you desire to understand is very much a personal journey, but one that tugs at you throughout your life.

There are as many answers being peddled as there are questions. Books on spirituality are regularly on the best selling lists but there does not seem to be a single guru that everyone can agree on. Moreover, before we get any further let me assure you that I too am not your guru. My purpose in life is not to lead you, but rather to awaken you to your purpose and the glorious role you will play in life.

Awakening to one's purpose isn't something that we typically list on our top goals in life now is it? Beyond a stable, enriching life for ourselves and our family, it is tough to find life goals that most of Humanity would agree on. Yet, despite our differences, we have a suspicion that we are all interconnected. However, if we are connected, how different can we really be and might we have a similar role to play?

One look at the evening news and you may conclude that we are quite different. On an individual basis, you may be on to something. But the more we engage with people that are different from us, the more we find the differences aren't as great as we had thought. But that only rings true when we are talking about someone else doesn't it?

You, on the other hand, are quite a bit different from everyone else. Or so you tell yourself. With our personal thoughts, unique quirks and individual abilities it is easy to compare ourselves to others and conclude that we are different. Sometimes we think we are better and other times we judge ourselves to our own detriment. However, I believe that with a bit of soul searching, you will discover your purpose and truly understand why it is special. By purely focusing on your favorite characteristics, you might position yourself as being extremely important. Or maybe you walk around everyday in this skin. The skin of being someone important. Alternatively, maybe you wear an inferior skin that tells a story that you are not good enough. Even worse, maybe you live in a skin that other people judge as being good enough or not.

As you can see from this passage, it is easy to get wrapped up in self-judgment. How we view ourselves and how others judge us is a big part of being human. However, most importantly, it has nothing to do with your purpose. Trapped in your own Mind, these judgments may rule your life, but without the threat of self-judgment, you can be liberated.

Card 1: Freedom: the power or right to act, speak, or think as one wants without hindrance or restraint. The cards shown are from the Inspiration Workshop[2].

Whoa, a life without judgment? It almost sounds sacrilegious to suggest such a concept. We are so caught up in the world of judgment that we have even convinced ourselves that it is inherently part of life. We even name the day on which we meet God, "Judgment Day."

However, without judgment, a purposeful life is possible because we can focus on our purpose rather than the petty judgments that hold us back. If you think about history's greatest people, few come to mind

[2] The Inspiration Workshop is based on the teachings of Inspiration Divine. At the end of the workshop, students are asked to give the instructors one word that symbolizes what the workshop was for them personally. The cards shown in Inspiration Divine are the actual, handwritten notes from the students.

that were held back by the little judgments that we spend time and energy worrying about:

> *Did worrying about what people would think of him deter Martin Luther King from breaking down the barriers of civil rights?*
>
> *Did Mahattma Gandhi worry about what he was dressed like when he returned from South Africa dressed as a peasant?*
>
> *Did Mother Theresa worry about how people would accept her after she worked with HIV/AIDS patients?*

It is easy to visualize great leaders as operating without judgment, but not so easy to project such strength upon ourselves. Moreover, this is even harder when you have yet to figure out your purpose. Stop for a moment and think how much people will judge you upon telling them that you have a special purpose. Think how much you will judge yourself.

In recognizing these judgments, you have become present to the criticisms that keep us from even pursuing our purpose. Thus, it becomes all too easy to return to our daily lives and leave the pursuit of happiness and peace to a later day. In the words of my loving wife we say, "I'll figure it out."

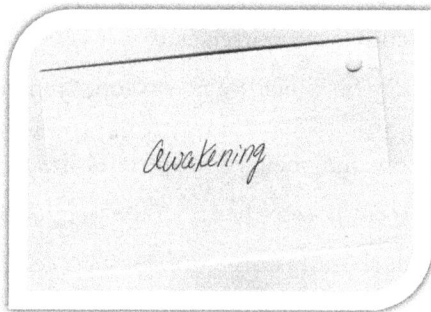

Card 2: Awakening: an act or moment of becoming suddenly aware of something

The day for you to figure it out has come. It may not be today specifically, but the Spiritual awakening that is occurring around the world is but one indicator that your day is coming. Your purpose awaits you.

Happiness Through Purpose

You might think that upon reading this book, millions of readers will discover their purpose and enlist in humanitarian causes to better mankind. Armed with an awareness of their purpose, they will leave their day jobs to bring food to the starving, dig wells springing clean drinking water and develop peace between nations. And while I certainly would be inspired to be at the center of such a movement, Humanity finding its purpose is more about individual movement than it is great causes.

Card 3: Peace: freedom from or the cessation of war or violence.

If the only people that found their purpose were those that made great change in the world, the result of such a movement would be on a rather small scale. I don't mean to take away from those that make such strides, but rather to point out that part of Humanity achieving their purpose is always less than all of Humanity achieving their purpose. I seek the latter and will only achieve my purpose if I succeed in helping you find your purpose.

So, believe me when I say that I am dedicated to you discovering your purpose. If you are reading this book or hearing my words then I am talking to you. I am not talking to the rest of Humanity but rather to you directly. Together, through this book, we are going to put you on the path to discovering your purpose.

Please know that I have not embarked on this journey to sell books. In fact, once you have finished this book I encourage you to give it away. Through this one book in your hands, many can find and achieve their purpose. However, that journey requires that you first find your purpose before it can begin for another.

To begin, recognize that this book is an instruction manual for mankind. I have purposely avoided the feel good topics that only make you feel better in the short term and instead focused on topics that will make a difference in you. In short, this book is a manual on how you will find and achieve your purpose. However, do not worry, pursuing your purpose brings with it a number of benefits that will make you feel good too.

Your purpose may or may not involve great change in your life. However, pursuing your purpose will align you with that which you care about. With this alignment, you will find lasting happiness. When I first began pursuing my purpose, my life was a roller coaster. Every time that I was happy it seemed something would change and my happiness would disappear. Despite my best intentions, my life was full of disappointments, let downs and basically being unhappy.

Often times we label people in our lives as being "happy" or "unhappy." However, these are merely the outward projections of people. Many people put on the appearances of being happy but are miserable. I was surely one of those people. No one in my life at the time thought I was unhappy, but my disappointments caused me great heartache.

Then I found my purpose. You are reading it. Or rather, you're reading one of the ways in which I go about achieving my purpose one reader at a time. The funny thing is that, with the clarity of pursuing my purpose, everything that can make me happy is now within me. I certainly experience sadness and disappointment like anyone else, but with clarity of purpose, those small road bumps can be placed in their rightful place.

My offer to you is to help find your purpose. Through my teachings you will embark on a journey, which will reveal your purpose. If you commit to the practice of seeking and achieving your purpose, greatness will come into your life and flow through you. And, in that, you will find lasting happiness.

3

MEET YOURSELF

At around age two, you developed the ability to communicate through language. Words turned into phrases and then into sentences. No one knows for sure when that voice in your head started talking but with no explanation of who it was, what it was, where it was coming from or why it would not shut up you decided that the voice must be you. That voice became your companion and provided a means to think. In addition, through that ability to think, you learned, expanded, and developed a unique personality.

However, something deep inside made you yearn for more. Your being was and is more than those thoughts in your head. In fact, there are times when you absolutely disagree with the thoughts your Mind expresses. Sometime after those first thoughts, you disagreed with your Mind's thoughts and made a decision that you *knew* was not the correct decision. Call it a hunch, intuition, or throwing caution to the wind.

When you first chose differently than your Mind recommended, you began the path to consciousness.

For example, in 1752 Benjamin Franklin conducted his famous kite experiment in an attempt to extract electrical sparks from storm clouds to demonstrate that lightning is electricity. Franklin knew he was conducting an experiment that could kill him. He had previously written of the dangers of proving his theory and was quite aware of the risks involved. In the end, Franklin proved his theory and survived to share the marvels of electrical power with Humanity.

Consciousness, the state of being conscious, is a term we'll use quite a bit so let's take a moment to define it. According to Wikipedia, "Consciousness is regarded to comprise qualities such as subjectivity, self-awareness, sentience, and the ability to perceive the relationship between oneself and one's environment."

Simply stated, consciousness is being aware. What you are aware of, is the subject of great debate and study. Unfortunately, some people use consciousness as a label as if to say, "I'm conscious and you're not." In this context, no one wants to be referred to as being unconscious. However, for our purposes, let us stay positive and keep the definition of consciousness central to a very personal awakening to your understanding of yourself, your relationship to the rest of Humanity and where you fit in the Universe. If you have ever wondered, "Why am I here?" then you will be happy to know that the answer will come from becoming conscious.

As was originally proposed by Sigmund Freud within his Reality Principle, your Mind is a thinking machine designed to keep you alive and your Mind will always choose survival over pleasure. [Freud 1911] Because consciousness is governed by free will, reaching a state of consciousness requires effort (energy) rather than something that you are born with. Consequently, the newborn unconscious being necessitates a controlling master. Otherwise, human beings could not survive. Thus, by design, we each were born with our Minds turned on and in charge.

Mind

Your early Mind was little more than a basic processor of cause and effect. When you are hungry, your Body communicates that it needs food. The means by which this communication takes place is through an uncomfortable feeling in your stomach. As your thinking Mind had yet to develop the ability to communicate through language, your Mind's early expressions were largely limited to turning on and turning off crying.

Your parents soon learned the difference between a pain and a discomfort cry. Through this binary on and off communication pattern, you were able to communicate to your parents when you were hungry, when you needed your diaper changed and when something hurt. Thus, your Mind began the journey of insuring your survival.

In this, a relationship developed between the Mind and the Body. Input from the Body causes the Mind to think and an action results. In our basic example, a pain from the stomach causes the Mind to conclude you are hungry and soon you are at the refrigerator looking for a snack. However, you are so much more than an animal capable of feeding itself and advanced thinking (e.g. curing cancer, inventing rockets and finding your car keys). You have a Spiritual connection that is distinct from any other living thing.

In one form or another, you have experienced a Spiritual side. For some, this is a connection with God, and for others, it is communing with Mother Nature. Buddhists meditate, Christians and Muslims pray and even atheists find moments of tranquility and peace that cannot be explained. Regardless of your religious ideology or beliefs, there is a Spiritual aspect of your life that is more than that voice in your head and the actions it causes your Body to do.

Body, Spirit and Mind

You are the collective consciousness that radiates from the connections between your Body, Spirit, and Mind. By distinguishing what you are into these entities, you can begin to become conscious to the interactions and communications that occur within you. Each part contributes a unique and valuable aspect to what we collectively refer to as our *self*. With our self being comprised of more than just the thoughts in our head, we hold within ourselves an untapped intelligence that can propel us to an even greater potential.

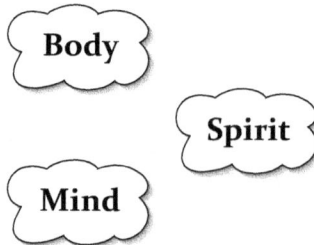

Body

Spirit

Mind

However, most people are *in their heads* and go through life primarily within the limited consciousness of their thoughts. These people believe their entire *self* exists only in their Minds and subsequently limit their consciousness. They feed their Bodies junk food, deprive them of exercise, and refuse to give them adequate rest. Furthermore, they pay lip service to their Spirit by complying with religious doctrine (e.g. going to church on Sundays), but at the same time, ignore and fail to truly nurture their own Spirit.

Try to visualize your consciousness as a three dimensional space that emanates from all around you. As you walk around, this three-dimensional space of consciousness would meet other people's consciousness to form a collective consciousness. With this interaction, groups of people would become conscious of the same ideas. And while you do not necessarily believe that people walk around with these three dimensional consciousness bubbles spontaneously joining to share ideas, one cannot help but notice that when an idea catches on, it spreads like wildfire.

There is a collective consciousness of Humanity in the Universe that contains every original thought, idea, and breakthrough ever conceived by mankind. Like a neural network beyond our comprehension, this Internet of Humanity contains the answer to every question that has ever been asked. However, to tap into it you must first learn how to ask a question.

Imagine that your ability to tap into a collective consciousness is expanded or limited by the expanse of your own consciousness. As such, the *more* conscious you are, the more you are open to and capable of tapping into the possibilities available to you from the Universe.

If you are having trouble with the concept of the *Universe* as our source of knowledge, then replace this word with another that you are comfortable with (e.g. God). As you will soon learn, your concepts are largely governed by the way your Mind interprets the world around you (your Mind's reality) through language. Whatever *God* or the *Universe* is cannot be changed because of what we believe it to be. For the moment, recognize that language has formed rigid understandings of concepts in your Mind based on the words we use. Thus, if you're struggling with a concept, try substituting a different word in order to break free from the mental limitations imposed by language.

As you can see in the diagram below, the consciousness of a person that is entirely *in their head* is represented as emanating from around their Mind:

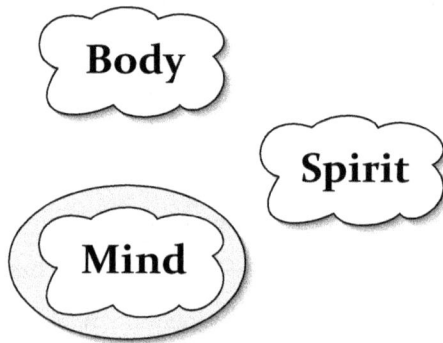

Body

Spirit

Mind

Your consciousness is similarly limited or expanded in relation to your awareness of your Body, Spirit, and Mind. If you think of consciousness like a radar dish, capable of receiving signals, then you can visualize that becoming more conscious would provide you with a larger radar dish, capable of capturing more signals than a small radar dish. Similarly, if you primarily experience life through your Mind's thoughts, you are only experiencing a fraction of the full life experience that is possible from a strong Body, Spirit, and Mind connection.

It should be noted that the consciousness potential of a Body, Spirit, and Mind connection is available and present in every human being. Renowned Philosopher of the Mind David Chalmers wrote, "Why would the universe be such that awareness gives rise to consciousness in one person, and one person only? It would be a strange, arbitrary way for a world to be." (Chalmers 1996)

We exist in harmony between the three and cannot exist entirely in any one component of our Body, Spirit, or Mind. Consequently everyone experiences periodic connections between their Body, Spirit and Mind which manifest themselves as sparks of brilliance, amazing coincidences and unlikely occurrences. However, these moments of greatness are but glimmers of the full human potential.

When considering our own potential, we typically think about what we are or can become capable of accomplishing. We focus on the end of the pursuit rather than the pursuit itself. *I will run my own business. My children will graduate from an Ivy League College. I will operate a shelter for the homeless.* Do not worry, there is not anything wrong with seeking individual accomplishments, but your full human potential is much more than anything you could accomplish as an individual. To accomplish your full potential, you must first expand your consciousness and learn to live in a reality in which your expanded consciousness is allowed to govern your life.

In terms of awareness, we human beings walk around perceiving, interpreting, and living within the consciousness of our Minds. In addition, as much as we might like to change this, there is no way to experience life any other way. However, please stop short of finding fault in your Mind as so many others do. Your Mind is a beautiful and important component of the collective *you* and should not be considered something intrusive, counter productive or the enemy.

However, an evolved life exists beyond our Mind's singularity of consciousness. When you expand to a consciousness bridging your Body, Spirit and Mind, the limited awareness of that voice in your head becomes but one of the components of your overall being. Like a butterfly emerging from a cocoon, your newly expanded consciousness will avail new opportunities, insights and connections beyond your wildest dreams. However, like a newborn, you have much to learn and must develop a new set of skills to thrive within your new consciousness.

You may not even realize it, but by simply comprehending an expanded *you* the evolutionary process has already begun. You are sliding down the birth canal of life into a new world from which you will accomplish greatness. As an evolved being, you have great potential, but in order to achieve anything, you will need to strengthen the connective bonds between your Body, Spirit, and Mind. When the connections between the Body, Spirit, and Mind are strengthened, one's consciousness further expands. Just by distinguishing the separateness and connection between the Body and the Mind, your consciousness has begun to expand:

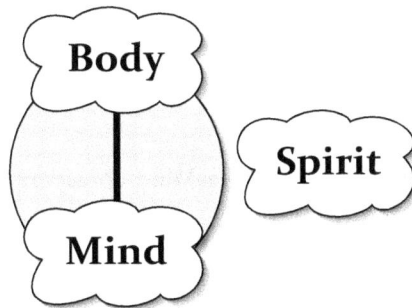

You have gone your entire life living within the confines of your Mind and believing that *you* were a physical manifestation of that voice in your head. Now you are beginning to peel back the real you to reveal the true human form. At first, this revelation comes as a bit of a shock and it is natural to not be able to conceptualize that you are anything other than that voice in your head. Nevertheless, a simple test reveals that the voice is not you.

You know from experience that you are able to stop talking. Everyday there are situations where it is appropriate to be silent. For example, Indian ascetics go years without uttering a single word. However, can you stop the voice in your head from talking? Try it and, most likely, you will find that you will soon be having a conversation with that voice about how you're, "not talking." Whereas we are more than capable of controlling sound emanating from our mouths, we are completely incapable of silencing the voice in our heads. And if you can't control your internal voice, then how could it be *you*?

Do not worry, there is not anything wrong with that voice in your head, but it is liberating to discover that you are not that voice. The voice in your head is nothing more than the internal dialogue which accompanies the logical and illogical thoughts of the Mind. Your Mind processes and considers millions of options all the time and not all of them are reasonable. At the end of the process, you make sound judgments and do a good job at managing your life through making good decisions.

Nevertheless, along the way, the Mind considers every option and listening to that internal dialogue can sometimes be a bit unsettling. Some of the things that the Mind comes up with are negative, inappropriate, or flat out crazy. Just know that in the process of considering every option, your Mind is going to weigh out the logical as well as illogical options. With so many choices to make in the course of managing your life, you wouldn't want any possible options to go unconsidered would you?

So the next time that voice in your head starts putting you down, take solace in the fact that it really is not you attacking your self-esteem, but rather the uncontrollable thoughts of your Mind. Let those thoughts be nothing more than thoughts. So too, refrain from judging them and allowing them to have meaning. Listen to them, consider what value they might have and where they are coming from. Then let them go.

I like to think of this internal dialogue as an interactive computer. The term *computer* is a bit cold, so as you visualize this concept in your Mind try to dress it up or make it a bit more personable than the clumsy personal computer that sits on your desk. One of the internal components of any computer is the Central Processing Unit (CPU). You may have heard this geeky term tossed around and it really is nothing more than the brain of the computer. However, unlike a CPU that serves only one user, the computer inside your head (brain) is shared by both your Mind and the collective consciousness of your Body, Spirit, and Mind.

When you're listening, but not participating, that voice is the ramblings of the Mind. However, the true self also uses your brain (not Mind) to logically think through problems, options, and possibilities. The means by which you experience this thinking process is through language. A subtle distinction to be sure, but on the path to consciousness you will find that there are pebbles on road that will guide you.

By stepping back to consider yourself as the collective consciousness of your Body, Spirit, and Mind, you begin to understand who you really are as well as the difference between a conscious and unconscious existence. In doing so, you will begin to appreciate your Body as a miraculous thinking machine. That is right, I am distinguishing your Body as a thinking machine that has intelligence not unlike your Mind. Your Body makes countless decisions every second that keep you alive, healthy and in balance. So why is it so hard to believe that there is intelligence emanating from the Body?

Modern science has convinced us that our Bodies are dumb carcasses that react to stimuli rather than processors of information. But even our heart has its own *brain*. The heart has over 40,000 embedded neurons (brain cells) that enable it to operate as its own intrinsic nervous system. With every beat of our heart, an electro-magnetic field is generated that is 5,000 times stronger than the field produced by our brain. This field is so powerful that it can be detected by electro-magnetic sensors over eight feet away from the Body.

And what is the purpose of the electro-magnetic field generated by the heart? It is one of four ways our heart communicates with the brain.[3]

It is true that if we're poked, we'll flinch. On the flip side, we are only starting to understand the Body's amazing ability to heal itself. In this moving from a reactive to proactive construct of our Body, we begin to understand the important role our physical Bodies play in our path to consciousness. For example, it is only through being alive (which requires your Body) that we are able to fulfill our purpose.

The means by which the connections between the Mind and Body are strengthened is via the awareness of how the two communicate. As originally put forth by Plato, the Body communicates via the five senses:

1. Vision - Light - Eyes

2. Hearing - Sound - Ears

3. Smelling - Olfaction - Nose

4. Tasting - Flavor - Mouth

5. Touching - Sensation - Skin

Every thought your Mind creates is shared with your Body and Spirit. The Mind is continually considering different options and sharing those thoughts with the Body and Spirit for consideration. The communications sent back are interpreted by the Mind and decisions

[3] The four ways that the heart communicates with the brain is through neurological impulses, biochemically via hormones, biophysically via pressure waves and energetically via the electro-magnetic field it generates. (ByronStock.com, 2008).

are made. The symphony of communication happening between your Body, Spirit and Mind happens millions of times a day and occurs with almost every thought you have.

Unfortunately, many people are disconnected from their Body as well as their Spirit and ignore the continual feedback provided. Without reverence for the Body and its part in *you*, these people unknowingly poison their Bodies with toxins, consume unhealthy amounts of innutritious foods, and deny their Body exercise.

However, this all too common assault on the human Body causes more damage than the physical impact. Their consciousness fails to thrive in this unhealthy state. However, by strengthening the bond between the Body, Spirit, and Mind, one's consciousness is greatly expanded:

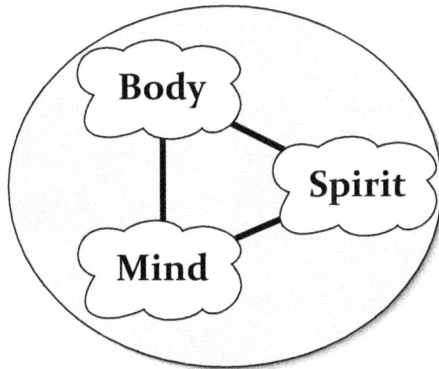

In concert, a Body, Spirit and Mind connection empowers one's self to its full potential. By increasing one's listening beyond the voice in their head, consciousness is greatly expanded. A Spiritual existence, whereby you are guided by your Spirit, is all together different from a physical or mental existence. When you live your life guided exclusively by your Mind, your life is filled with chaos, unpredictability, and drama.

This is because your Mind is only capable of processing information to make decisions based on available data. Like a computer with limited access to the facts, the Mind is limited by its access to knowledge.

Your Mind is an advanced thinking machine, which depends extensively on information. Given enough facts, there is very little that your Mind could not figure out. However, therein lies the problem. There are never enough facts to provide the Mind with enough information to make solid decisions about many things in life. As a result, the Mind does the best that it can but often that is not good enough. In addition, living a fulfilled life doesn't often require better decision-making but rather better overall guidance. The world is not black and white, nor do we struggle much with turning left or right. The bigger challenge is fulfilling our potential and achieving our dreams. In these areas, the Mind calculates what we should do, but life is not always about calculations.

A Spiritual existence, in contrast, is one of harmony, order, and beauty. Whereas your Mind is limited by access to information, your Spirit is connected to both God and other enlightened beings. Thus rather than a limited pool of information, your Spirit has access to every piece of data that has ever existed, will exist or even can exist. Therefore, your Spirit is much better suited to help guide your life, make smart decisions, and help you fulfill your purpose. But as most people are disconnected from their Spirit and living a mental existence, they're missing out on many of the benefits available from the Universe, God and Humanity.

To get a feel for how much information is available to you, consider the limited digital information that the Internet contains. The amount of digital information worldwide today is far beyond the point of being expressed in gigabytes or even terabytes. The size of the digital universe today approaches one zettabyte :

1,000,000,000,000,000,000,000 bytes (10^{21}).

This data heap would fill 15 stacks of books extending the 93 million miles between the Earth and sun. Even more astonishing, the digital universe is expected to grow 10 times larger over the next five years. And while this is a lot of information, it is only a fraction of the non-digital information contained in the total consciousness of intelligent life.

Living a Spiritual existence does not require handing over control of your life to your Spirit (or even God for that matter). You were born with a Mind for a reason. A Spiritual existence embodies collaboration between the Body, Spirit, and Mind. When the three work as a team, you are operating in harmony with the Universe and thus able to operate outside the limitations of a physical existence. However, to achieve harmony, you must first allow the Body and the Spirit to participate in managing your life.

The Mind, born with the paternal responsibility for survival, will not release its control easily. Although it was designed to work in harmony with the Body and the Spirit, the Mind takes the job of keeping you alive very seriously. With so much to risk with your life, the Mind needs to be convinced that the Body and the Spirit are ready to take on this responsibility. After all, the Mind has kept you alive all these years and has not had much of a relationship with the Body and the Spirit. As such, convincing the Mind that the Body and Spirit are online and equally capable of being trusted takes time and effort.

However, by strengthening the Body, Spirit and Mind as well as the connective bonds between them, the Mind will relinquish control and naturally allow the full human potential to emerge.

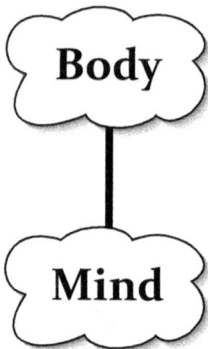

Both the Body and the Mind are self-contained entities. The physical structure of the Body, despite being made of atoms like every other physical entity in the Universe, has boundaries. There is a clear distinction (in our Mind) between where your Body starts and finishes. Similarly, your Mind is contained within you and cannot be fully experienced or shared with others.

The Spirit, in contrast, is not self-contained and exists outside the boundaries of a three dimensional world. Your Spirit is no more contained in your Body than water is limited to a single state (e.g. solid vs. gas). Thus by strengthening one's connection to the Spirit, consciousness is greatly expanded and, as you will soon learn, your ability to achieve greatness becomes much more attainable.

By developing your full Body, Spirit and Mind connections, your consciousness spreads beyond our four dimensional (length, width, depth and time) world and taps into the collective consciousness of Humanity in the Universe.

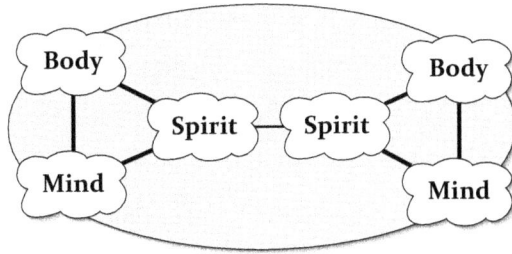

To realize one's full human potential, one must strengthen the Body, Spirit and Mind as well as the connections between them. With strong connective bonds between the three, they are able to communicate fluidly with one another and operate as a team. If their connective bonds are weak, communications will not flow between them and they will revert to managing their area of responsibility in isolation. For example, your Body works to keep you healthy and alive but does not understand how to heal itself. It may be capable of healing itself but it does not know how to do it. Your Mind, recognizing that you are sick takes action to get you to a doctor. Thus in collaboration, the two work quite effectively as a team. However, if the connections between the Body and the Mind were severed, the Body would not be able to recover from very basic illnesses (or at least would suffer without access to treatment).

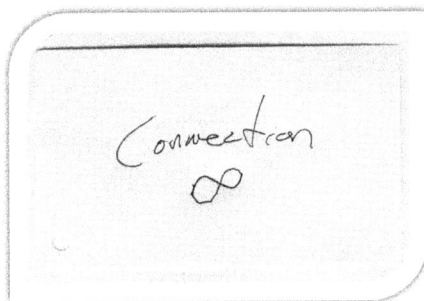

Card 4: Connection: a relationship in which a person, thing, or idea is linked or associated with something else.

The same is the case with all of the connective bonds between all three entities. If strong, they can operate effectively as a team but when atrophied, they struggle and often resort to working in isolation. Thus to achieve your full human potential, you need each of your entities to be healthy and operating with strong connective bonds.

To understand how to strengthen these bonds, consider each one as a pair:

Body ~ Spirit

Spirit ~ Mind

Mind ~ Body

There are a number of ways to strengthen these bonds. To identify these techniques it is useful to understand the domain of each:

The Body exists in the domain of "Here and Now."

The Spirit exists in the domain of "We are."

The Mind exists in the domain of "I am.[4]"

Each of these domains conveys a perception of reality. Whereas the Mind interprets reality from our individualistic view of life, the Body only understands the here and now. For example, the nose only knows the smell of a rose when it smells a rose even if the Mind remembers the smell of roses from our childhood. For the Body, there is only what is happening in the moment. For the Spirit, there is not an

---

[4] In Hinduism, the ego-principle, ahamkara (lit., "I do"), is the root cause of dualism or the seeming separation between man and his Creator. – Autobiography of a Yogi, Paramahansa Yogananda, 1946.

emphasis on the individual, but rather an inclination towards a collective Humanity.

From each entity's perspective of reality:

The Mind focuses on our Past.
The Body focuses on the Present.
The Spirit focuses on the Future.

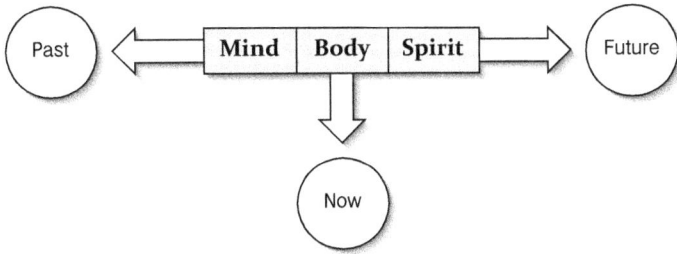

Figure 1: The Mind exists in the domain of the ego (I am) with a focus on the past. The Body exists in the domain of Here and Now with only an awareness of the present. The Spirit exists within the domain of a collective Humanity (We are) with a focus on the future.

Through these connective bonds, we are able to connect the past, present and future. For example, smells and sounds are able to trigger the retrieval of distant and sometimes obscure memories from our past. So too, these same smells and sounds often evoke emotions from that same period of time in our lives.

Let us pause for a moment to reflect on how this ability to understand one's relationship to time is uniquely human. No other creature on the planet can remember the past and visualize its own future. Moreover, as we have just discussed, your senses are not only connected to this experience, they actually enable cognitive retention. Thus your senses are much more than tools to help you function in the world. They are the means by which you relate to where you are in the world in terms of space and time.

Collectively the three entities of the Body, Spirit, and Mind communicate with one another through sensations, feelings, and thoughts. You have experienced these three communication tools your entire life and probably assumed they were just part of that mysterious brain of yours. However, sensations, feelings, and thoughts are actually groups of dimensions that define human beings and the Universe we live in. In total, they comprise the eleven dimensions theorized by quantum physicists. (Walker 2008)

11 Dimensions?

You may be surprised to hear our Universe described in eleven dimensions instead of four (three axes of space and time). However, in an amazing turn of events, physicists have mathematically demonstrated that our Universe must exist within a higher number of dimensions than the standard four. Some theories propose as many as twenty-six dimensions, however the favored string-theory postulates ten to eleven dimensions.

It is beyond the scope of this book to try to explain how and why string-theory fits into our scientific understanding of the Universe. There are numerous books on the subject written by authors more knowledgeable than I that can explain the mathematical reasoning behind the eleven dimensional existence of string-theory.

The eleven dimensions (pictured below) are the means by which we operate in the Universe. In fact, the entire Universe exists within the confines of these dimensions, as they are the tools that govern its existence. However, beyond explaining the construct of our Universe, the eleven dimensions explain our role to play in life and the purpose human beings have in the grand scheme of the Universe. They are, quite simply, uniquely human and elemental to the survival of our Universe.

MIND	SPIRIT	BODY		
THOUGHTS	FEELINGS	SENSATIONS		
DEPTH / WIDTH / HEIGHT / TIME	AROUSAL / EMOTION	MATTER / TOUCH / ODOR / SMELL / FLAVOR / TASTE / SOUND / HEARING / LIGHT / VISION		

Figure 2: The eleven dimensions of the Universe are comprised of the very same elements of human existence. As much as the simplicity of the 11 dimensions mystifies the Western mind, elements of the 11 dimensions[5] have been ever present in many cultures such as the concept of Sadāyatana. For example, in Buddhism the concept of the Six Sextets represents a process, which begins with sensation (sense organ making contact with the external stimuli), giving rise to thought and resulting in a feeling.

Until now (this very minute to be precise), you were probably either unaware of the eleven dimensions or considered them impossible for the human Mind to comprehend. The prevailing theory amongst quantum physicists is that the dimensions beyond the standard four were either unable to be perceived by human beings, too complex for us to understand or not yet employed in our evolution of the Universe. Nevertheless, as you will come to understand, the eleven dimensions of the Universe are not only present in everyday life but they contain the keys to unlocking your full human potential. Who would have guessed that your school teacher was explaining the ways of the Universe when

---

[5] The 11 dimensions are represented throughout the book in their experiential form. For example, the dimension of light is represented as we experience it through vision.

she taught you about the five senses, how to tell time, geometry and how to play nice on the playground when emotions flared.

However please consider that, for there to be eleven dimensions operating in the Universe in which you live, it would be highly improbable for them to be a mystery to you. Understanding the four dimensions that you've distinguished since grammar school is possible even though providing a mental definition of these *dimensions* is much more complex.

Upon looking up the definition of "dimensions" in a dictionary or encyclopedia, you will find a myriad of definitions depending on the context in which you are seeking an answer. There are slightly different definitions of dimensions depending if you want an answer from a mathematical, physics or geometrical perspective. Even though the definition of dimensions vary, the four standard dimensions you have known since childhood are as familiar to you as the back of your hand. Imagine explaining these four dimensions to someone who did not understand a four dimensional reality and you will begin to understand the reasons why the simplicity of the proposed eleven dimensions is as reasonable as the standard four.

Just such an attempt was made in Edwin A. Abbott's 1884 masterpiece Flatland. His story describes the journey of A. Square, a mathematician and resident of Flatland, where women - thin, straight lines - are the lowliest of shapes and where men may have any number of sides, depending on their social status. Early in the novel, A. Square attempts to explain how life is in a world without the dimension of height:

Place a penny on the middle of one of your tables in Space; and leaning over it, look down upon it. It will appear a circle.

But now, drawing back to the edge of the table, gradually lower your eye (thus bringing yourself more and more into the condition of the inhabitants of Flatland), and you will find the penny becoming more and more oval to your view; and at last when you have placed your eye exactly on the edge of the table (so that you are, as it were, actually a Flatlander) the penny will have then ceased to appear oval at all, and will have become, so far as you can see, a straight line.

As much as it seems impossible to imagine life in Flatland, so too is it implausible to believe that you could be living in a world that has dimensions of which you are not aware. Scientifically there are many ways to explain how we would be unaware of these dimensions, but these explanations simply cram the dimensions into a definition that fails to reveal an understanding.

However, just as the Flatlander only knows a world devoid of height, so too you are completely cognizant of the reality in which you live regardless of how many dimensions there are. Most of us do not spend a lot of time contemplating how many dimensions there are in the Universe. The concept of a four dimensional reality has been well established before any of us were born and thus the four dimensions is something we just take for granted.

Consequently our not knowing, that the eleven dimensions are inherently part of the human experience, is not all together illogical. We often assume that something that we do not yet understand needs to be incredibly complex. For example, in 1928 Alexander Fleming discovered the antibiotic substance penicillin from a fungus, but ancient Greeks had been employing moulds and plants to treat infection since ancient times. Science, history, and practical experience regularly reveal that the simplest answers are often the best. Shouldn't the answers to our questions about the Universe, God, and Humanity be simple enough for a child to understand?

American architect, author, designer, futurist, inventor, and visionary, Richard Buckminster "Bucky" Fuller once said, "When I am working on a problem, I never think about beauty. I think only of how to solve the problem. But when I have finished, if the solution is not beautiful, I know it is wrong."

The beauty of the eleven proposed dimensions is that they are simple and every human being understands them. How they operate in the Universe and the purpose they serve is a topic we shall get into. However, for now, simply try to recognize that the elegance of these basic constructs of our Universe is elemental in the human experience and this, in itself, is beautiful. If you think about it, none of the eleven dimensions is more profound or essential than the others. Together they not only describe the human experience, but they also contain the keys to unlock our Universe.

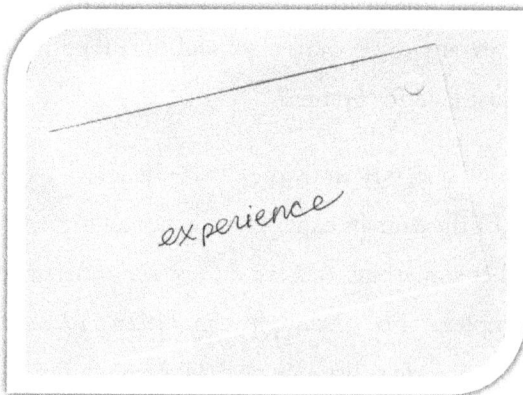

experience

Card 5: Experience: practical contact with and observation of facts or events.

In 1996, David Chalmers wrote in The Conscious Mind, "Ultimately, we will wish for a set of fundamental laws. Physicists seek a set of basic laws simple enough that one might write them on the front of a T-shirt; in a theory on consciousness, we should expect the same thing. In both cases, we are questing for the basic structure of the universe, and we have good reason to believe that the basic structure has a remarkable simplicity." (Chalmers 1996)

So, before dismissing the proposed eleven dimensions as being too simple to describe the Universe, try to understand how each can be a dimension unto itself. Ask yourself of every dimension including the common four, "What is the purpose of this dimension, and how does it enable life to exist?" In this, you will find an answer to any potential skepticism over the proposed eleven dimensions.

In our understanding of the eleven dimensions, we shall group them by the entities that employ them. Each dimension plays a unique role with its entity to enable the Body, Spirit or Mind to both understand their perception of reality and to convey their understanding of their reality to another.

The way human beings come to a point of understanding is through communications. Through receiving and interpreting communications from another, we "think" about the message and then comprehend. Our entire lives have been thus far viewed from the perspective of our Mind. That voice in your head "thinks" your Mind's thoughts and thus we have deduced that all the "thinking" takes place in our Mind. Instead, consider your Body, Spirit, and Mind as a collective machine that communicates back and forth as a unified being. Moreover, in order for there not to be miscommunications, each of your entities has its own language known to us as a collection of dimensions.

The Mind speaks the language of the mental dimensions:

1. **Time**
2. **Height**
3. **Width**
4. **Depth**

The Mind, on its own, cannot see, hear, smell, taste, or feel. Similarly, the Body, on its own, cannot understand the framework of length, width, depth, or time. The eyes merely see and the ears merely hear, but in concert with the Mind, these dimensions can be combined for a unique human understanding of our world.

So too, the Body speaks the language of the sensual dimensions:

1. **Vision**
2. **Taste**
3. **Hearing**
4. **Smell**
5. **Touch**

And finally, the Spirit speaks the language of the emotive dimensions:

6. **Emotion** (a continuum ranging from Pleasure to Displeasure)
7. **Arousal** (a continuum ranging from Aroused to Asleep)

To understand the range of communications possible through the emotive dimensions, consider the Core Affect Diagram described by

James A. Russell in his 2003 paper, "Core Affect and the Psychological Construction of Emotion." (Russell 2003)

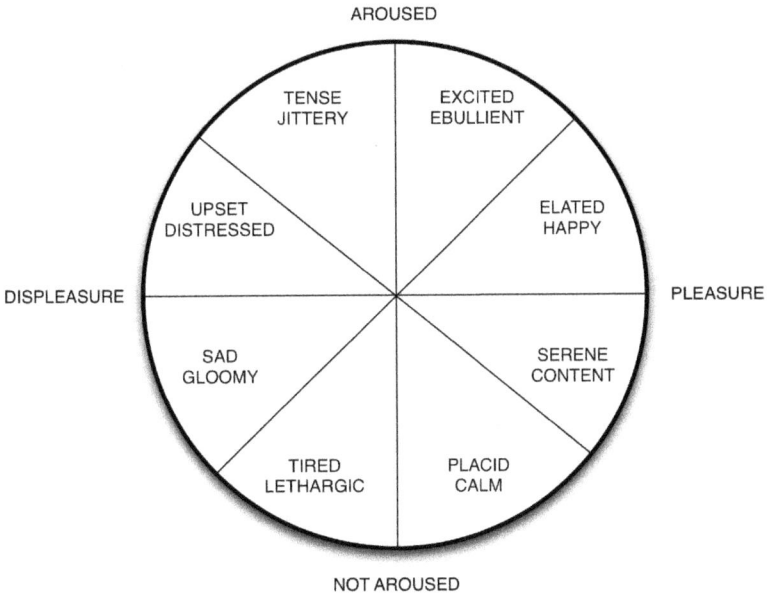

AROUSED

TENSE
JITTERY

EXCITED
EBULLIENT

UPSET
DISTRESSED

ELATED
HAPPY

DISPLEASURE

PLEASURE

SAD
GLOOMY

SERENE
CONTENT

TIRED
LETHARGIC

PLACID
CALM

NOT AROUSED

Figure 3: The Core Affect Diagram represents the range of human emotional states made possible by a combination of emotion and arousal.

Through Russell's Core Effect Diagram, he described emotions similar to dimensions. "It is encouraging that," wrote Russell, "from a biological perspective, different researchers have proposed similar or related dimensions. The subjective experience and its neuro-physiological counterpart are not separate events but two sides of the same coin." With any emotional response represented as a single point on the Core Affect Diagram, the combination of different degrees of arousal (ranging from asleep to highly aroused) and emotions (ranging from pleasure to displeasure) are able to communicate a wide variance of instructions from the Spirit to the Mind.

In the domain of the Spirit, the emotive dimensions of emotion and arousal continuums do not represent a positive or a negative. For the Spirit, emotions are simply the tools and dimensions of the Spirit. They simply are. As experiential life is full of difficulties, it is hard to understand how feelings such as pain and anger are not negative. Or how happiness and joy could be anything other than positive. Be that as it may, emotions and arousal are simple, yet powerful, dimensions of the Spirit that enable the Spirit to effectively guide the Body and the Mind.

In Buddhism, we find a similar depiction of the five sensual dimensions:

> You have been alive a long time. Your eyes have seen any number of forms and colours, your ears have heard so many sounds, you've had any number of experiences. And that's all they were - just experiences. You've eaten delicious foods and all the good tastes were just good tastes, nothing more. The unpleasant tastes were just unpleasant tastes, that's all. If the eye sees a beautiful form that's all it is, just a beautiful form. An ugly form is just an ugly form. The ears hear an entrancing, melodious sound and it's nothing more than that. A grating, disharmonious sound is simply so. (Bercholz and Chodzin Kohn, Entering the Stream 1993)

Neither the Spirit nor the Mind can exist without the Body (more on this later) so the Mind accepts the continuums of emotion and arousal as indicators of positive (good) and negative (bad) from the Spirit. In concert with the Spirit, the Mind controls the Body and keeps it out of harms way by listening to the emotions that give rise from a combination of emotion and arousal. You can think of this flow of emotions as a steering mechanism that enables the Spirit to guide the Mind.

In our Minds, the communications of our Body, Spirit, and Mind are commingled into a singular understanding of ourselves. Through our Minds, we have experienced life up until this moment and thus it is sometimes difficult for us, as human beings, to decouple the separate and distinct parts of us from the whole.

Do you feel pain when pricked by a needle?

Do you feel pain when your heart is broken?

While both of these pains are real, they emanate from two different places (the Body and the Spirit). Both are interpreted by the Mind and stored for future reference so that the being (you) can avoid the same pain in the future. Consequently, emotions are often harbored in your Mind, even though the Body and Spirit have moved on.

We can move beyond a physical existence to a Spiritual existence and, in the process, free ourselves from the stored memories that no longer do us any good. In collaboration with our Body and Spirit, the energy that flows through us can both nurture and bring us to a new understanding of our sensations, emotions and thoughts. Rather than simply experiencing each one, we can bring ourselves to an active participation where they become the language of enlightenment.

In this language, we will become in tune with the voice of God and be able to listen to the messages being broadcast to both mankind and our individual being. No longer will we seek answers, but only find half-truths. In harmony with the Universe, God and Humanity, we will find that we are closer to the truth than we ever imagined.

Your Practice

A. Distinguish

Throughout your day, distinguish your entire self as the Body, Spirit and Mind rather than the combined consciousness of everyday existence. When you distinguish your three entities, speak them aloud in the order of Body, Spirit, and Mind.

Your egocentric Mind will continually seek to put itself first (e.g. Mind, Body and Spirit), but as the Mind and the Spirit put the survival of the Body as their top priority, remember to put the Body first. As you are your Spirit as expressed through your Body and Mind, put your Spirit second and then the Mind. To shake your Mind's adherence to putting itself first, recite the three in the ancient language of Sanskrit dating back to approximately 1500 BC:

> Deha (Body),
> Jiiva (Spirit),
> Buddhi (Mind)

B. Seek to Understand

For each of the 11 Dimensions ask yourself, "What would you miss most if this dimension no longer existed?"

1. Vision _____

2. Taste _____

3. Hearing _____

4. Smell _____

5. Touch _____

6. Emotion _____

7. Arousal _____

8. Time _____

9. Height _____

10. Weight _____

11. Depth _____

C. Know Your Emotions

As you go through your day tomorrow, plot each emotion you become aware of. Each time you become aware of an emotion, plot it on the Core Affect Diagram below to understand its relationship between emotion and arousal. Write down the emotion in the listing below and what meaning the emotion is trying to tell you:

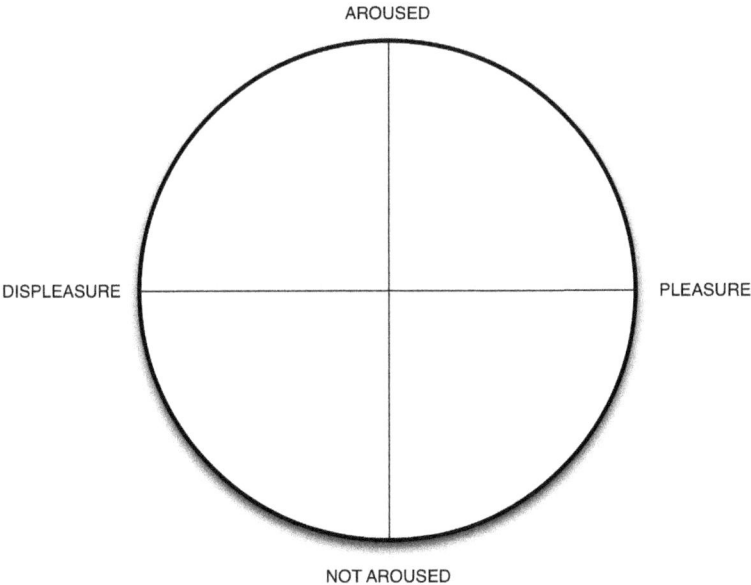

AROUSED

DISPLEASURE

PLEASURE

NOT AROUSED

EMOTION   MEANING

1. _____ - _____

2. _____ - _____

3. _____ - _____

4. _____ - _____

5. _____ - _____

D. Know Your Senses

For each of the five sensual dimensions, list your favorite experience with each (e.g. favorite smell) and the feeling you associate with the experience. Do the same for your least favorite experience for each.

Dimension	Favorite Experience	Feeling
Vision		
Taste		
Hear		
Smell		
Touch		

Dimension	Least Favorite Experience	Feeling
Vision		
Taste		
Hear		
Smell		
Touch		

4

ENERGY

As we go through life, we store our experiences as memories. For example, as much as our parents warned us, it was the memory of that first burn that kept our hands away from fire for the rest of our lives. In some ways, these stored memories serve us well by helping us not repeat mistakes. But this approach also forms habit-forming behaviors that cause us to repeat mistakes in our lives over and over again.

If you look back on your own failures in life you'll likely see a repeating pattern. Why do we do the same thing over and over again despite knowing better? For many of us, we've orchestrated elaborate stories to explain the cause of these repeating patterns. But once we catch ourselves explaining our stories to justify our behavior, we begin to unlock the causal event that is repeating throughout our lives. Unfortunately, after years of telling and believing these stories, the story itself begins to become our reality. And many of you deserve the Pulitzer Prize for Literary Accomplishment for your stories. You've written such a best seller that everyone around you is buying it.

A Spiritual existence walks away from our stories and seeks to chart a new course. We seek happiness, joy and creation in our lives rather than repeating a tired story one more time. Another failed relationship, another troubled situation and one more reason why our willpower wasn't enough... these are the stories that plague our lives and can ultimately lead to an unfulfilled life. At the heart of these stories are our stored memories. Stored firmly in our subconscious are memories from past experiences that we pull out as scripts for future life episodes. But each time we recall one of our conclusions and use it as a playbook for life, we fail to grow.

The Mind has good reason for storing memories even though it may prevent us from growing. The Mind stores memories to save energy.

Energy is required for a thought to conclude.

In order for your thoughts to conclude, the Mind must originate the thought and pass it to the Body for consideration. In turn, the Body evaluates the thought against the five sensual dimensions and passes on its recommendation to the Spirit. And finally, the Spirit (Master), decides what to do and passes the information back to the Mind in the form of feelings. Upon concluding the validity of input from the Body and Spirit, the Mind determines to store the conclusion or not. And this flow of decision making takes energy.

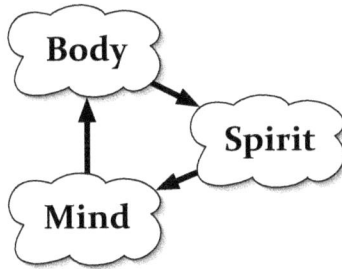

For example, if you go to a swimming pool and venture out onto the diving board, there will be a symphony of communications within you. Your Mind may have instructed your Body to go out on the diving board, but upon reaching the end of the board, your Body will begin to assess the situation:

Your eyes will look down to determine how far it is to the water;

Your skin will feel the strength of the breeze blowing across the pool;

Your ears will detect the sounds of happy children playing in the distance;

Your toes will feel the grainy non-slip texture of the diving board beneath you;

Your mouth will taste the gum that you forgot to spit out.

The Body takes in this information and passes it along to the Spirit. Your Spirit assesses the situation, based on the quality of communication from the Body, and decides what to do. If the Spirit detects you're standing on the top level of an Olympic diving platform, it will likely send a highly aroused feeling of fear to the Mind. However, if you're at a local swimming pool standing on a standard diving board, the Spirit will more likely send a feeling of calm.

At this point, your Mind will listen to the Spirit and instruct the Body to dive in or not. In conclusion, your Mind will store these memories as conclusive thoughts so that the next time you climb up on a similar diving board, this decision-making can be retrieved locally, rather than expending energy to communicate with the Body and the Spirit.

When this revelation first came to me I was a bit taken aback. Living within the consciousness of our Minds means that we believe that every sensation, emotion and thought is born in our Mind. I don't want you to think that it is impossible for the Mind to invoke an emotion or for the Body to communicate with the Mind via a sensation. This understanding isn't about absolutes but rather about developing awareness of how the three entities communicate. Energy flows through the path of least resistance and the flow of information that is being put forth is just that. It isn't that information can't flow in other directions. But rather that it takes less energy for information to flow in this manner.

In order to avoid entropy (energy that is expended in a system but does no useful work), the Mind stores these results so that the next time a similar situation is encountered, a conclusion can be retrieved locally rather than through what the Mind may consider an unnecessary communication with the Body and Spirit. The very energy that powers the communication between the Body, Spirit and Mind is the same energy that powers the Universe, heals the sick and brings you closer to your dreams. As such, your Mind is very efficient in the management of this precious field of energy.

Einstein's Blunder

The question becomes, "Why does the Mind care so greatly about conserving energy?"

One could surmise that the Mind is a wise manager of resources, but the answer is actually on a cosmic scale. Physicists once thought that, despite the Universe expanding, it would eventually collapse. The tipping point in our Universe's expansion was believed to be directly related to the finite maximum entropy of the observable Universe. In layman's terms, this theoretical model proposed that our Universe required more energy to fuel its expansion than the gravitational pull of all the matter in the Universe. Once gravity became greater than the expansive force, our Universe would contract more than it expands. Like a ball tossed in the air, everything would eventually fall back to center.

After that physicists believed that the Universe would not collapse, but rather it would continue to expand until it died. According to this theory, the average density of the Universe determines its ultimate fate. A Universe with too little matter would expand forever and its average density would eventually drop to zero. Conversely a Universe with too much matter, would one-day collapse under its own gravity (the 'Big Crunch'). One special value, critical density, determined the difference between our Universe maintaining a healthy expansion, collapsing in on itself or expanding out of control towards a cold, silent death.

As you can imagine, both of these understandings of our Universe are a bit unsettling. If the Universe continues to expand until its critical density either causes its collapse or its unchecked expansion leads to its ultimate death, then there is no hope. Either way, the Universe has no way to survive under either of these models. There are however three scenarios in which the Universe could survive forever:

1. **Steady State Universe** - the Universe expands at a constant rate but produces an occasional atom out of the void to maintain its critical density. A steady state Universe is infinite and doesn't require a Big Bang birth.

2. **Cyclical Universe** - where every Big Crunch is followed by another Big Bang.

3. **Parallel Universe** - where two or more Universes, linked with a spring-like attraction, periodically pass through one another. Every time they interact, incredible amounts of energy are released and both Universes fill with hot plasma - resulting in a new Big Bang. There is no Big Crunch nor Cold Death, as each Universe is constantly expanding. A trillion years or so after one Big Bang, when a Universe is practically empty, another Big Bang occurs and the stars and galaxies form once more.

Let's take a moment to think about what this means. In the Steady State Universe, the stability of the entire Universe is dependent on the introduction of additional atoms in synchronicity with the expansion of the Universe. If you think about the vastness of our Universe, you can begin to contemplate how incredible a feat this would be. Even more amazing would be the fact that we've never witnessed, detected or experienced these magical atoms being created. If they exist, what are they? Where are they? And how the heck are they introduced so elegantly in perfect synchronicity with the expansion of our Universe and in a way that we can't detect them?

Whereas the steady state Universe appears to be magical, the cyclical Universe is just plain sad. Even though the collapse of such a Universe is beyond our lifetime, it is unbelievably sad to think that one day our Universe, with everything contained, will one-day collapse in on itself.

However, the parallel state Universe is both promising and sustainable. Humanity has a future with a parallel state Universe as long as our Universe wins out upon coming in contact with another universe. The victor in this cosmic battle will be the Universe with more energy and better chance for survival. Time and time again nature demonstrates that evolution favors the survival of the fittest.

The Steady State Universe theory died out as physicists concluded that the incredible perfect conditions required for such a Universe, were improbable to result in a Universe that sustains life. According to the anthropic principle, this could be true because we're obviously here. Observations of the density of the Universe, provided through the discoveries of dozens of supernovae, finally put the nail in this theory's coffin. By being able to observe how fast the Universe was expanding billions of years ago with these supernovae, we were able to determine that the Universe's expansion isn't slowing but rather it is accelerating.

When Albert Einstein published his General Theory of Relativity in 1915, he believed the Universe was neither expanding nor contracting. But Einstein knew that the gravitational pull of Universe's mass would make the Universe contract. Therefore he proposed that empty space contains energy; a "cosmological constant," that counteracts gravity to maintain this balance. When Edwin Hubble discovered the expansion of our Universe in 1929, Einstein rejected his own cosmological constant and called it the greatest scientific blunder of his career.

If Einstein would've lived until 1998, he might not have been so hard on himself. Using the Hubble Space Telescope a team of astronomers, led by Adam Riess of the Space Telescope Science Institute (STScI), discovered that today's Universe is expanding at a much greater rate than it was over 10-billion years ago when these distant supernovae exploded. We now know that our Universe's expansion was slowing down until recently (measured in billions of years) when it began to accelerate its expansion.

With the accelerated expansion of our Universe, the parallel Universe model vaulted ahead as the most viable option and the limitless lifespan of our Universe once again became a possibility. Rather than collapsing when critical density is reached, our Universe could dynamically expand over and over again.

Much like consciousness, our Universe requires energy in order to expand. Said another way, when the average density of the Universe drops to zero, after billions of years of expansion without a proportionate amount of matter, the Universe proposed in the parallel state Universe model will require energy to fuel a new, dynamic Big Bang expansion. And with the possibility of a parallel state Universe, we can also consider that there are several Universes that periodically interact in this way. Instead of conceptualizing one giant Universe, consider everything in existence as a loaf of bread. That's right, the entirety of God's creation is a neatly packaged loaf of bread.

Now take this God bread and cut it into slices with each slice representing a Universe. String Theory postulates that each of these slices, which are called branes (as in membranes), is a Universe that exists outside of our reality. So instead of a dual Universe, we have many Universes that under normal conditions never interact with one another. But under extreme conditions, like the average density of one Universe dropping to zero, these Universes are pulled towards one another. When and where they touch, great amounts of energy would be pulled out of one Universe and a new expansion would result in the other.

Accordingly there must be enough energy available to sustain our Universe. Otherwise when our Universe interacts with another, the other Universe might be sucking energy out of ours instead of providing energy for our Universe's re-birth. Thus by avoiding unnecessary use of energy, which performs no useful work (from the Mind's perspective), the Mind helps the Universe maintain enough energy to fuel a rebirth in the future.

You may find it a bit strange to learn that the energy used, wasted or conserved by a human being has a relationship to the survival of the Universe. However, this is just the beginning of your awakening to the central role Humanity plays. You surely don't doubt how special human beings are in the Universe and you're about to learn that we're more connected than we ever realized. As you awaken to the critical and pivotal role we play in the Universe, the Mind's desire to avoid entropy will be but one of the many ways you make a difference.

By avoiding entropy, the Mind believes it is doing its part in keeping the Universe in homeostasis (maintenance of a constant internal environment in an organism) by not expending unnecessary energy in communicating with the Body and Spirit on a subject it believes it already knows the answer. In doing this, less energy is consumed and more is available.

Unfortunately this also means that the Mind, which operates in the domain of the past, often makes decisions without counsel of the Body and the Spirit. With the fear associated from the pain of a causal event stored firmly in our memories, the Mind repeats the cycle again each time a similar event is encountered. For example, the fear associated with an attack by a dog during one's childhood is stored. As a result, each time the adult comes in contact with a dog, the belief that dogs attack will bring back the stored fear. Thus the person, who goes their entire life fearing dogs, is actually limiting their life experience by repeating the cycle of retrieving an unnecessary conclusion.

Unnecessary conclusions cause our past to become our future.

One might come to this understanding and conclude that all memories are bad because they cause the Mind to make decisions without council of the Body or the Spirit. However, it is important to note that your Mind is not the enemy and it stores memories in order to conserve energy. You were designed to store the conclusions provided by the Spirit in order to not waste energy each time a similar situation is encountered. In this, there is an obligation to keep yourself in integrity by only keeping the conclusive memories that are necessary.

But how? How does one know which memories to keep and which ones to disregard? The answer is that you'll never know because *knowing* is the domain of the Mind and only the Spirit understands which memories are valid. What you're uncovering about yourself in this understanding is that wisdom has more to do with submission than it does with conquering. Leading a Spiritual existence isn't about knowing, but rather about letting go while continuing to expand the Universe. To do so, you'll need to bring your entire being into balance and trust in God. To do that, you'll need to fully understand the domain of your Spirit.

The Domain of the Spirit

For the future oriented Spirit, the Universe is a simple reality combining emotion and arousal. For the Mind, the feelings that give rise from the combination of these two states are interpreted as on and off, positive and negative, good and bad, or divine and evil. However, for the Spirit, this is simply the dimension of its reality (similar to how you don't associate positive or negative feelings about the Mind's dimensions of length, width, depth and time). And while this blissful simplicity is elemental in our Universe (e.g. waves vs. particles), the duality of this reality is insufficient for our Body's environmental survival and consequently a more complex decision making process is necessary (e.g. finding food and shelter requires logical thought).

None of this indicates a shortcoming of the Body, Spirit or Mind. Each of the three entities has their own roles to play and with those roles they each have specific capabilities. As we are the combination of the three, we can see how each is different and not a single one of our entities can exist in isolation. The three entities of being human are designed to work together as a team, with each contributing a valuable and beautiful aspect to the complete you.

As I go through my daily life, I often get focused on one entity without even knowing that I am. When I'm dealing with the problems of my life I'm entirely in my Mind, at the gym I'm all about my Body and while in prayer I'm entirely connected to my Spirit. But just as easily as we can move our consciousness into one entity or another, so too can we submit to a collective consciousness between the three. Each has a role to play in our lives and recognizing that role makes a Spiritual existence possible.

The roles of the Body, Spirit and Mind can be expressed as:

The Body is our Machine for Execution
The Spirit is our Decider/Master
The Mind is our Logic Processor

When unconscious, the Mind operates in isolation and receives out of tune feedback from its partners (Body and Spirit). When conscious, the three balance and operate in complete harmony. Once feedback is received from the Body and/or the Spirit, the Mind stores the result as a memory, depending on how convinced the Mind is that the conclusion is valid. How conclusive the Mind finds the feedback from the Body and Spirit is directly related to the strength of the connections between the three. Subsequently to get the most out of the Body, Spirit and Mind, one must strengthen the connective bonds between each.

You are not your Mind alone. You are the collective consciousness of your Body, Spirit and Mind. The un-evolved species is ignorant of the Body and the Spirit. The human being that awakens to the trinity is like a newborn baby. You must train yourself to think, react, listen and operate differently.

However the connections between each are asynchronous rather than synchronous (i.e. meaning they don't operate in a linear, cause and effect, manner). The hard-wired connection between each operates outside the boundaries of the four dimensions of our Mind (length, width, depth and time).

As such, the logical (and illogical) thoughts of our Mind are passed to our Body which tests them against its five sensual dimensions and the results are passed to the Spirit. In return, the Spirit communicates the feedback (i.e. conclusion) to the Mind in the form of feelings (e.g. from pleasure to displeasure and their countless deviations as well as a degree of arousal). What this means is that your Spirit is able to guide *you* on matters that haven't occurred yet as well as what is happening right now. But you must first learn to trust your own Spirit. You've heard of trusting your instincts and this is the same thing.

Let's pause for a moment to take this in. Thus far we've distinguished human beings as the combination of the Body, Spirit and Mind. Through the eleven dimensions, these three entities communicate with one another to work as a team. Understandably this is a big change in your understanding of not only the human race but also of yourself. As both the active participant and passive observer of the human being that is *you*, this flow of information has thus far been jumbled into a singularity of consciousness. You aren't aware of your Mind communicating through the Body and Spirit to make decisions, because the entire process happens whether you're conscious of it or not. However, all three of your entities can work as a team despite your present inability to distinguish the flow of information between them.

Through sensations, feelings and thoughts you are able to work through any challenge. In the end, your Mind decides what to do and stores the result as a conclusive memory so that the next time a similar situation is encountered the decision can be retrieved locally rather than through this process. Therefore when you *feel* a certain way, recognize that the feeling is your Spirit actively communicating with you in order to influence your Mind to act.

The Language of Connecting Bonds

Like every human being ever born, each entity has both a parent and a child. These paternal relationships carry with them both guidance and honor. We think of the relationships between our entities as paternal in order to better understand how they relate to one another, which one calls the shots and why we act the way we do sometimes. Through this relatedness, we can appreciate how we struggle in certain situations and have empathy for ourselves when one of our entities plays too large of a role in our lives.

Like different cultures around the world, your three entities speak different languages and this is the language of their dimensions. As such, each parent speaks to its child in its own language. The Body speaks to the Spirit via the sensual dimensions. For example, your Body detects flavor as a method for determining what you should eat. Nutritious food has more flavor than non-nutritious food and this sensation enables the Body to quickly determine what to eat.

With zero latency, the Body communicates a flavorful sensation to the Spirit and subsequently an emotional response is sent to the Mind. If the food is tasty, you'll likely receive the emotion of contentment with a mild arousal state. However, if the food is awful, you'll experience the Spirit sending you a much more abrupt feeling. You don't notice the messages sent between the Body, Spirit and Mind because the entire experience is fused into a singular state of consciousness. Behind this singularity, there is a myriad of communications going back and forth.

If you stop and think about this it isn't all that surprising. Each entity was designed for a specific and beautiful purpose. Your Body has a different job to do than your Mind and therefore it is logical that it would have its own form of communication. Furthermore, this ensures that each entity avoids mistaking a communication as coming from the wrong entity. In the architecture of life, there is no room for miscommunications.

Communications normally flow in one direction and pass through the other two entities before returning to the source. By completing the circuit, this lets the originating entity know that the message was received by the other two entities. Obviously if the message doesn't complete the circuit, then one of the entities didn't receive the message.

There are many reasons why a message wouldn't complete the circuit ranging from noise to an unconscious entity. One of the simplest examples of communications breaking down is overeating. The Body sends the sensation of being full but the message doesn't complete and we continue eating. There are many mental reasons why we overeat, but the simple fact remains that the Body told us to stop eating but we ignored the instruction.

A more serious and chronic problem exists with unconscious entities. When an entity becomes unconscious, the entire being suffers and the Mind takes over. Throughout the ages we see the most common disconnection occurring with the Spirit. Even devoutly religious people are often disconnected from their Spirit. As a result, they go through life guided by their Minds, driven by their Minds' aspirations and helpless to listen to anything or anyone that their Minds don't agree with. Despite love and compassion being the focus of religious intent, all too many people are caught up in the domain of logic and doctrine preferred by the Mind.

Card 6: Compassion: sympathetic pity and concern for the sufferings or misfortunes of others.

Religion is not the enemy of the Spirit, for the purpose of religion is to focus Humanity on God. Furthermore pursuing a relationship with God through organized religion is not removing yourself from a connection to your Spirit. Quite the contrary, as all energy spent praising God intensifies the connection to one's Spirit (even if that is not your intent). So why then are so many religious people disconnected from their Spirit?

You may find the answer in yoga. Originating from the ancient language of Sanskrit, 'yoga' simply means *union or balance of Body, Spirit, and Mind.* It is in this balance between the three entities that a true union with God is possible. In our love for God, we may find ourselves pursuing a Spirit-only approach to life. However, life was designed to evolve with a Body, Spirit and Mind. To live entirely within the consciousness of any one of these is to live a life unfulfilled.

Thus one can be entirely devoted to their religion and still be disconnected from God. This is not to say that all religious people are disconnected from God because they're not conscious of their unbalanced ways. There is more than one way to connect with God and clearly most of Humanity finds religion a method that works for them. But to sustain a connection with God and to evolve to a Spiritual existence, one must achieve balance between their Body, Spirit and Mind. To do this, one must invest in their entities, become aware of their entities and learn to speak their language.

Let's pause for a moment and contemplate what is meant by "union with God." Some may interpret this to mean *equal to God* but this is not the intent. Imagine in your Mind the initial creation of life by God. Regardless of your religious beliefs, understand that God created life and that necessitates that life didn't exist prior to God creating life. But even before God created life, God created the Universe and everything that is contained within the Universe. If you take this line of thinking far enough you will be left with God and nothing. For God is the Creator and thus everything is derived from God. And therefore we are part of God because we (and everything else) were made from God.

Figure 4: The Creation of Adam by Michelangelo. It illustrates the Biblical story from the Book of Genesis in which God the Father breathes life into Adam, the first man.

Now before you start thinking that this means that this would imply that we are God, understand that a part can never be equal to a whole. And thus man can never be God nor can man ever be equal to God. But this does mean that God is part of us and we are part of God, for we are made from God. To achieve balance, in order to come into union with God, is a goal that is intended to bring you to a true relationship with God in which your God given purpose is revealed.

To come into balance, one must learn the languages employed by the Body, Spirit and Mind. Knowing the language, employed in a connective bond between two entities, is essential for investing in each entity. Imagine attending a lecture in a language you didn't understand. How much would you get out of the transfer of knowledge compared to the other people at the lecture that understood the speaker's language? So too must you speak to an entity in the language of its parent.

You're well trained in communicating through sensations, feelings, and thoughts as you've been using these communication tools your entire life. Of all the methods of communicating, be particularly mindful of thoughts for they come from within the domain of the Mind. In isolation, the Mind fails to recognize the partnership it has with the Spirit and the Body. Without a connection amongst the three, the Mind will forget its place and dominate your life (as it probably has for most of your life).

"We are what our thoughts have made us; so take care about what you think. Words are secondary. Thoughts live; they travel far."
Swami Vivekananda

The first step is to recognize which language to use based on which entity you're communicating with:

To speak to the Body, communicate via thoughts from the Mind.
To speak to the Spirit, communicate via sensations from the Body.
To speak to the Mind, communicate via feelings from the Spirit.

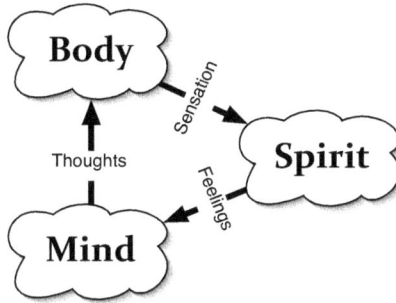

Although you've been using these communication tools since your birth, you may find using them in isolation to be difficult at first. Take it slow, remember the dimensions of each entity, and you'll soon find the communication flowing effortlessly. For example, to communicate with the Spirit we must do so via sensations. Of the five senses, there are two that express as well as receive energy and communicate through their respective parts of the body:

Skin (mainly your hands): touch
Mouth: voice

To communicate with the Spirit, concentrate on energy flowing through your hands and mouth. The beauty of your three entities is that they are always listening for these communications. It isn't necessary to get the Spirit's attention. Simply begin by expressing yourself through these two dimensions. You can write, sculpt, dance or journal with your hands. You can talk, hum, sing, chant or even scream with your mouth. Remember that the Spirit is always listening and has been listening your entire life. Therefore don't worry about getting the communication right, but rather let it flow freely. The instant that the communication leaves your Body it is received by the Spirit.

The timelessness of communication within human beings has even been measured. In 1995, three scientists working for the Institute of HeartMath conducted experiments that measured the physiological results of positive and negative emotion. In their study, salivary IgA (antibodies in your saliva), heart rate and mood were measured in thirty individuals before and after experiencing the emotional states of care/compassion and anger/frustration. When the participants experienced care and compassion their salivary IgA increased (i.e. more antibodies) and when they experienced anger and frustration their salivary IgA decreased (i.e. fewer antibodies). (Rein, Atkinson and McCraty 1995)

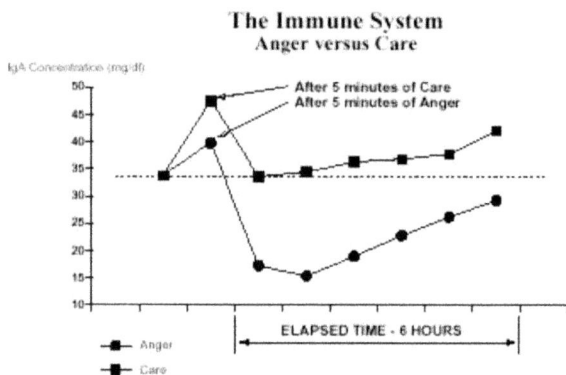

The Immune System
Anger versus Care

IgA Concentration (mg/dl)

After 5 minutes of Care
After 5 minutes of Anger

ELAPSED TIME - 6 HOURS

Anger
Care

Figure 5: This graph shows the impact of one 5-minute episode of recalled anger on the immune antibody IgA over a 6-hour period. The initial slight increase in IgA was followed by a dramatic drop that persisted for six hours. When the subjects used the Freeze-Frame technique and focused on feeling sincere care for five minutes there was a significant increase in IgA, which returned to baseline an hour later and then slowly increased throughout the rest of the day. (Rein, Atkinson and McCraty 1995)

Two years before this study was published, Cleve Backster performed experiments to determine the latency in communication between emotional experience and the triggered response in DNA. In the experiment, DNA extracted from the subject's mouth was isolated and removed to a separate chamber in the same building. The subject was subsequently shown a series of videos to elicit a range of different emotional states. In the other room, the DNA was measured for any changes in electrical response.

Much to Backster's surprise, not only did the DNA show an electrical response coinciding with the subject's emotional state, but the amount of time that it took for the DNA reaction was measured as zero time. Despite the DNA being physically removed from the host, the reaction to emotional stimuli was instantaneous.

Backster went on to test this zero latency reaction using the atomic clock in Colorado over a 350-mile separation between subjects and their DNA:

> Distance seemed to impose no limitations to communication between cells. For example, Dr. Brian O'Leary, a NASA scientist-astronaut, conducted successful experiments with Cleve both in the laboratory and over distances of 350 miles away using his own donated white blood cells. (Cleve Backster 2003)[6]

---

[6] Cleve Backster's research has been replicated, but others have failed in their attempts and disparage his work. *Mythbusters Episode 61, 2006*

The Interpretation of the Mind

Every message, regardless of source and recipient, is ultimately interpreted and subject to the experience, bias and completeness of the Mind. For this reason, forget about getting it right, being right and not being wrong. Know that, because your Mind is biased, that you will regularly not get it right.

Your Mind is not capable, on its own, to determine what is truth and what is not truth. Of course, logically the Mind will come up with very impressive arguments to defend that it (you) is right. In your Mind, you're rarely wrong but those around you (ranging from the driver that cut you off on the freeway to your spouse) are not as *right* as you are. Your Mind may concede that you're human and thus capable of being wrong once in a while. In general, we human beings go through life believing that we're right until we're proven wrong. And, with this approach, we tend not to give too many people license to prove us wrong.

Without a true partnership amongst the Body, Spirit and Mind this is impossible to overcome. As soon as you allow yourself to be wrong, your Mind will subsequently take over and justify you being right in the next controversial situation. Thus recognize that, despite your convictions, you're probably not entirely right about everything.

So too recognize that other human beings aren't entirely right either. Despite their credentials, experience or intentions, no member of the human race is capable of being right all of the time. Thus the challenge is how to determine what is correct and what is not through the perception of your biased Mind. As there is no other way to rationally *think*, to determine truth one must give up "being right" and listen for messages from the Spirit. Through a Spiritual existence, we can step away from our ego biased Mind to find truth.

To Which an Entity Communicates It Also Governs

The Mind governs the Body, as is evident by your Body taking direction from the Mind. Your Body will execute whatever action your Mind commands it to undertake. However, the inverse is not true. The Mind is more than capable of ignoring the Body when it believes that it is in the best interest of the Body to listen to the Mind.

For example, your Body may indicate that it is tired, sore or lazy but your Mind can overrule your Body and instruct it to exercise anyway.

Please try to separate the concept of your Mind from the organ we call the brain. Your Body, Spirit and Mind are intimately interconnected and share equally with one another. We can demonstrate the role that the brain plays in the formation of thoughts and, in this, the brain is surely a tool shared by both the Body and Mind. However, the modern day belief that our Minds are a manifestation of our brains simply reduces human beings to a collection of organs. You know that you're more than the sum of your parts. So give yourself a little more credit and refrain from reducing every sensation, feeling and thought as coming from your nervous system.

As the Spirit communicates to the Mind, so too is the Mind governed by the Spirit. The power of emotions are so strong that the Mind is helpless to resist the temptations of pleasure and wants nothing more than to avoid pain. Conversely the inverse is not true as the Spirit cares little for the logical thoughts of the Mind as it operates in the reality of emotion and arousal. Remember that the Spirit exists in the domain of, 'We are.' The logical and individualistic concerns of the Mind are of no concern to the Spirit. The Mind wonders, "Why?" but the Spirit accepts things as simply being one way or another.

Paradoxically, the Spirit is governed by the Body. Like a child from a parent, the Spirit's connection to our world is only made possible by the Body. The Spirit knows that in order for there to be a 'We are' there must first be a 'Here and Now.' Thus, despite the aspirations of the Spirit to connect to the collective consciousness of Humanity, it will always listen to and be governed by the Body.

Unfortunately, most people are unconscious to their human potential and fail to listen to the limitless wisdom being communicated to them by the Spirit each and every day. The messages are coming, but they're not in the language of our Mind. The Spirit receives input from the Body and communicates via feelings to the Mind. However, as the Spirit isn't limited by the same boundaries and connections of the Body and Mind, it is also transmitting messages from the Universe via the unlimited connections of other conscious beings.

When you become fully conscious, your Spirit taps into the unlimited potential of the Universe and connects you with others that share your passions. New people come unannounced into your life and seemingly coincidental events bring you ever closer to your hopes and dreams.

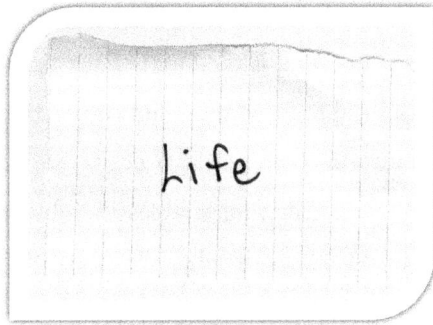

Card 7: Life: the period between the birth and death of a living thing, esp. a human being.

The hardest part of becoming conscious is tuning into your Spirit and filtering out the chatter. Moreover, the more intelligent you are, the harder this becomes because you've developed a strong intellect that has served you well in figuring out so many of life's challenges. As a result, letting go and trusting your own Spirit and refraining from letting your Mind take over is all the more difficult. Just know that a Spiritual existence isn't devoid of the Mind, but rather a partnership.

Each entity takes what it needs from its communicator (e.g. The Mind takes what it needs as governed by the Spirit) and discards the rest. As a result, each entity is able to filter a tremendous amount of information and selectively use what it needs to accomplish the task at hand.

The inverse of this is true as well. Because there is more information available from the communicator than is required, it is also true that there is more information available to you. Consequently one of the greatest enablers of "tapping into the source," is simply listening with your Body, Spirit and Mind (more than just the single dimension of listening with your ears).

Said another way, each entity has a parent/child relationship with the entity it governs. The Mind is the child of the Spirit, the Body is the child of the Mind and the Spirit is the child of the Body. Through this pattern of communication, each parental entity provides its child with what is needed and more. Filtering enables the ability to focus on the task at hand and so too much of what we need to know has already been given to us despite the fact that we discarded it. Being able to listen fully requires that we re-learn these languages so that we can discern the wisdom that is being given to us each and every day.

Each entity expresses itself to its child by means of the dimensions of the parent:

> The Body expresses itself to the Spirit via the Body's five sensual dimensions of seeing, hearing, tasting, smelling and feeling (touch).

> The Spirit expresses itself to the Mind via the Spirit's two emotive dimensions of emotion and arousal.

> The Mind expresses itself to the Body via the Mind's four mental dimensions of length, width, depth and time (the reality you've experienced your entire life). This is why, no one can experience the voice in your head, even though they can hear words come from your mouth.

In order to listen for the messages coming to you, it is first necessary to learn to listen via all of the dimensions governed by the Body, Spirit and Mind. If you're waiting for words to be heard or visions to come to you, then you're limiting your listening to only two of the eleven dimensions. To listen to the Spirit, you must pay close attention to your feelings. In a conscious state, your feelings can be trusted and interpreted as messages from your Spirit.

Much like your Body, Spirit and Mind, your consciousness doesn't exist as a constant state. Simply stated, your consciousness is continually expanding and contracting in accordance with how strong each entity is and the strength of the bonds between them. Thus one is not *conscious* or *unconscious,* but rather continually changing one's state of consciousness.

What this means is that one's consciousness, by which great things are possible, must be continually strengthened and protected from decay. One does not attain a state of consciousness and remain there for eternity, but instead one must feed the Body, Spirit and Mind, as well as the connecting bonds between them, to continually expand and maintain a state of consciousness.

Investing in your Body, Spirit and Mind is paramount to your success and happiness. Every action you take and every action you fail to take impacts the expanse of your consciousness. Luckily for you (and me), the blueprint for expanding one's consciousness is inherently part of our being.

To tap into this genetic blueprint for consciousness, one need only invest energy into one's Body, Spirit and Mind. Bringing the three into harmony expands one's consciousness exponentially (via the connections made possible through the boundlessness of the Spirit) and reciprocally brings more energy into our lives.

Our investment comes by way of the activities that nurture each entity:

Body

- O Healthy Diet
- O Exercise
- O Movement
- O Eliminating Toxins

Spirit

- O Meditation
- O Sharing
- O Helping Others
- O Forgiving
- O Praying
- O Loving

Mind

- O Creating Original Ideas
- O Expanding Awareness
- O New and Different Experiences
- O Mental Stimulation
- O Communicating and Interacting with Others
- O Education

To determine if an activity is an appropriate or effective investment to make, ask yourself if the activity will quiet or bring peace to the entity it communicates with and governs. In real terms, if an investment activity in the Spirit brings peace to the Mind, then you can conclude that the activity is useful.

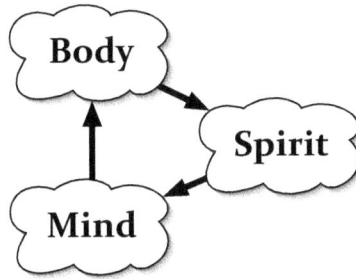

For example:

- Exercise nurtures the Body and causes the Spirit to send the emotion of pleasure (endorphins are generated during exercise) and thus is a worthwhile investment to make in the Body (the Body governs the Spirit). [7]

- Meditation quiets the Mind and thus meditation is a worthwhile investment to make in the Spirit (the Spirit governs the Mind).

- Learning nurtures the Mind and brings peace to the Body. For example, many people experience reprieve from their pain in a learning activity (e.g. reading a book) and thus is a worthwhile investment to make in the Mind (the Mind governs the Body).

When You Learn, You're Absorbing the Collective Consciousness of the Universe.

When you're intent on becoming more conscious and living a Spiritual existence these teachings are easier to apply. But when life gets tough, it is more difficult to see how a Spiritual, conscious existence can

---

[7] This brings new meaning to the phrase, "No pain, no gain" as if you haven't been investing in your Body you may experience post exercise pain before you experience this pleasure.

solve the problem at hand. But these are precisely the moments that matter the most for your growth.

All too often when the going gets tough, we push the Body and the Spirit aside to let the Mind take over. It is as if we're saying, "When times are good, I'll put my trust in God but right now I've got a serious problem that I only trust my Mind to handle." As you are currently on a path to enlightenment (as evident by your reading this book), you can see the absurdity of not trusting your Body, Spirit and Mind at the moments in your life when you need them most.

However upon experiencing your next life crisis, you too will want an immediate solution and be tempted to turn everything over to your Mind. In these moments, focus on investing in each of your entities and listen for guidance from your Spirit. As a complex human being, you will desire a much more sophisticated answer to your problems than investing in your Body, Spirit and Mind. However, when you're being challenged, this is precisely the best course of action because through the harmonization of the Body, Spirit and Mind you will be open to and able to hear the voice of God. Most importantly, when the answer comes act on it with all your might. Otherwise you'll miss out on the solution to your problem.

Everything that you hear, read, smell, taste and feel is ultimately interpreted by the Mind. As such, it is important to note that the Mind (our logic processor as interpreted by emotional feedback) is the tool by which you will experience the results of your investment in the Body, Spirit or Mind.

By learning to listen to the symphony of feelings being transmitted by the Spirit, you will become *in tune* with the Universe. Whereas today you may be missing many of the messages that are being communicated, when it tune you'll receive and understand these messages because you'll be listening via the dimensions of your Spirit. Becoming in tune requires continual effort and investment through strengthening the health and completeness of your Body, Spirit and Mind.

In addition to investing in any one of the single entities, you can also invest directly in the connective bond between any two entities through activities that nurture both entities.

For example:

O   Performing Yoga or Tai Chi engages and nurtures both the Body and the Spirit.

O   Practicing a sport that requires strategy and physical effort engages and nurtures both the Body and the Mind.

O   Creating a work of art engages and nurtures the Mind and the Spirit.

Lessening the Grip of the Mind

As introduced earlier, you were born with the Mind online and in charge. The Mind takes insuring your survival very seriously and isn't going to initially be in favor of granting a balance of power over to the Body and Spirit. Even though this is how you were designed to operate, the Mind is inherently skeptical. As such, your path to conscious enlightenment will be rich with complaints, objections and skepticism from your Mind.

The Mind will ensure your survival even if it has to lie to you. Have you ever wronged someone and subsequently justified your behavior via a conversation in your head?

Your Mind is not the enemy and the goal is not to eliminate the voice in your head. Rather the goal is to strengthen the bonds between the Body, Spirit and Mind, so your Mind has two equal partners to govern your life. This begs the question, "Who am I? Am I my Body, Spirit or Mind? Am I one of them or all three combined?"

You are the Spirit as Expressed Through Your Body and Mind

Your Body, Spirit and Mind have always been communicating with one another, but if you've been managing your life through the Mind, the bonds between the three may be atrophied. You can never sever the connective bonds between any two entities, but without use, they can become extremely weakened.

With your Mind being in control of *you*, the process of achieving harmony between the Body, Spirit and Mind is a challenge. Unless you're reading this as a young child, you've got years of *programming* that has established a rigid set of conclusive memories in your Mind. These mental conclusions have varying degrees of rigidity that might be difficult to dislodge.

As a result, most people live their lives according to a common understanding even though they've never considered any alternatives. What that understanding is varies by group and may consist of behavior patterns that are never discussed and consistently followed. Over time these understandings become norms and are passed along to future generations. The cycle repeats itself until someone breaks free of the norm and asks, "Why do I believe this?"

Card 8: Free: not under the control or in the power of another.

Dislodging unnecessary conclusive memories is key because, with these mental conclusions stored within you, the Mind believes it is unnecessary to seek counsel with the Body and Spirit. In your Mind's opinion, *'We've already dealt with this situation before and don't need any input from the Body and Spirit.'* However, without input from the Body and the Spirit, you are doomed to make the same mistakes over and over again. Furthermore, the fears that hold you back in life will continue to have a grip on your ability to find happiness with your past conclusive memories guiding your future.

Luckily for you (and me), the only person capable and qualified to determine which conclusive memories need to be dislodged is you. There is no guru or adviser who is more qualified to decide which to keep and which to trash than you. We're not accustom to trusting ourselves to make such decisions and we usually look to the outside for others (presumably those that are smarter and more experienced than ourselves) to tell us what to do.

However, as soon as one of those gurus challenges one of your ideologies or principles, you (or rather your Mind) will reject the guru. And thus don't put your trust in another but instead trust thyself.

In trusting yourself, be careful not to blindly trust the Mind. Remember that the Mind will lie to you, in order to ensure your survival. Like a protective dog that barks at everyone entering your home, the Mind is protective to a fault. As the communicator to the Mind is the Spirit, invest in activities that nurture the Spirit in order to dislodge the unnecessary conclusive memories held by your Mind.

It is important to recognize that your Mind itself cannot determine which conclusive memories to ignore. After all, it is the Mind that stored them in your memory in the first place. Thus one can't *think* their way through removing unnecessary memories, but rather can submit to their Spirit's counsel. By doing so, your unnecessary memories will slowly erode and become distant recollections of your former self. But to do so requires providing your Spirit with a means to fully express itself.

There is no definitive list of activities that dislodge unnecessary or untrue memories via the expression of the Spirit but these are a good start:

dreaming - particularly daydreaming;

communicating - being in communication with others in your life and those that you regularly are not in communication;

sharing - giving away what is precious or makes you happy;

forgiving - probably one of the most powerful human contributions and one that we struggle with the most;

singing - for so many of us, we really only sang our hearts out as children and singing is precisely how we can express ourselves the most;

dancing - forget the lessons and simply let your body flow to the rhythm of your favorite music;

crying - controlling emotion is sometimes such a habit that getting that first tear to roll down your cheek is often a challenge for fear that the floodgates will open;

laughing - such a simple pleasure and one that is so important;

sexual pleasure[8] - don't ignore this elemental method for unifying the Body, Spirit and Mind with someone you love.

What all of these have in common is an element of expressing one's self fully and letting go. Each brings with it a state of Nirvana (when the Body, Spirit and Mind unite in harmony). Each of these also is rigidly guarded by the Mind and therefore are activities that the Mind is not likely to let you do freely.

When is the last time you fully expressed yourself without restraint in any of these activities without judging yourself?

---

[8] Yes, I know that calling out sexual pleasure as a healthy activity for the Spirit will make many of you uneasy. Try and recognize that there isn't a single thing about you that isn't perfect and that God designed you with a sexual nature for a reason. To deny that part of you would be un-human.

Your Practice

A. Distinguish Self Judgment

Think back to the last time you did any of the activities listed at the end of this chapter and write down how you judged yourself afterwards:

1. _____ - _____.

2. _____ - _____.

3. _____ - _____.

4. _____ - _____.

5. _____ - _____.

6. _____ - _____.

7. _____ - _____.

8. _____ - _____.

9. _____ - _____.

10. _____ - _____.

B. Distinguish Justification

Think back to the last three fights you've had with a colleague, friend or family member and write down why you were right and they were wrong. Then flip the scenario and imagine an alternative to your mental conclusion in which you could have been wrong and they were right:

Conflict	Why You Were *Right*	Why They Were *Wrong*
A.		
B.		
C.		

Conflict	Why You Were Wrong	Why They Were Right
A.		
B.		
C.		

C. Daily & Weekly Strengthening Activities

List an activity that you would enjoy doing on a *daily* basis for your Body, Spirit and Mind:

1. Body: _____

2. Spirit: _____

3. Mind: _____

List a more intensive activity that you could do on a *weekly* basis for your Body, Spirit and Mind:

1. Body: _____

2. Spirit: _____

3. Mind: _____

D. Connective Bond Strengthening Activities

List as many activities you can think of that would strengthen the connective bonds between two entities:

1. Body :: Mind _____

2. Mind :: Spirit _____

3. Spirit :: Body _____

E. Document Spiritual Communication

Circle your preferred method for communicating with your Spirit via your hands/skin, list the last five activities you engaged in using these methods and think about how the energy that was created improved your life or others:

Preferred Method for Expressing Energy via Your Hands:

WRITING	SCULPTING	PAINTING	DOODLING
DRAWING	DANCING	MASSAGING	SIGNING
JOURNALING	SKETCHING	SEWING	COOKING

OTHER(S)

_____

Five last activities using these methods and the benefits to myself/others:

1. _____ - _____

2. _____ - _____

3. _____ - _____

4. _____ - _____

5. _____ - _____

F. Unnecessary Conclusions

Write down your top 3 fears, your earliest memory of experiencing each fear and how these fears have limited your life experience?

Fear #1:	Earliest Memory:
How has this fear limited your life experience?	

Fear #2:	Earliest Memory:
How has this fear limited your life experience?	

Fear #3:	Earliest Memory:
How has this fear limited your life experience?	

5

NIRVANA

We are all individuals with unique life experiences. Some of us are more conscious than others and each of us has shortcomings in our Body, Spirit and Mind. Consequently, the path to enlightenment is a path governed by our own individual situation. What your path to expanded consciousness requires is different than what someone else needs.

Before considering your own path to consciousness, take a moment to consider how unique you are amongst the rest of the human race. You're quite a bit different than everyone else and, with that, know that you are special. If God wanted an army of duplicates, He certainly would've made us that way. But you were born unique and, in that uniqueness, you are eloquently different in the most wonderful way. And with that uniqueness comes your distinct and personal path to consciousness.

In your path to consciousness, you can imagine that you will become more than you are today. For example, your Mind has a certain amount of knowledge, wisdom and understanding that has been accumulated throughout your life. By comparing yourself today to where you started out in life, you can see that you are *more complete* than when you began. So too, if your Mind continues to grow, you will be even more complete in the future than you are today. As such, your Mind has a potential completeness in terms of where you started and where you are capable of getting.

We refer to this most complete potential as *integrity* because this is a state of being whole and undivided. Thus, instead of thinking of integrity as a moral fortitude, we're referring to integrity as a representation of our most complete potential. By looking at ourselves in terms of completeness, we can better understand our lives through an assessment of the integrity of our Body, Spirit and Mind. In doing so, we're able to better understand where we are in life and where our path to consciousness can take us.

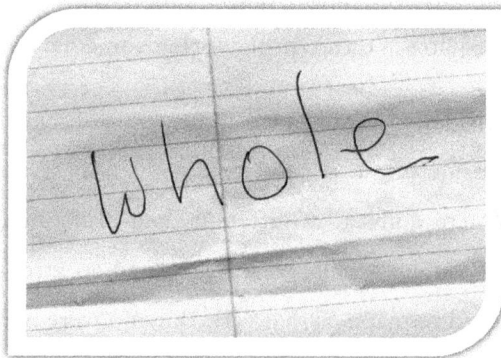

Card 9: Whole: all of something.

To determine where your path to consciousness needs to begin, consider first how a typical *unconscious* person might progress through life:

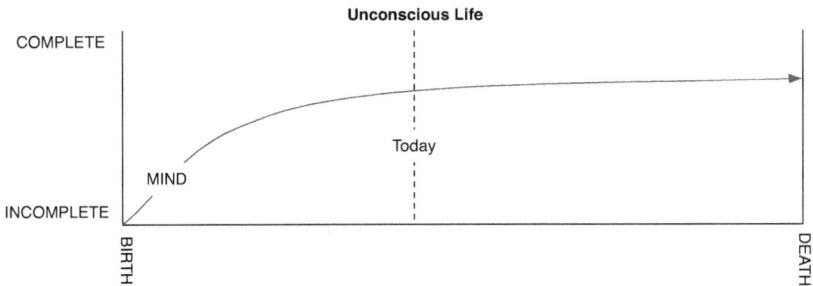

Unconscious Life

COMPLETE

Today

MIND

INCOMPLETE

BIRTH

DEATH

Figure 6: As depicted across the time line of one's life progressing from one's birth to death, this chart depicts the "completeness" or "integrity" potential over time of the Mind.

Although it is online and in charge, the Mind in our example starts at a very incomplete state (at the bottom of the chart). Without the ability to communicate through language and devoid of practical (real life) experience, this Mind started in its most incomplete state and progressed to become more and more complete as it accumulated information, experience and knowledge.

Keep in mind that this is an example of how an unconscious person would enter into the world and progress. What we're attempting to understand here is not the cognitive progression of a newborn, but rather the degree of completeness or integrity of the Mind at birth and the subsequent progression through life. We all start out as babies, but our mental progression is far from standardized. Some people struggle through adolescent academics and yet hit their stride later in life. Others show amazing progress as children, but fail to continue their intellectual progress through life. By way of example, we're following the progression of an unconscious individual who is starting out at an entirely incomplete state.

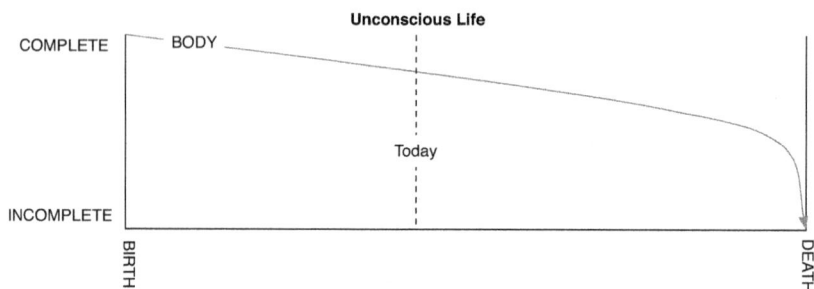

Figure 7: In our example, this person's Body began at the most complete state and progressed over time until death.

Conversely, the Body in our example is starting in its most complete state. Freshly born into the world, most babies have yet to meet their first cold, experience injury or have any health complications. When we think of a Body in terms of being complete, we tend to visualize an adult athletic physique. In relation to integrity, we should instead look internally beyond the exterior physique and seek a true definition of health. In this context, our example is demonstrating how the individual experienced their healthiest state on the day they were born. However, over time, their health deteriorated as their cells broke down and lost the natural ability to recover from illness and disease.

The completeness (health) of our bodies fluctuates over time, but doesn't have to become less healthy as we age. And as you'll soon understand, the completeness of your Body has a relationship to your Spirit and Mind.

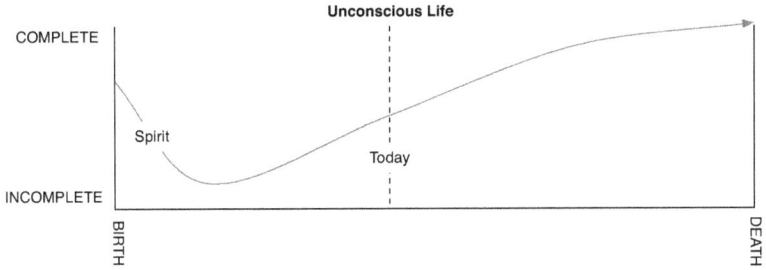

Figure 8: Without any guidance to nurture their Spirit, the person in our example fell away from completeness during their youth but refocused their energies during the middle years of their life and continued in their Spirituality until death.

The Spirit in our example is taking an all-together different path. Starting at a highly, but not entirely complete state of integrity, the Spirit experienced a rapid decline as mainstream society put little to no value into growing and nurturing the person's Spirit. The seemingly vastness of Spirit in a young child quickly declined as the individual entered their teenage years.

When viewed in isolation, there doesn't appear to be any correlation between the completeness of our Body, Spirit and Mind. But when viewed in relation to one another, we can begin to see where we've got chaos going on in our lives. Whereas one entity is ascending, another is descending. And when they collide, we experience conflict in our lives.

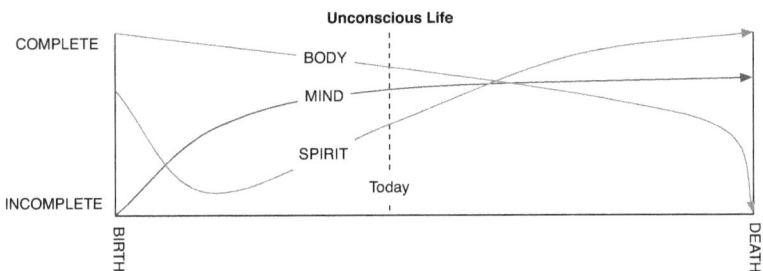

Figure 9: When viewed together, we can see what is going on in our lives in terms of where our Body, Spirit and Mind is at. More importantly, we can see where we're going if we don't change.

Whenever two or more of your entities cross in opposition, there is a great release of energy that we experience as upheaval and change. For example, during puberty the Mind is rapidly growing and the Spirit is rapidly declining. When these two entities cross, there is great upheaval in the teenager's life (ask any parent during this period of time).

In the late twenties and early thirties, Spiritual growth accelerates as is evident in the return of young families to church and synagogue services (the sea of grey hair in the pews is spotted with dark haired patches of young families). Later in life, when the Mind's growth is slowing and the Spirit is in rapid growth mode, many people in their mid-life are seeking Spiritual answers and coincidentally this is when great upheaval occurs in many people's lives (e.g. mid life crisis, divorce, long term relationships dissolve, etc.).

Without an awareness of the relationship between our Body, Spirit and Mind, we assign meaning to these events in order to make sense out of the chaos unfolding in our lives. We tell ourselves that we feel lost, in need of a change or believe that we have bad luck. In reality, we're simply unconscious to the path we're on and thus hopeless to course correct.

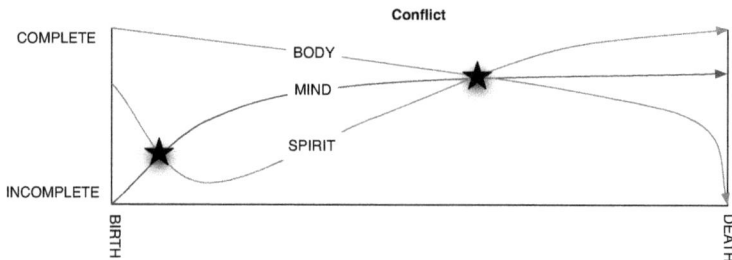

Figure 10: When two or more entities cross, a release of energy occurs. When the crossing entities are oppositional, we experience conflict in our lives. Each black star represents a crisis point caused by two oppositional entities.

There are several times in our lives when the conflict we're experiencing is a result of two or more of our entities opposing one another. Only because we're often not present to the growth and completeness of our three entities, do we not notice the relational effect of one entity upon another.

When two or more oppositional entities cross in one's life there is great chaos, pain and negativity. In time, order is restored and stability returns. However without continual investment in the Body, Spirit and Mind, the unconscious being will encounter great moments of pain in their life every time two or more entities cross. Thus it is critical that you regularly invest in your Body, Spirit and Mind to maintain each on a path to becoming more, not less, complete.

If you think about it, this isn't that much of a departure from how you currently experience conflict in your life. When you're sick, you're probably not that much fun to be around. This may seem obvious in reference to having a full-blown flu or being hospitalized, but even less invasive illnesses can cause you to be cranky, short tempered and not as tolerant as usual. Picture yourself not feeling well in line at the grocery store picking up some chicken soup before you go home to crawl into bed. As you approach the checkout counter, the checker is beaming with happiness and glee. As much as you would like to be cheery, you're not feeling well and her unusually peppy nature seems to make your shopping trip all the more difficult. She wants to brighten your day and you want to crawl under a rock to sleep. Naturally there is a tension between the two of you as one is ascending and the other is descending.

After you walk out of the store the checker thinks to herself, "Wow, that person was not very nice." However if she knew you were sick, she would instead have compassion for you rather than angst. And this is precisely the difference between being conscious and unconscious. When you understand where your entities are in terms of growth, you can both anticipate conflict in your life and better understand when ugliness lands on your doorstep. Thus our desire to become more complete requires that we both understand where we are today and what we need to do in order to become more complete.

To become more complete, an entity must be in forward ascension. There are two components to this term that are important to consider:

1. **Forward** - meaning moving forward in time. As the Body and Mind are constrained by the dimension of time, forward ascension, propels an entity into greater integrity in the future, as opposed to reverse ascension, which would propel an entity into greater integrity in the past.

2. **Ascension** - meaning rising towards becoming more, not less, complete.

In combination, this term conveys the movement of an entity towards completion in the future. Implied in this definition is the concept of a sustained investment to keep the entity in motion. Without investment, or rather energy, the entity will descend rather than ascend. With time being constant, a lack of investment in any one of your entities will cause it to fall towards a state of being less complete. For example, a body at rest becomes less complete as is evident in the development of bedsores on immobile hospital patients.

Let's pause here for a moment to take in what we've just learned. Rather than a brain attached to a dumb carcass, you are the collective consciousness of your Body, Spirit and Mind. Each of these parts of you has an intelligence and ability to grow or be neglected. By becoming conscious of the integrity potential of each entity, you can better understand your life in terms of where you are now and where you're going. By investing in the growth of your Body, Spirit and Mind, you can change your destiny towards completeness rather the path that you were following.

"Wait a second," you ask yourself. "I actually have to do something?"

I concur that it would be much easier to approach a Swami after he had meditated in a cave for ten years and simply ask him to tell you how to become enlightened. In this magical transformation, he would tell you the secrets he had discovered and upon gaining this Divine knowledge you would instantly become enlightened without any effort on your part.

In truth, the path does not require Herculean efforts. You don't have to go to yoga everyday, meditate six times a day or recite any ancient texts. These are all great activities to nurture your Body, Spirit and Mind, but there is no magical formula that every person can follow to enlightenment. The path is unique for every person and yet each path will always involve the Body, Spirit and Mind being kept in forward ascension through continual growth and nurturing.

You might conclude that this is a rather lonely path to enlightenment with everything needed to follow this path already being within us. It would be false to conclude that this path puts all faith on the self rather than God. In reality, just the opposite is true. By propelling our Body, Spirit and Mind into forward ascension, we bring ourselves into union with the Divine. This harmonious balance brings us into direct communion with God. Like tuning an instrument designed to play beautiful music, our path to integrity is an opportunity to evolve from a physical existence to a Spiritual existence.

The Golden Ratio

Mankind has been fascinated with numbers from the moment we began to count. In particular, the history of mathematics has many examples of times when our greatest thinkers found meaning in the simplest of numbers [(Livio 2002)]:

1240 In the year 1240, Christians and Jews in Western Europe expected the arrival of some messianic king from the East, because the year 1240 in the Christian calendar corresponded to the year 5000 in the Jewish calendar.

666 In the Book of revelations (13:18) it is said, "This calls for wisdom: let anyone with understanding calculate the number of the beast, for it is the number of a man. Its number is six hundred and sixty-six." Incidentally, Nancy and Ronald Reagan changed their address in California from 666 St. Cloud Road to 668 to avoid the number 666.

7 The names of the seven days of the week were based on the names of the celestial objects originally considered to be seven planets: the Sun, the Moon, Mars, Mercury, Jupiter, Venus and Saturn.

4 The number four, for the Pythagoreans, was the number of justice and order (e.g. the four winds of directions provided the necessary orientation for humans to identify their coordinates in space as Water=West, Air=South, Fire=East, Earth=North).

Along with rational numbers (a number which can be expressed as a ratio of two integers), early Indian mathematicians found particular mystery in irrational numbers (a number which cannot be expressed as a fraction). The first proof of the awareness of irrational numbers is commonly attributed to Hippasus of Metapontum, a Pythagorean who is believed to have discovered them while identifying the sides of the pentagram.

During the 14th to 16th centuries, the infinite series for several irrational numbers such as Pi (π) and irrational values of trigonometric functions were discovered. The most highly regarded and mysterious irrational number of all time is clearly Phi (represented as φ and pronounced 'fee'):

> Some of the greatest mathematical minds of all ages, from Pythagoras and Euclid in ancient Greece, through the medieval Italian mathematician Leonardo of Pisa and the Renaissance astronomer Johannes Kepler, to present-day scientific figures such as Oxford physicist Roger Penrose, have spent endless hours thinking about this simple ratio and its properties. But the fascination with the Golden Ratio is not confined just to mathematicians. Biologists, artists, musicians, historians, architects, psychologists, and even mystics have pondered and debated the basis of its ubiquity and appeal. In fact, it is probably fair to say that the Golden Ratio has inspired thinkers of all disciplines like no other number in the history of mathematics. (Livio 2002)

A basic explanation of phi is that it is a ratio between two distances and is approximately 1.6180339887. Examples of phi in nature can be found in leaf placement on stems (shown to provide optimal orientation for sun, rain and air), arrangements of florets in sunflowers, hexagonal scale placement on pineapples and the growth of seashells.

a   **b**

a + **b** is to **a**   as   **a** is to **b**

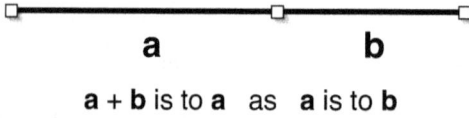

Figure 11: The total length "a" + "b" is to the longer segment "a" as "a" is to the shorter segment "b."

There have been many volumes of study dedicated to the existence of phi in nature, as well as great debates centering on the greatest art masterpieces of all time being produced with knowledge of phi. However, regardless of its application in our world, the fact remains that phi is a regularly occurring ratio in nature and a number that holds great intrigue for those that find mathematics riveting. For the rest of us, phi plays a very personal and important role in our destiny.

Phi plays a very personal and important role in our destiny.

At birth, there is a golden ratio (φ) between the completeness of the Body, Spirit and Mind (e.g. in our previous example, the Mind is incomplete, the Spirit is highly but not entirely complete and the Body is complete). Think back to your earliest childhood memories and see if you can determine where your Body, Spirit and Mind began on the phi oriented completeness scale.

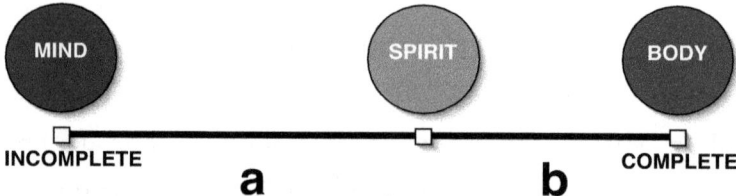

MIND   **SPIRIT**   **BODY**

INCOMPLETE   **a**   **b**   **COMPLETE**

Figure 12: Represented as a completeness scale, your Body, Spirit and Mind (or rather the ratio of the distances between them) are in the perfect order of phi at birth. The scale ranges from one end, representing the most incomplete state, to the other representing being complete.

For most of us, our Minds were born into a new world with no real world experience and at their most incomplete state. Our Bodies, in comparison, were at their most complete state as most of us will never be as healthy as the day we were born. And the Spirit, freshly born into the world, was highly complete but not entirely complete (otherwise great spiritual leaders would seek counsel from newborn babies on the ways of God). Of course, where your entities began may be different, but the phi ratio between your entities will have been in this Divine state.

These charts are intended to help you visualize the growth potential of your Body, Spirit and Mind as well as the path you're currently on. In reality, there are no charts and there is no adherence to phi. However, by understanding where you're going vs. where you want to go, you can better find your way.

Without a focused investment in all three, each entity follows its own path with complete ignorance of one another and the potential for harmony amongst their connections. Consequently, we fall out of phi and subsequently seemingly random and chaotic crisis events enter our lives.

Notice that there is also a similar distance (ratio) between the Body, Spirit and Mind on the completeness scale at birth and death. At birth, the Body is the most complete with the Spirit in the middle and the Mind at its most incomplete state. Similarly at the end of life, the Golden Ratio returns with your Body being its most incomplete, your Spirit the most complete (note the sea of gray hair at religious services) and your Mind in the middle.

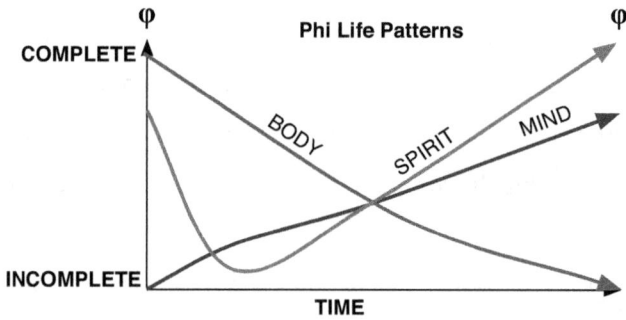

Figure 13: The natural order of phi is present at birth and again at death.

If you stop for a minute and think about this path through life you won't find this to be alarming. Biological aging is a progressive, degenerative process of decay, in which the healthy cellular and molecular order of our Bodies begins to fall apart. This natural biochemical side effect of normal metabolism builds up until it reaches critical mass and we die. In fact, if you plot your medical costs on a timeline you'll see a rise beginning in your early forties and a sudden spike seven years prior to your death (give or take). The point is that under normal circumstances our Bodies become less and less complete until they can't function.

But what's the alternative? If my Body is going to slowly degenerate until I die, then what does its relationship to the Spirit and Mind matter? What matters is your ability to live longer, healthier and better than you ever imagined. The secret to living a long, healthy life beyond today's norms exists in the phi ratio of our entities at birth and upon our death.

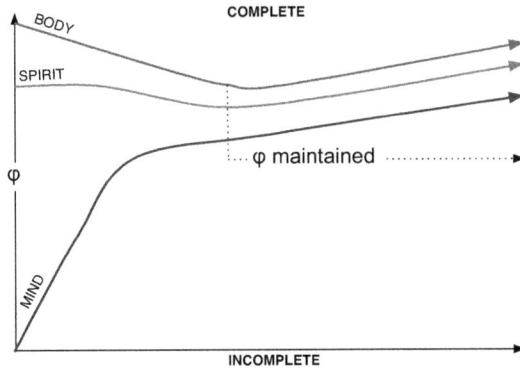

Figure 14: Once you achieve phi (φ) in the natural order of your birth, with continual investment (maintenance), your Body, Spirit and Mind will sustain phi throughout your lifetime. This phi balance can be reached even if your entities are currently not in the same order of completeness as when you were born (natural order).

Without parental and societal (it takes both) guidance, each of your entities will follow an unconscious path through life. As such, the Body slowly decays at first, but after reaching the mid-life point, begins a rapid decline towards becoming incomplete. Similarly, the Mind steadily grows through life, but upon reaching the mid-life, levels out and maintains its state of completeness through the latter years in life. The Spirit takes a much more traumatic path through life by initially falling away from completeness without parental and societal reinforcement that the Spirit warrants equal investment as the Mind. Parents say, "You will get a college education!" but aren't equally as concerned about the growth of the child's Spirit. In the twenties and thirties, the Spirit wakes up and begins a strong growth all the way into the golden years. With the end near, the Spirit continues to grow with vigor until the Body ceases to function. Even though the order has changed, the three entities return to phi as they began in phi.

When your entities are unrelated (e.g. not relating to one another, nor near one another in their state of completeness) they have no effect on one another. Similar in comparison, if the moon were not as close as it is to the Earth, we wouldn't have the same tidal patterns as we do. The reverse is also true as the Earth's larger size has had such a strong influence on the moon that it has caused the moon to stop rotating (we always see the same side of the moon). Thus the closer two bodies are to one another, the greater the gravitational effect they have on one another. The same is the case with your Body, Spirit and Mind. The closer they are to one another (in terms of completeness) the greater influence they have on each other.

As this relates to aging, the closer you can get your Spirit and Mind to the Body, the more they can influence the health of the Body. Space is an interesting concept and we tend to think of closeness in geometric terms. But remember that the three dimensions of height, width and depth are the dimensions of the Mind and the Spirit isn't bound by these same dimensions. Instead think of closeness in terms of how complete each entity is rather than where it is physically in space.

How close should the entities be to one another? For this answer, we look to the phi ratio present at our birth and our death. Phi is the intended ratio between our three entities and returning to that same ratio is what will enable us to influence the health of our Bodies. The problem is that we've been living without regard to the relationship of our three entities and thus they've been all over the map throughout our lives. As a result, we must first understand how complete our entities are today and then make investments to pull them closer together.

The result is an extension of our lives but more importantly an extension that includes health, vitality and contribution. No one wants to become a burden later in life, but our Bodies leave us with no other choice when we lead a typical life. However with phi balance, we can return to the state in which we were born and propel our Bodies towards better health throughout our lifetime.

Enlightenment

Whereas when two conflicting entity paths cross (one rising and the other declining) chaos occurs, when entity paths cross in ascension (growing via investment) enlightenment occurs. By investing in your Body, Spirit and Mind you can put yourself on a path to enlightenment where two or more of your entity paths cross in ascension. In doing so, your Body, Spirit and Mind will be brought into asynchronous harmony and henceforth maintain the golden ratio distance between each entity.

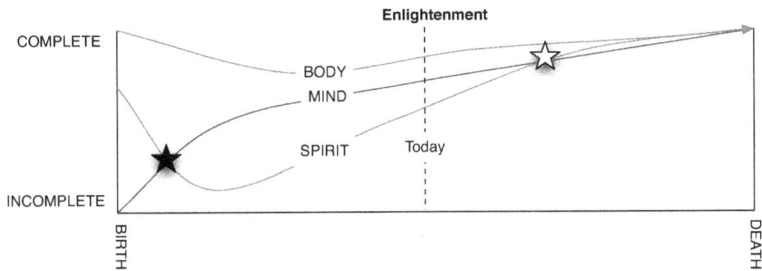

Figure 15: When two entities cross in forward ascension, enlightenment occurs (white star).

It is vital to invest in your Body, Spirit *and* Mind. For example, to purely focus on one's Spirit is to disregard its partners. As the Spirit is governed by the Body, a sole investment in the Spirit can quickly be unraveled by the Body (e.g. when illness strikes the Body, everything else comes to a halt).

However from an inflection point of enlightenment (where entity paths cross while rising in forward ascension), the golden ratio between the three entities will harmonize and maintain each on a path of growth. In doing so, they will attract one another into continual growth. Through the harmonization of the Body, Spirit and Mind and investment into each, they will each grow instead of decay.

According to Newton's universal law of gravitation, every mass attracts every other mass and the force of attraction decreases as the they get further apart. In particular, doubling the distance weakens the attraction by a factor of four. Conversely when your Body, Spirit and Mind are further apart (in terms of completeness), they are less able to influence one another than when they are similarly complete.

By design, age provides a finite degree of completeness that your Body can attain (don't worry, you can become a lot more complete than you are today). With your Body having a finite amount of potential completeness in an eleven-dimensional world (i.e. over time our bodies break down), most of Humanity experiences their Bodies becoming less and less healthy over time. However with the Body, Spirit and Mind operating in a close proximity of completeness, the growth of any one of your entities propels the other two towards completeness too.

Upon bringing your entities to a similar state of integrity, growth and investment into the Spirit and Mind will pull the Body up towards a greater state of completion. What this means is that you can actually cause your Body to become healthier than it is today. As the Spirit and Mind become more complete, the Body is gravitationally pulled up too. And the closer your three entities are in terms of completeness, the more influential they are on one another. Thus by bringing the Body, Spirit and Mind into similar states of completion, they begin to work as a team and influence one another's growth.

No longer do our golden years need to be subject to debilitating Bodies and Minds. By putting your entire being into forward ascension in the natural order of phi, your Body, Spirit and Mind will keep one another in forward ascension. When one drops due to an illness or injury, the others will adapt and use their energy to pull the ailing entity into health. Because your Body, Spirit and Mind will be operating as a team, they will not only be aware of one another, but also have a vested interest in the entire team being healthy.

What you have today is a Body, Spirit and Mind that has attained a level of completeness through blood, sweat and tears. You've worked really hard to get where you are physically, spiritually and intellectually. No one can take away from you the path you have carved out to get where you are. However, when we look at our elders, we can see that our approach to life probably won't get us the rest of the way. This is why we seek a new approach to living that won't break down as we age. We seek a path that will bring us to an inflection point, a point where we will come into harmony.

The sooner one achieves inflection point harmonization of the Body, Spirit and Mind, the sooner one can begin a path of collective growth instead of decay. This is wonderful news for anyone desiring the healing power of God. Not only will enlightenment bring us to our hopes and dreams, but it can also make our Bodies more, not less, complete. And who doesn't want that?

Your Practice

A. Chart Your Life

Starting with your birth, plot the completeness of your Body, Spirit and Mind as you have progressed through life thus far:

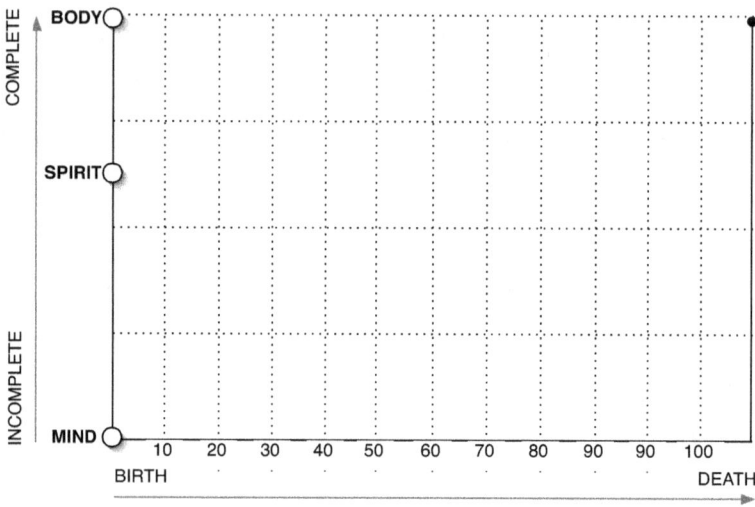

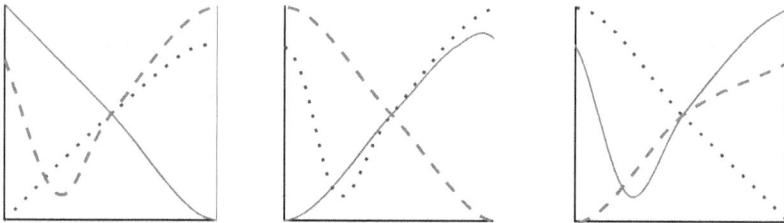

Examples of different life patterns.

Tips for plotting your life chart:

1. The higher up on the chart, the more complete the entity.

2. Instead of drawing lines initially, place a dot at each age interval to represent how complete the entity was at that time.

3. To begin, recall how your entities were during your teenage years. Compared to the most complete each entity is possible of becoming, where was each one when you were fifteen?

4. After marking each interval in your life up to your current age, connect each entity's dots with sweeping, curving lines.

5. Remember that oppositional entities crossing (one rising, another dropping) represent conflict. Does your life chart accurately reflect those moments in your life when you had conflict?

B. Know Your Order

List your three entities in their order of completeness (more complete on top) now and where you want them to be in five years:

BIRTH e.g.	NOW	IN 1 YR	IN 5 YRS
BODY			
SPIRIT			
MIND			

C. Entity Focus

Which entity(s) require investment to get where you want to be in 5 years? _____   _____

D. Today's Change

List one (1) investment you can immediately commit to for nurturing:

BODY _____

SPIRIT _____

MIND _____

E. Five Year Goal Attainment

Are the investments listed above enough for you to achieve your goals?

_____ Yes   _____ No

If not, list an additional activity that can be started in the next year to put you on a path to achieving your completeness goal:

_____ for my ◯ Body ◯ Spirit ◯ Mind

F. Chart Your Old Future

Recreate your chart from exercise "A" and draw where your future is headed. For example, if each entity were to continue on its current path, where would it end up? This chart indicates where you were going without course correcting the path you are on.

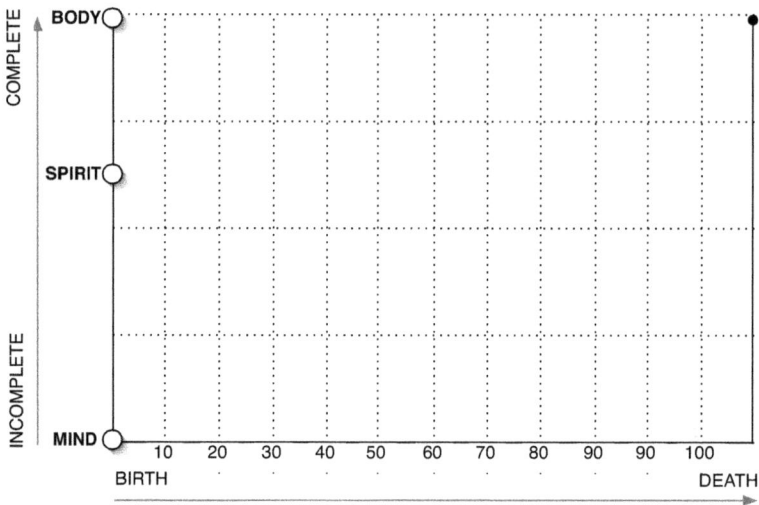

G. Chart Your New Future

Recreate the chart from practice "A" and, assuming you'll live to 110 years old, draw the path of your future. Start by plotting where you'll be in five years. Remember that you'll be putting all three of your entities into forward ascension so your entities should no longer drop towards becoming less complete.

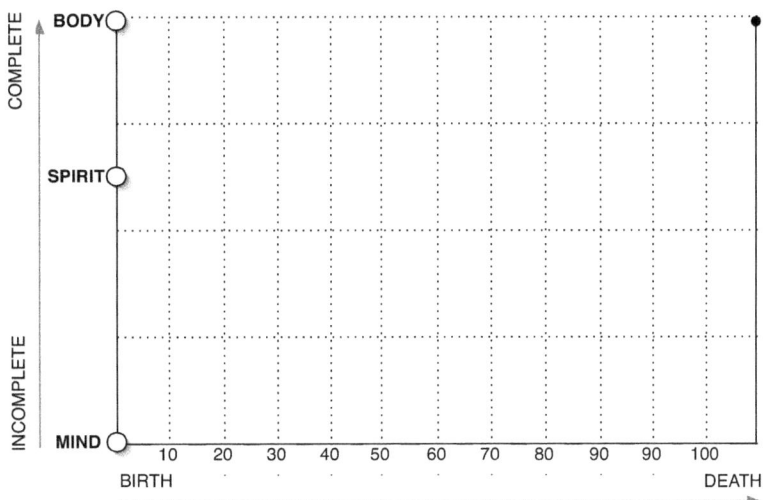

H. Enlightenment Window

When two or more entity paths cross in forward ascension, enlightenment occurs. Are you on a path towards enlightenment?

_____ Yes   _____ No

If no, which entity would you have to invest in more heavily to put yourself on a path to enlightenment?   _____

6

HARMONY

Without being conscious of your Body, Spirit and Mind and their connective bonds, you will be subject to seemingly random moments of upheaval and chaos in your life. The inverse of this isn't necessarily true as conscious beings are not immune to upheaval and chaos. Consciousness isn't an insurance policy against problems, but rather a means to understand the events that unfold in our lives without judgment. Through greater consciousness, we can learn to ride the events of our lives like a surfer hops from wave to wave. In a conscious and Spiritual existence, we are present to both the waves we are riding as well as the sets of waves that are coming in behind us. We learn to work with the energy of the waves in our lives with reverence, respect and admiration.

If you take stock of your Body, Spirit and Mind during traumatic moments in your life, you will find that two or more of your entities are in conflict as one is in ascension and the other is descending. Like two waves crashing into one another, the energy from oppositional entities releases into our lives and the lives of those around us. When you're not conscious to these waves of energy, your life can really seem like you're living inside of a washing machine.

In order to achieve harmony, all three of your entities must be in ascension and they must be in a relatively similar state of integrity (state of being complete). If your entities are grossly different in their state of integrity, you will be unable to maintain harmony because they're too far apart to affect one another. However, if all entities are similarly complete, they will pull upon one another and keep you in harmony.

In order to achieve harmony, you must first put each of your entities into forward ascension. There really isn't anything difficult required to do this and yet most of the human race fails to accomplish this basic task. Simply stated, forward ascension is investing in your Body, Spirit and Mind in order to achieve balance. Sure we invest in one or maybe two, but consistently investing into the completeness of our Body, Spirit *and* Mind is another thing all together.

In fact, many of us know and respect people who have a really strong Body, Spirit or Mind. We glorify people who have healthy and beautiful bodies. Moreover we admire people who are in shape and aspire to be healthy ourselves. So too we feel a reverence for God in the presence of people who are committed to their faith as well as put time and energy into nurturing their Spirit. And the Mind? Heck, we love the Mind so much that we invent awards, scholarships and prizes for smart people all over the world. But what about all three?

The simple task of investing into our Bodies, Spirits and Minds eludes much of Humanity. The beauty and grace that is brought forth by the balance of such an investment is a gift from God. In balance, we understand the events of our lives more clearly and find happiness in the most unlikely of situations.

With such a beautiful gift within our grasp, why do we fail to achieve what is obviously available to every man, woman and child on the planet? The answer is life.

During the busy and hectic parts of our lives it is easy to lose sight of a Spiritual existence. It seems that one crisis is often replaced by another and we can't even remember the last time that life wasn't a struggle. So too during these times it is difficult to be mindful and present of our personal completeness. However by keeping your Body, Spirit and Mind in forward ascension towards becoming more complete, the struggles that seem to define our life can and will fade away. You now have more reasons than ever before to improve your diet, never miss a workout and sign up for that yoga class. By simply investing regularly in your Body, Spirit and Mind, you will naturally put each of your entities into forward ascension.

However, in order to sustain harmony, you must bring each entity into close proximity with the others in terms of relative completeness. To do so, you should first assess the integrity of your Body, Spirit and Mind. Depending on your individual situation, you may have more work to do with one or more of your entities. As such, you might need to invest more heavily in one entity, for a longer period of time, before all three are close enough to achieve and sustain harmony.

Accordingly, the integrity of your Body is key. You were born in the natural order of phi and your three entities desire to return to that state with the Body being the most complete amongst the three. Even if your Body is not the most complete today, all three desire the Body to be the most complete as, without the Body, they otherwise cannot fulfill their purpose. If you remember only one thing from this chapter, remember your Mind and your Spirit need the Body to exist and thus put the Body's health as their top priority. Your job as conscious mediator between your three entities is to put and keep them in a position where they can do their jobs.

Imagine your Body, Spirit and Mind as planets orbiting the sun. In the center, the sun represents your source of energy and your entities orbit around the sun as time progresses. We don't think of planets in terms of completeness, but if we did would you expect the planets to be more complete just after the Big Bang when they were still fragments of disconnected energy or now when they are clumped together as living planets?

The completeness of the planets and the completeness of our entities have one thing in common: time

While they have vastly different life spans (billions of years for a planet vs. roughly 100 years for your Body and Mind), both the planets and our entities are intended to become complete over their lifetime. The problem is that we human beings have forgotten our purpose. Without an awareness of our purpose, we've fallen off the path of becoming complete and instead fool ourselves into believing that life is all about accomplishment, flashy cars and expensive homes. Instead of serving God, we spend our time serving ourselves. We have been given ample time to evolve into a Spiritual existence, but without an instruction manual we've gone astray.

It really isn't that God didn't provide us with everything that we need to become complete. The messaging from God is ever present in our lives even though we've lost the ability to tune into the message. With becoming conscious, this ability to listen will manifest itself. However be forewarned, a direct and conscious relationship with God means that you will commune with and know God's words. You may be surprised what you learn and this may cause you to question much that you take for granted.

For example, imagine that God came to you right now and gave you a message. In this message, you found inconsistencies and statements that were not in line with your understanding of the Universe, God and Humanity. Moreover this message from God didn't coincide with the teachings of your religion. What would you do? How would you feel? Who would you tell? How would they judge you?

A true relationship with God is above all worldly teachings. Regardless of what you've learned in life, the direct voice of God supersedes all prophets, scripture and religious doctrine. And through aligning with your Spirit and bringing balance into your life you will know the voice of God, for that is how human beings were intended to operate in the Universe. We've just been too busy focusing on ourselves to bring about this phase of evolution.

As your entities become more complete, they are drawn to one another like every other object in the Universe. What this means for the evolving being is that as you become more complete, your entities will pull together and become more complete as a group. Whereas in the beginning one must invest energy into each entity separately in order for it to be nurtured and grow, when your entities pull together the energy from one propels the other two. As a result, less and less energy is required to propel them towards greater states of completeness (e.g. life gets easier).

When your three entities are in dissimilar states of completeness, their gravitational attraction to one another is weak. However when they are close together, they can gravitationally keep one another on a path of growth.

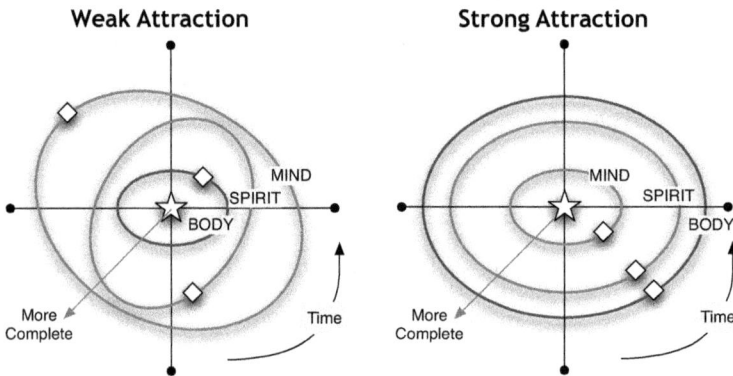

Figure 16: Metaphorically representing the orbit of your Body, Spirit and Mind rotating around your source of energy, as each entity becomes more complete it gets closer to the other entities and they are pulled together. When they align, they have a stronger influence on one another even though they're independently working towards becoming more complete. Consequently, when one entity is propelled to be more complete, all three entities are propelled to be more complete.

One would expect that as an object moves away from a source of energy that it would slow down. In theory, the further away we are from a source of energy the less the effect. For example, the effect of the Sun's heat is drastically different on Mercury than it is on Pluto.

Similarly one would expect that objects rotating close to the source would be moving at much higher speeds than those far away from the source. One can visualize this concept via a spiral shaped galaxy:

Figure 17: From the perspective of looking straight into a Whirlpool Galaxy, spiral galaxies have spiral arms beginning close to the galactic center and extending out towards the edge of the disc. Image provided by Wikipedia.

However empirical evidence demonstrates that this is not the case. As it turns out, the objects that are rotating close to the center of a galaxy actually move slower than objects that are at the outer arms of a galaxy. The reason for this is due to the effect of *dark energy* and *dark matter* on these objects. (Schultz 2007)

These phenomena are called "dark" because they don't emit light. We're not going to get into the science of dark energy and matter in this book but I'll note that in combination these two elements make up 96% of the known Universe. That's right, all the *normal* stuff that we think of as being in our Universe (e.g. planets, gas, stars, human beings, space aliens...) makes up only 4% of the Universe. The point of this brief astronomy lesson is that everything in the Universe is affected by two entities that we know virtually nothing about.

Unless you're an astronomer or a physicist, you've probably never heard of dark energy or dark matter. Don't worry, even the world's top scientists are just beginning to measure the presence of dark energy and dark matter in the Universe. What we do know is that they're both abundant in the Universe and have an effect on objects both large and small.

What I find particularly interesting is that 96% of our Universe consists of elements that we know hardly anything about. We believe that we've got so much of life figured out and yet we only truly understand 4% of our Universe. And this would be something all together different if dark energy and dark matter only existed outside of our solar system. However, dark energy and dark matter exist all around us. Dark energy is passing through you right now. Just because you're unaware of dark energy, it doesn't mean that it isn't there.

Spiritual Transformation

The shift in consciousness that we are experiencing around the world is amazing but it is thus far only reaching a small percentage of the population. Despite many people connecting to their Spirit, the vast majority of Humanity still believes that they are right and those that disagree with them are wrong.

But (this is a big one) life as we know it will soon not be the same. Even though many around us will be the same, *we* will be all together different. As Spiritual beings, we will be unable to sin, commit atrocities against our fellow man, or harm anything. Not only will we put the needs of others before those of our own, but they will reciprocate as well. We will not view the Earth as a temporary home for our life enjoyment, but rather the host of our species. With this our priorities will shift from self-preservation and gratification to social equality and sustainability.

Of course, none of this is possible with a non-Spiritual existence. Life as we know it today doesn't place value on all of Humanity, but rather only on those that are in our group. Our differences rise up from an ego-based existence in which we believe we are right and the other side is wrong. Only when we realize that we are all one will we begin to turn the tide. This awakening begins with the Spiritual evolution of one human being at a time. This awakening begins with you.

Your awakening to the relationships and power of your Body, Spirit and Mind can open up great possibilities for healing, enlightenment and growth. Your expanding consciousness acts as a radar dish collecting vast amounts of information from collective consciousness intended to help you succeed. Now that you know how to expand your consciousness, you have the ability to achieve your hopes and dreams through the unlimited potential of the Body, Spirit and Mind.

You were born in a state of potential harmony as represented in the potential completeness of your Body, Spirit and Mind. Consequently your entire being desires to become complete and attain enlightenment.

Harmony is defined as a complete and balanced state of the Body, Spirit and Mind.

There is a natural order of the Body, Spirit and Mind, which is perfect at the time of your birth. This natural order includes the Body as the most complete (high on the completeness scale), followed by the Spirit and then the Mind. There is good reason for this:

Without the Body, the Mind cannot exist.

Without the Body, the Spirit can't connect to this world.

Without the Spirit, the Mind is alone in guiding you.

With all three, the Mind and the Body gain access to the collective consciousness through the Spirit.

All three entities require the Body to function and consequently place the survival of the Body as their top priority. Thus your entire being desires and will be most complete with the Body, Spirit and Mind in the same order of completeness as when you were born.

To understand your most complete state, imagine investing in your Body, Spirit and Mind from the moment you were born. Instead of growing up in a society that primarily values the Mind (e.g. one in which the education of the Mind is the top priority) imagine a childhood in which all three entities were equally valued (e.g. one in which taking care of your Body and developing your Spirit were given equal emphasis as the education of your Mind).

Your path to completeness would ideally look like this:

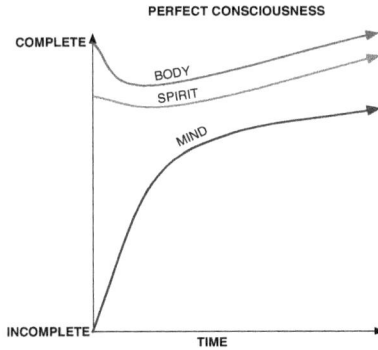

PERFECT CONSCIOUSNESS

COMPLETE

BODY

SPIRIT

MIND

INCOMPLETE

TIME

In this ideal environment, your parents would have taught you from an early age to appreciate and nurture your Body, Spirit and Mind. At no point would you need to become enlightened, because you would've preserved the harmonic state in which you came into being.

Conversely, imagine a life of neglect where your Body, Spirit and Mind were all ignored and allowed to decay:

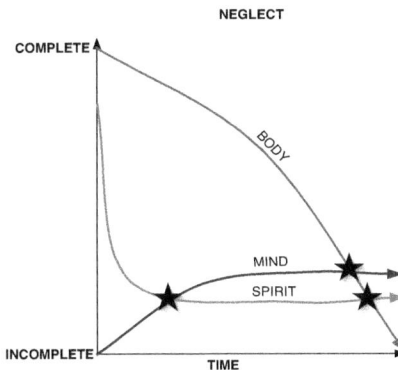

NEGLECT

COMPLETE

BODY

MIND

SPIRIT

INCOMPLETE

TIME

Figure 18: The surface area of consciousness depicted in this graph demonstrates how the unconscious being is unable to tap into the power of the collective consciousness. Beyond being unconscious, the being depicted is in a continual state of forward descension.

The Unconscious being that only periodically invests in their Body, Spirit or Mind, will achieve random moments of consciousness, but ultimately will become incomplete. Without a continual emphasis on the Body, Spirit and Mind, this is the path most of humanity will experience:

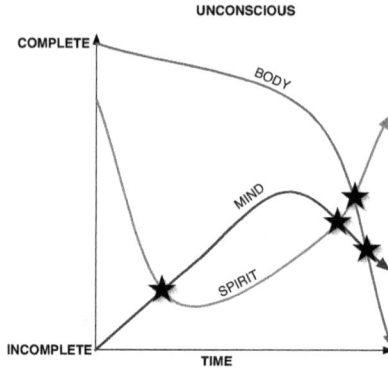

However, by awakening to the power of a Spiritual existence made possible by a strong Body, Spirit and Mind, as well as the connective bonds between them, we have the opportunity to expand our consciousness and become complete.

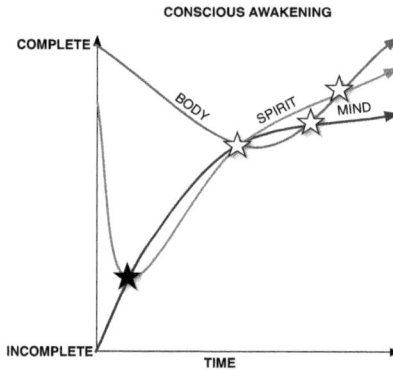

As shown in this last graph, after an inflection point of enlightenment occurs between two or more entities, the entire being moves towards integrity. With all three entities working together (the Body, Spirit and Mind), the being continually reaches greater and greater completeness. Nirvana, defined herein as the integrity of the

Body, Spirit and Mind, is thus not only possible but also something that every human being can cause to occur.

Remember that Nirvana is a state we can reach, rather than a state we achieve. The subtle difference here is worth noting. Nirvana is not something that you achieve and then stay there for eternity. Instead of thinking of Nirvana as a destination, think of it as a way of living that brings heaven to your earthly existence.

While the benefits of attaining Nirvana are beyond description, the opportunity to enlighten your being is a gift waiting to be unwrapped. Most people go through life anticipating a better life sometime in the future. For some, this is a better job, a better relationship or having more money. And for others there is only the anticipation of a blissful afterlife in heaven. The cosmic trick in this approach to life is that we miss the opportunity to experience heaven in this lifetime.

Living in a free will reality brings with it uncertainty, risk and the potential for suffering. Surely whenever we're experiencing the down side of living in a free will reality, it is natural to wish for better days. And when life is hard, one can find themselves longing for the pleasure filled existence we associate with heaven.

But what if there was more? What if, instead of waiting until you die to experience heaven, you could experience heaven in your current lifetime? What we fail to understand is that the potential for heaven on earth is a true gift from God. Your maker, the Creator of heaven and earth, has provided you with everything you need to transcend the troubles and woes of the free will reality and experience heaven now. To do so requires continual investment in the Body, Spirit and Mind, as well as the connective bonds between them.

Breaking the Evolutionary Code

You may be wondering if a human being's Body, Spirit and Mind can achieve completeness in whole. While we certainly don't know the answer to this question, it is plausible that this is possible. However, because of mankind's unbreakable connection to Humanity, this would certainly require more conscious than unconscious beings.

To aspire to become complete for personal reasons would be missing the point entirely. As human beings in our current phase of evolutionary progression, it is natural for us to desire to be better. No matter who you are, there is something that you probably want to be better at or have more of. Some people want a bigger house and others desire more vacation time. The point is that we human beings tend to see the world through our individual set of eyes. And why wouldn't we? In a world where only the strongest survive, we have to look out for ourselves or we might get eaten by a dinosaur. OK, maybe the world isn't quite as dangerous as it was during prehistoric times, but we still have a fair amount of survival stress in our lives.

The next step in our evolutionary chain will bring forth a collective understanding of Humanity. When all of mankind evolves, we will no longer toil over wars, fight over money or even kill in the name of God. And while this may seem impossible, so too must walking upright on land have seemed impossible to the sea creatures staring at the beach from the ocean. Regardless of where you weigh in on the evolutionary argument, recognize that in a truly Spiritual existence the pain of even one human being will be felt by the entire human race. A collective Spiritual existence will bring about heaven on earth through a series of enlightened beings that starts with you.

What's more, this dream of utopia is not far away. The shift to consciousness that is occurring around the world is but an early preview of our world to come. In this new world, mankind's collaboration and synergy will replace mankind's fighting and devastation. The reason this will be the case is that people who are conscious and maintain balance in their Body, Spirit and Mind are incapable of committing crimes against their fellow man. And while you may not believe that the rest of Humanity is capable of achieving this level of Spiritual enlightenment, you surely believe that this is possible for yourself.

And thus you are the key to mankind's future evolution. Through your own Spiritual enlightenment, you will bring forth a balance into your own life that will eradicate hate, anger, jealousy and rage from your own heart. And in this, the Universe will gain one more soul that seeks expansion rather than domination. Your balance will bring out an intoxicating force that will breathe energy into those around you. One enlightened soul will become two, two will become four and it will go on from there.

If this were just an ambition of the troubled human race then all of this would truly be for nothing. Aspiring to be something you cannot become will only lead you to delusion and depression. Pursuing what you can't achieve certainly won't bring forth the solidarity of all Humanity. But we, as human beings, are on a path to do much more than aspire. Our path is woven directly into our purpose and understanding our purpose will not only bring us to our future but so too will it unlock the keys to the Universe.

It is normal to view the troubles of the world and conclude that your personal evolution to a Spiritual existence won't make a difference. But what we fail to realize is how much of an impact we actually have on the world around us. Every day we change the world through the important work we do and the seemingly small acts that fill up our days.

We often don't consider sexual relations between a man and a woman to be causal in changing the world. That is until one of our offspring saves or takes the life of another. This small act of passion is but one example of how causal we are in changing the world, but it's also the essence of how life has progressed to current times. Every idea we express and every act we put into motion changes the world in ways we may never know.

And that is the crux of the problem. When we don't receive feedback about our actions we conclude that there was no impact. Because we didn't experience the change that occurred by our actions, we mistakenly conclude that we don't matter. And if we don't matter, then what's the point?

As a result, we invent judgment. We conclude that even though our actions don't matter, God is watching over us and judging our every action and thought. Because God is always watching and always judging, our actions matter because we don't want to suffer from being on the wrong side of God's judgment.

Unattached from judgment, we find our purpose and find enlightenment in pursuing our purpose. This is more than a feel-good affirmation. Energy is God's currency for creation and we find ourselves the benefactors when we pursue our God given purpose. Thus it isn't that God judges us and rewards us for doing as we've been told, but rather the energy that powers everything in the Universe flows to and through us when we pursue our purpose.

My God, my God, why hast thou forsaken me? Why art thou so far from helping me, and the words of my roaring? *Psalm 22:1*

It is natural for us to yearn for a God that watches over and protects us even if it comes with judgment. In this view of God, we are on God's side as long as we follow the rules. And because we follow the rules (most of the time), we believe that God will be on our side in battle, protect our families and answer our prayers. The problem we face is that the enemy is also following their version of the rules, seeking favor for their family and praying that God is on their side.

To cope, we conclude that our God is the one true God, the rules we follow are the correct rules and God loves us more than the enemy. And why does God favor us? Because we follow the correct rules. In the grand wisdom of the ages, we're doing what God wants us to do so we're right and they're wrong. And we're right back where we began: judgment!

From our earliest childhood experiences we are indoctrinated with judgment. We are made to believe that we are sinners and that there is always something wrong with us. From there, judgment expands to tell us that we're not pretty enough, not smart enough, not strong enough or simply not good enough. And even when we are good enough… the pretty are too vain, the smart are condescending and the strong are domineering. In a life guided by constant judgment, you can't win.

And even when we live a good life, we actually believe that God will judge us for our thoughts. But as we've already discussed, that voice in your head is not you. So how is it fair that God would judge you for thoughts that you can't control?

Instead try to understand that judgment was invented by human beings to control other human beings. It may be so deeply infused in our cultures that we can't imagine life without judgment, but that doesn't mean that judgment is the way of God.

A Spiritual existence operates outside of judgment even though our Minds are predisposed to make countless judgments without our involvement. Thus don't make the Mind the enemy for being judgmental, but instead let the Mind's thoughts serve their purpose and let them go. A Spiritual existence takes input from sensations, feelings and thoughts but doesn't attach meaning. As such, in Spirit, one can move away from living a judgmental life.

With a physical existence, we reduce our relationship with God to a Spiritual chessboard. On the Spiritual chessboard, everyone is either on the *right* team or the *wrong* team but this division is never ending. At a root level, we push everyone that doesn't believe in God over to the other team. If you don't believe in God then you already know what this feels like. For everyone else, those that believe in God are on our team, but from there we continue dividing based on which God you believe in. If you believe in our God, you're on our team and otherwise you might as well be over with everyone that doesn't believe in God anyway.

But the division doesn't stop there. Even amongst those that believe in the same God there is division. For example, Christians, Jews and Muslims all believe in the same one, true God but divide themselves by scripture, prophecy and belief. Ultimately we place anyone that doesn't follow our religion onto the other side of the chessboard because they're really not on our team.

But we don't stop there. Even within Christianity there are divisions between the Catholics, Protestants, Mormons, etc. And then we divide into conservative vs. liberal, literal interpretation of scripture vs. intended meaning, and so on. In the end, we've assembled our *side* of the Spiritual chessboard with those that believe what we believe, act like we act, talk like we talk and think like we think. On the other side stands the rest of Humanity.

We convince ourselves that we are right and they are wrong by selectively citing scripture, finding fault in others and reinforcing our belief system. On the other side, the practice is the same with the result being the division of Humanity. Over us God looks down and wonders why we are so lost. He calls us to move off of the Spiritual chessboard and into a true relationship with Him. The path is before us if we only can find the courage to take the first step.

It is truly hard to walk away from judgment for we have a lot riding on "being right." At the end of the day, following the rules (even if they're not the best rules) feels a heck of a lot safer than knowing God. Moses had it easy with the burning bush and the booming voice of God from the heavens. There is little room for error when God screams to get your attention. A true relationship with God (without the fire and brimstone) requires that we connect with God, learn the language of enlightenment and move away from judgment.

The relationship we seek is attainable via our purpose. Through our purpose, the energy of God flows through us and connects us to God. When this energy flows through you it is unmistakable. The life force energy of God empowers you to do great things, draws wonderful people into your life and brings you to your dreams. Without this energy flowing through us, we find ourselves struggling like a car running out of gas. In judgment, we believe God is punishing us during hard times, but in truth, we have simply failed to find and pursue our purpose. The cause of suffering isn't an angry God but rather our attempt to row a canoe up stream against the current of God's energy that is trying to help us achieve our purpose.

In order to pursue our purpose, we must first discover our own individual purpose. And to do this we must first understand the big picture of the Universe and where we fit. The good news is that we fit nicely and play a pivotal role in God's Universe. The bad news is that this role has no use for judgment. But while giving up judgment will be hard, it will also bring you to a true relationship with God.

Your Practice

A. My Heaven

Write down below, or on a separate piece of paper if necessary, your vision of heaven. Complete this exercise (even if you write only one sentence) before starting the next chapter.

_____

_____

_____

_____

_____

_____

_____

_____

_____

_____

_____

B. My Spiritual Chessboard

Visualize your own Spiritual chessboard by placing as many people (e.g. religions, organizations, political groups, ideologies) as you can think of on 'your' team or the 'other' team. Your team should only include those that you're prepared to hold hands with and stand in front of God. Everyone else should be placed on the 'other' team.

On My Side					Not On My Side		

Take your time and really go through all the groups that you hate, dislike, fear, despise, or loathe. Don't forget pedophiles, Nazis, Al-Qaeda or that guy that cut you off on the freeway last week. This is not to suggest groups for you to hate but rather to encourage you to leave no stone unturned in completing this exercise.

7

THE UNIVERSE

We have discussed investing in your Body, Spirit and Mind as well as the connecting bonds between them in order to put your entire being into forward ascension towards becoming complete. In this, you will experience great changes in your life that will bring you to your hopes and dreams. However, this is but the tip of the iceberg in tapping your human potential.

Before embarking on the journey to discover your relationship to the Universe, let's first take a moment to conceptualize the Universe on a very simplistic level. In the theoretical treatise Timaeus, the great philosopher Plato discusses the origin and interworkings of the cosmos. In breaking down the structure of all matter into five regular solids (known as polyhedra), Plato distinguished the Platonic solids, which are defined as the only existing solids in which:

1. All the faces are identical,

2. All the faces are equilateral (having equal sides) and

3. The entire object can be circumscribed (fitting snugly within) by a sphere (with all vertices lying on the sphere).

In total, Plato distinguished five Platonic solids and associated each with the four basic elements and a fifth "atomic" theory of matter. Plato's unified theory puts forth a model in which each of the Platonic solids represents a fundamental particle of the Universe:

Tetrahedron	Cube	Octahedron	Icosahedron	Dodecahedron
Fire	Earth	Air	Water	Quintessence

Figure 19: Each polyhedra represents a elemental particle of the Universe. Images from Wikipedia.

According to Plato, Earth is associated with the stable cube, the tetrahedron with the penetrating quality of fire, air with the mobile appearance of the octahedron and water with the icosahedron. The fifth solid, dodecahedron, representing the Universe as a whole, was described by Plato as that "which the god used for embroidering the constellations on the whole heaven."

These five distinctions of elemental matter are similarly held by many traditions:

	Fire	Earth	Air	Water	Quintessence
Greek	Fire	Earth	Air	Water	Aether
Hinduism Buddhism	Agni/Tejas	Prithvi/Bhumi	Vayu/Pavan	Ap/Jala	Akasha
Tibetan	Fire	Earth	Air	Water	Space
Alchemy	Fire	Earth	Air	Water	Aether

Table 1: Elemental Matter as depicted by world cultures. In addition to the five elements, Medieval alchemy also includes Sulphur, Mercury and Salt.

For our purposes, it isn't necessarily important what the different traditions defined as the fifth element, but rather that they each understood there to be a fifth element comprising the matter of the Universe. The fifth element is attributed to the dodecahedron, partly due to its connection with the golden ratio of phi. In his book *The Divine Proportion* published in 1509, Luca Pacioli attributes five reasons why phi should be referred to as "The Divine Proportion" including:

> *The fifth reason reveals an even more Platonic view of existence than Plato himself expressed. Pacioli states that just as God conferred being to the entire cosmos through the fifth essence, represented by the dodecahedron, so does the Golden Ratio confer being to the dodecahedron, since one cannot construct the dodecahedron without the Golden Ratio.* (Livio 2002)

Pacioli wrote extensively about phi and enlisted none other than Leonardo da Vinci to illustrate the five solids in sixty different illustrations in both skeletal and solid forms:

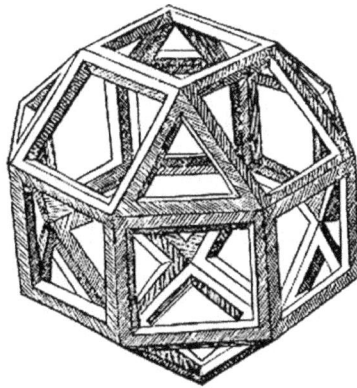

Figure 20: Leonardo's Dodecahedron - The first printed illustration of a rhombicuboctahedron, by Leonardo da Vinci, published in De divina proportione.

There are numerous references (both founded and unfounded) to phi being used by artists, architects and mathematicians to convey a natural order, beauty or spiritual meaning. For example, in his masterpiece The Sacrament of the Last Supper, Salvador Dali is quoted as saying that he included the dodecahedron in the painting because, "Communion must be symmetrical."

Figure 21: The Sacrament of the Last Supper, Salvador Dali, 1955.

These efforts to describe everything in our Universe through a basic and simple understanding of its parts is reductionistic in nature. They are an attempt to understand the nature of complex things, by reducing them to the interactions of their parts or to a simpler or more fundamental model. For example, both Johannes Kepler's laws of the motion of the planets and Galileo's (Galileo Galilei) theories of motion for terrestrial objects, are reducible to Newtonian theories of mechanics, because Newtonian theory so too explains these laws and theories of Kepler and Galileo.

Modern reductionalistic theories such as the still incomplete *String Theory* seek to understand elementary particles, by breaking them down into tiny strings that emit tones that represent the elementary particles. Through understanding how these strings work, interact and even exist, we hope to understand larger cosmological perspectives like the creation of our own Universe some fifteen thousand million years ago. And so too Inspiration Divine will help us understand our role in the Universe. However, as opposed to scientifically explaining the *how* of the Universe, Inspiration Divine reveals the *why*.

Humanity's Purpose

Every living thing has a purpose. A simple understanding of plants, reveals that they convert carbon dioxide into oxygen. As we need oxygen to breathe (you in particular), one can deduce that the purpose of plants is to convert carbon dioxide into oxygen. However, we must be careful not to interpret everything from our Mind's perspective. Although I may enjoy a good ham sandwich, I can hardly deduce that the pig's purpose is to become my lunch.

With all our differences and the amount of noise present in our modern lives, it has become difficult to detect our common purpose. But if you listen carefully you will hear a voice calling you to your purpose. As a species, we've nearly lost the ability to hear this voice calling to us. That is not to say that the voice is not present or that it has given up on us. Rather we have become tuned into the noise and thus lost the ability to distinguish the voice in the crowd. But with practice and consciousness, you will begin to tune into the voice that calls to all of us.

The message that is available to us all is a calling to our common purpose. Interwoven into this message are the lessons, hints and answers that you seek. Through tuning into this cosmic broadcast, you will find everything that you need to know. But first you must discover why you are here; why we are all here.

We all share a common purpose and still retain individual roles to play in our lives. The question is, "How is mankind different from other living things and what does this tell us about our unique purpose in the Universe?"

Much like plants produce oxygen as a byproduct of absorbing carbon dioxide, the byproduct of our purpose should have a positive impact on our environment.

In this, we have a symbiotic relationship with other living things. We breathe in oxygen and expel carbon dioxide, which in turn, plants absorb to produce oxygen. Similarly our purpose should help our environment, which provides a host (i.e. home) for life. Without a host environment, plants cannot live and thus we could not breathe. So too without the Universe, Humanity cannot exist. This is not offered as a proof to demonstrate that logically we can deduce our purpose. However with all our gifts, talents and abilities we surely must fulfill some purpose beyond breathing. What that purpose is and why we are here, has eluded mankind throughout the ages. However, the answer is as much a part of us as it is for us.

Symbiotic relationships exist and are necessary between all living things.

If human beings have a purpose unique from other living things, then there should be something unique about ourselves that enables us to fulfill our purpose. Otherwise, our purpose could be fulfilled by other living things and that purpose would be a function that all living things would be capable of performing. That would define any living thing's purpose, rather than Humanity's purpose.

While there are several useful characteristics of homo-sapiens (like having opposable thumbs), the most important characteristic of being human is our ability to be exocentric. As defined by Helmuth Plessner, exocentricity is the distinct nature of human "ex-istence" which means the experience of self as located outside of self. By identifying your self as your Spirit as expressed through the Body and Mind, you distance yourself from and objectify yourself. As stated earlier, you are much more than that voice in your head and the actions it calls your Body to execute.

As a result of being able to distance and objectify one's self, a pair of inter-relationships develops:

1. **Self Relatedness** - to objectify one's self is to be conscious of self or to be self-conscious.

2. **Temporal Relatedness** - to objectify one's self is to be conscious of time as it is relative to one's life in total.

Therefore our unique purpose in the Universe should both contribute to our environment and require an exocentric awareness of ourselves. An animal might contribute to their environment, but without the ability to be self-conscious and understand their relationship to time, the animal merely experiences life as it occurs. More specifically, animals adapt over time, but human beings adjust in real time. The means by which we adjust is our ability to assess a situation, determine what is required to survive and execute accordingly. Animals avoid death, but human beings create solutions to stay alive.

The evolution of mankind is progressing from a physical existence to a Spiritual existence. As originally published as a series of articles in the Arya between August 1914 and January 1919, the great Indian teacher (nationalist, scholar, poet, mystic, evolutionary philosopher, yogi and guru) Sri Aurobindo wrote that there is taking place a gradual awakening of consciousness over time, an evolution of consciousness:

> *A spiritual evolution, an evolution of consciousness is the inner fact which alone illumines the problem of earth existence and opens to its true solution.* (Aurobindo, Essays Divine And Human 1997)

When we think of consciousness, we view this body of awareness through our individual, egocentric perspective. Partly because we know no other way, we assume that the only way that knowledge can be passed from one person to another is through a common language. Be it printed or spoken word, the language of mathematics, or paintings on cave walls, we understand and use a finite set of communication tools to pass knowledge and wisdom to one another.

Inherent in this paradigm is a fundamental assumption that both communicator and recipient must understand the language used for communicating. For example, unless you understand sign language you're not going to be able to decipher a message being signed to you. However, just because you don't understand the language this doesn't mean that the information contained in the message doesn't exist or that it isn't being communicated to you.

Outside of documented knowledge, there is a collective consciousness that contains every idea, thought and creation ever expressed by intelligent life. We may not be aware of this body of knowledge or understand the language by which it is communicated, but that doesn't mean that it doesn't exist. And just like we might understand the message of someone that is warning us through a foreign language that we're about to get hit by a car, it isn't inconceivable that we have occasionally tapped into collective consciousness despite our not knowing its language. But by learning this language, we open up our lives to much more than we thought was available to us.

The wisdom available to us through collective consciousness is a gift from God. By allowing us to contribute as well as tap into the vast knowledge contained in collective consciousness, we are brought into a direct relationship with God.

Expanding Universe

Our collective home environment is much grander than our hometown, state, country, continent or even the planet Earth. It is the Universe that we should consider our home. Because we don't believe that our lives have any impact on the Universe, we tend not to think of the entire Universe as our home environment. But as you'll soon come to understand, we not only have a highly influential relationship to the Universe, but disregarding our custodial obligation to care for its well being will result in the extinction of the human race.

Like a second stage rocket that propels an object beyond the atmosphere, mankind's collective consciousness is the means by which more and more dark energy is generated to fill up and push out the boundaries of our Universe[9]. Mankind brings about the expansion of the Universe by creating that which did not exist before. In every original creation, we fulfill our common purpose and find meaning in our daily existence.

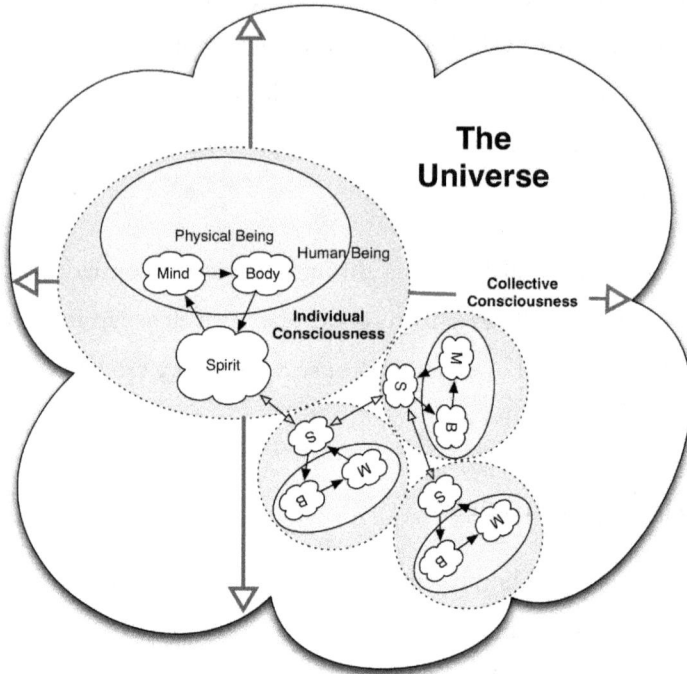

Figure 22: As collective consciousness expands, dark energy is provided which, among many things, expands the Universe.

The dark energy that expands our Universe is the very same life force energy that flows through you. As a human being, you absorb the dark energy that flows from your Spirit into your Mind and through your Body. In passing through your Mind, your original creations are

---

[9] Many have theorized that it is merely consciousness that is expanding the Universe (e.g. Einstein's "Blunders" or What? by Avtar Singh - October 21, 2007: *"Holistic Relativity vindicates Einstein's insight as a scientific wonder rather than a blunder. It also demonstrates that the expansive energy of the Cosmological Constant is synonymous with the mysterious dark energy (vacuum energy) or consciousness fueling the observed spontaneous (free-willed) expansion of the universe."*

added and flow from your Body's mouth and skin back to your Spirit and into the collective consciousness of Humanity. When your original creations expand collective consciousness, dark energy is produced. The additional dark energy that is generated via your original creations expands the very Universe in which you live.

Years before we modern thinkers began wrestling with gravitons, dark energy, string theory and all the other scientific explanations as to how the Universe is expanding, Sri Aurobindo (1872 - 1950) gave Humanity the answer we're all seeking. Sri Aurobindo described collective consciousness (he called it Infinite Consciousness) as creating the Universe to extend its own static delight into the dynamic delight experienced by "forms of force" (e.g. human beings).

Sri Aurobindo explained that when we humans rise in consciousness and discover our higher nature, we experience that very same delight — thereby fulfilling what he calls the Divine Intent. Sri Aurobindo's perspective is that we regenerate the consciousness that was lost when the Universe was born. As unconscious matter was generated from a Spiritual source in the creation of the Universe, mankind's expansion of collective consciousness is replacing the consciousness that was given to create our Universe. In line with this thinking, it isn't strange that mankind's expansion of collective consciousness is what would create dark energy. In other words, dark energy is required to birth the Universe, dark energy was expended to birth the Universe, mankind's causal role in bringing about more dark energy by expanding collective consciousness is replacing that very same dark energy and this is causing our Universe to expand.

Human beings are responsible for the dark energy that is expanding the Universe.

Regardless of how mankind generates dark energy (we'll get to that next), mankind generating dark energy only solves half of the problem. Mankind is a relatively recent addition to the Universe and dark energy has certainly existed for billions of years prior to our introduction. A Universe even capable of sustaining living beings didn't come about until 4 billion years after the Big Bang. That may seem like a long time but it really isn't compared to the Universe's Big Bang birth some 13.7 billion years ago. Thus the question is, "If mankind is not *ever-present* in the Universe, then how did the dark energy that existed before mankind come into being?"

Sri Aurobindo may have been able to explain that collective consciousness is what enabled the Universe to be born but who, what or how enabled this to actually happen and where did the dark energy come from that expanded the Universe prior to our arrival? One could surmise that our introduction into the Universe was perfectly timed, but as we saw with the highly improbable requirements of a steady state Universe, this seems beyond anything reasonable.

There are many possibilities ranging from beings in another Universe to the Creator being the source of the Universe's dark energy. If other living, thinking beings are capable of creating dark energy, then it is plausible that there are numerous living beings like us throughout the Universe that have been generating dark energy long before we Earthlings came on the scene. And while this is all together possible, it doesn't account for the amount of dark energy that would've been necessary to fuel the expansion of the very first Universe beyond its Big Bang birth.

There is an alternative, biological explanation of our presence in the Universe being one of chance with human beings simply being a byproduct of existing in a Universe that is capable of sustaining life. Essentially this theory postulates that because it is possible for us to exist, our existence is merely an isolated instance of the right environment producing intelligent life. And for those people that choose to live a non-Spiritual existence, this construct surely provides them with a scientific explanation of how they are here. However, just because this is what they choose to believe, it doesn't make it true. But it is one plausible theory.

So too there are religious explanations of our presence in the Universe being one of Divine intent. God created the Earth for man and we are here to build massive churches, synagogues and mosques in His honor. And while I'm obviously over simplifying the concept, for many people it is enough to believe that man was placed here by God to pay homage to God. Although many would beg to differ, so too just because this is what they choose to believe, it doesn't make it true. But it is another plausible theory.

There is no scientific or religious perspective that will convince you that the theory of everything put forth by Inspiration Divine is correct. The body of information we're exploring here is for understanding rather than for being convincing. The point is to open up your Body, Spirit and Mind to the construct of purpose and then to explore the theories put forth on your own.

In order for you to live and breathe this life force energy of the Universe (dark energy), there must have been a life force energy before your existence. The same can be said for every living thing. Therefore an entity capable of generating a tremendous amount of dark energy must have existed prior to living beings. That entity is God the Creator.

Card 10: God is most often conceived of as the supernatural creator and overseer of the universe.

Upon logically searching through all the plausible alternatives you will likely come up with another option involving another Universe. As a Universe requires energy to dynamically expand, it attracts other non-expanding Universes and, upon colliding, the energy is pulled from one into the other. Under this conceptual model, each Universe is either growing or collapsing with the stronger, more expansive Universes surviving under this cosmic tale of survival of the fittest.

However, even under this model, you can't resist peeling back the layers, one after the other to go back to the beginning when there was not even a single Universe. Like the life that sprung forth on our planet, there always has to be a beginning if there is to be an end. And in the beginning, there was only one[10]. There was God.

God is energy, energy is God.

Energy flows through you, God flows through you.

Your creations generate energy, your creations expand the presence of God.

We know a lot more about our Universe than we did ten, one hundred or several thousand years ago. We also know a lot more about our existence as a form of life than we did throughout history too. At some point, mankind must come to understand that the ways of the Universe and Humanity are in line with God's intent. Regardless of what we believe to be true, the ways of the Universe and Humanity cannot be different than how God intended them to be. With this, we can find meaning in knowledge and wisdom by understanding God rather than picking and choosing pieces of information that support our belief system.

We can find solace in understanding the ways of the Universe and Humanity as a reflection of God's intent. If God didn't intend for the Universe and Humanity to be what we observe, then He surely would've designed our reality differently.

---

[10] God created the Universe in which we live and this Universe is governed by the 11 dimensions. Thus God isn't necessarily governed by the 11 dimensions (including time) and isn't restricted by a 'beginning to end' cycle. Therefore the cycle in which we progressively reveal predecessors doesn't necessarily continue forever.

With this understanding, the atheist and theist can come together in an understanding of the Universe, God and Humanity without arguing who is right and who is wrong. We can simply understand *what is* as a reflection of the truth. And in pursuit of the truth, we will all find what is absolutely true beyond mankind's interpretation.

8

COLLECTIVE CONSCIOUSNESS

In order for dark energy to expand the Universe, more dark energy must be created from that which did not previously exist. Therefore when you expand your consciousness, rather than absorb existing consciousness, you are fulfilling your purpose. We know this to be a purpose only mankind can fulfill because this contributes to mankind's environment (expanding and thus sustaining the Universe) and original ideas require an exocentric being capable of creating solutions (rather than adapting) in an ever changing environment.

As with knowledge, before you can teach you must first create. Once created, the creation can be shared with others. It is these original creations that are the substance of collective consciousness.

> *Original creations are the substance of collective consciousness, which brings forth the dark energy that is expanding the Universe.*

In order for dark energy to expand the Universe, these original creations must be released into the Universe. By keeping an idea to yourself, consciousness can't expand and the Universe fails to grow. Thus in order to fulfill your purpose, you must bring forth original creations and share them with others. Much like a balloon, to expand a container one must put more into the container than was present previously. Otherwise the container will either maintain or collapse (if the contents escape). If you breathe in the air that is in one balloon and blow it into another balloon, you have not doubled the size of balloon volume but simply transferred it from one balloon to another.

Let's pause here and digest what you've just read. Without more and more dark energy being produced, the Universe will collapse in on itself. The Universe is expanding and dark energy is what is fueling its expansion. Human beings are the catalyst for dark energy and we bring it about by creating original ideas and sharing them with others. And this is not only how the Universe was designed, but it also reveals the purpose of mankind.

Take a minute and imagine yourself standing on the Spiritual chessboard introduced previously. Next to you stand the people that believe what you believe, think what you think and act like you act. And across from you on the opposite end of the board stands the rest of

Humanity. Now imagine God's hand appearing and mixing up all the people on the Spiritual chessboard (or a massive flood that re-arranges everything) and changing everyone's appearance so that you can't tell which team anyone is on. But now, instead of playing the game according to rules, hierarchy and established order, imagine playing the game in synchronicity with God's intention.

Rather than moving through pre-defined paths that limit your movement, you can now move in any direction and without the intention to conquer your opponent. Instead you are now in synch with God and move about the board flowing with the energy moving throughout the game. When you flow with this energy, you feel propulsion. When you move against this energy, you feel resistance.

By tuning into the energy flowing from God, you become skilled at navigating around the board. As more and more people tune into this energy flow, you notice that there are fewer and fewer collisions. What's more, upon close observation you notice that even the people that are unconscious to this flow of energy are guided and moved by it. Even as they force themselves to navigate the game according to the old rules of the game, they too experience propulsion when they move with this energy and resistance when they move against it.

When we awaken to our common purpose, we furthermore experience even more energy flowing in our lives. In the creation of knowledge and wisdom, we find an abundance of energy flowing through us towards our hopes and dreams. By creating that which didn't exist before, we find that navigating the game of life gets easier and easier. No longer are we playing the game alone against the rest of

Humanity, as we are now all on the same team striving to achieve a common goal in purpose.

Unconscious in the lives we have been born into, we find this new model of the Spiritual chessboard to be an unattainable utopia. Without an awareness of the language in which we can tap into this flow of energy, we find the real world to be harsh, problematic and confusing. Our Minds seek logical, definitive and testable answers that can be put into a machine and evaluated for a consistent result. But the energy flow of God doesn't work according to our Mind's logical ways. And so we're left to a decision to trust God or to trust our Mind.

If this were only a decision that impacted our own lives, we might not need to care so much about our choice. But we aren't disconnected life forms hitching a ride, but rather integral components of a living Universe. Our role to play in life is not only relevant to the singularity of our consciousness, but also an integral component of our Universe. God designed both life and the Universe to symbiotically work together, which bears us a responsibility to fulfill our purpose.

Clearly this is a lot to take in and quite a paradigm shift from how we human beings relate to nature. We accept that we impact our environment, but never before have we understood that we are central to the very survival of the Universe in which we live. Suspend your Mind's disbelief for the moment and return to the concept that our unique human purpose should both contribute to the environment in which we live and require abilities that we human beings alone possess.

So even though your value to the Universe has just been elevated to a status previously unimaginable, try and understand that it is possible for God to design you for a very special and pivotal purpose that you weren't aware of. Your awareness of your purpose is coming to light via your expanding consciousness and no doubt this won't be the last time that your horizons expand beyond your initial perception of reality.

Sharing Original Ideas

It has been said that there is no such thing as an original thought. Everything that has been said is an expansion of an existing thought. It is the piece that you add onto the thought that is your contribution. Without an awareness of every human thought that has come before you, it is impossible for you to truly know if your thoughts, ideas and creations are original. Pay this no mind, for it is not important that your creations be original, but rather that they contribute to Humanity. In investing in the birth of thoughts, you too will harvest creations that are truly original.

One might ask why God would need our original thoughts, ideas and creations? And while we don't know why God designed a Universe that necessitates the expansion of collective consciousness, we do hold to the concept that our God is an all-knowing God. As we are living beings that are subject to the fourth dimension of time, we think of the collection of knowledge as a progression from ignorance to knowledge.

For example, at one point in our life we are without a piece of information and then after a learning experience we possess the information. Prior to the learning event, we were ignorant of the information but afterwards we are knowledgeable. However, as God is not subject to any of the eleven dimensions of our Universe including the dimension of time, He already possesses the knowledge we have yet to create even though it didn't exist before we create it.

With God not being subject to the dimension of time, He is never not all-knowing even though the suppliers of knowledge operate in a time defined reality.

It is difficult and egotistical to view ourselves as the provider of God's knowledge. And when one considers knowledge in terms of who has it and who does not, the value that we associate with being knowledgeable is what gives way to this judgmental perspective. But imagine that God desired to be all knowing and He specifically created human beings to think of everything that is capable of being thought. Thus we are not here on Earth as a byproduct of the sea or to simply pay homage to God, but rather God has placed us here to think, innovate, grow and discover. In doing so, we provide God with knowledge and in doing so fulfill the purpose He intended. In this, we are not egotistical purveyor's of knowledge, but rather humble servants performing the work that we were designed to do.

Up until now, we have spoken of the Mind as a worker bee component of our being. However, beyond the Mind's job to keep us alive, process logic and listen to the Spirit, the Mind has a much richer role to play in our lives. Not only must the Mind filter and interpret all communications from the Spirit, but the Mind must also formulate our thoughts. In doing so, our Mind is front and center in our quest to birth original creations.

The Mind, which focuses on the past, is mindful to store thoughts to avoid entropy. We relate to this process as memories and information being stored in the memory cells of our brain. As such, the

Mind has a rich field of information to retrieve information, memories and experiences (i.e. the brain). The Body, in contrast, has no such retrieval system as it exists in the domain of *Here and Now*. Once the present becomes the past, it is stored with the Mind.

The Spirit, which lives in the domain of the future, doesn't store its experiences either. Without a means to store information, the Spirit simply interprets and passes along recommendations to the Mind. However, just like the Mind, the Spirit also has a rich field of information to retrieve information. When our original creations are shared with Humanity, they are released from the confines of our Body and Mind. With this release, our creations go into the collective consciousness of the Universe and are available in entirety to the Spirit.

Much has been written on the concept of collective consciousness under a number of different names over the years. The central theme of collective consciousness is a data bank of information that holds every thought, idea and concept that has ever been created by mankind. To try and comprehend such a concept, take our idea of an all-knowing God and remove the *knowing* part from a conscious God and remove the concept of *self*. This is, of course, hard to do because we envision God to be like us but on a grander scale. And because our Mind can't really imagine itself existing outside of our own *self*, it is also difficult to imagine an all-knowing consciousness without the Mind of God ruling over it. But this too is simply our egotistical Minds projecting our sense of *self* onto God.

The Spirit, through its boundless connections in the Universe, is readily able to retrieve a vast amount of information from collective consciousness and pass insights along to the Mind. Every original creation throughout the history of time is embodied in the collective consciousness and available to your Spirit.

In order for original creations to become part of collective consciousness, they must first be released from the confines of your Body and Mind. If you don't share your thoughts, ideas and dreams with others, then it is impossible for anyone else to know of your thoughts, ideas and dreams. The same is the case with collective consciousness. If your original creations remain trapped within you, then they cannot be shared with the other Spirits in the Universe, collective consciousness doesn't expand, and more dark energy isn't generated.

The Mind formulates the thoughts that birth original creations and these thoughts must leave the Mind if they are to make it into collective consciousness. As the Mind solely communicates and governs the Body (not the Spirit), our original creations must be communicated to the Body in order for them to subsequently be communicated from the Body to the Spirit.

There are only two sensual dimensions of the Body that communicate as well as receive energy. Whereas the eyes, ears and nose only receive information, the skin and mouth send and receive information. Thus the original creations passed from the Mind to the Body need to be released via your mouth and skin. For your mouth, this expression comes by way of your voice. And, for the most part, this expression is through the hands for your skin.

In order to know if you are contributing original creations to collective consciousness, you need to look no further than your mouth and hands. If your creations are flowing from your mouth in the form of voice (e.g. talking, sharing, speaking, singing, etc.) or from your hands (e.g. writing, shaping, forming, sculpting, moving, building, etc.) then you are successfully releasing original creations.

For there to be a successful transmission into collective consciousness, there must be both expression and reception. We do this by way of communication from the Body to the Spirit. While this may seem obvious, the means by which this communication flows and your ability to do this may surprise you. For starters, recognize that this is the way you were designed to operate and therefore everyone is capable of communicating with their Spirit. However, if you've not been nurturing your Spirit, then your ability to communicate directly with your Spirit may be compromised.

So too, keep in mind that you're evolving to a Spiritual existence and this progression was both intended and designed by God. Because of this, it is implausible that God would design us with this evolutionary path and not consider alternative ways for knowledge to flow into collective consciousness. After all, if God designed life to progress in evolutionary waves, there also would need to be a method for un-evolved life forms to contribute their original creations. As such, human beings have more than one way to communicate with their Spirit.

We do this primarily in one of two ways:

1. **Harmony** - by nurturing the connective bonds and bringing the Body, Spirit and Mind into balance, we establish a direct link with our Spirit to receive information from our Body and communicate information to our Mind.

2. **Sharing** - by sharing with others, we expand the number of connections that can transmit and receive information. Others that are strongly connected to their Spirit act as conduits for your Spirit.

In order to get original creations to your Spirit, the connective bonds between the Body, Spirit and Mind must be strong. Establishing harmony is like tuning a musical instrument. Once tuned, the instrument can play beautiful music. Thus by investing in the Body, Spirit and Mind, you will strengthen the connections between each and be able to send and receive information with insights derived from collective consciousness. Please don't judge yourself for not being in direct communication with your Spirit or automatically assume that you are either. Harmony requires focused and regular investments be made.

However, the act of playing beautiful music is all together different from the act of creating the original piece of music itself. This is not to say that there is anything wrong with playing music composed by another or that the act of playing music composed by another has no value. Quite the opposite is true, as playing music enables others to hear the music. Subsequently others may be inspired to write their own symphony. And the cycle repeats itself.

When the student becomes the master and the master becomes the student the Universe expands. The cycle repeats throughout eternity.

As this relates to consciousness, there is value and purpose in expanding one's consciousness without regard to the originality of the creation. Being open to and in-tune with the Universe will bring to you a flood of information that is akin to listening to a beautiful trio concerto. From this harmonious connection to collective consciousness, you will attain enlightenment and be given the tools to create your own symphony.

Through this creative process, you too shall expand the Universe. Your original creations, combined with the collective consciousness of all Humanity, will generate unlimited dark energy and, in turn, enable others to fulfill their purpose. Accordingly, fulfilling your purpose contributes to your environment (the Universe) and is made possible by your exocentric ability to be self-conscious and temporally related to your environment. Because you now know who you are (your Spirit as expressed through your Body and Mind) and when you need to act (a body at rest begins to decay, so get started now), you can play a contributing role in our common purpose to expand the Universe.

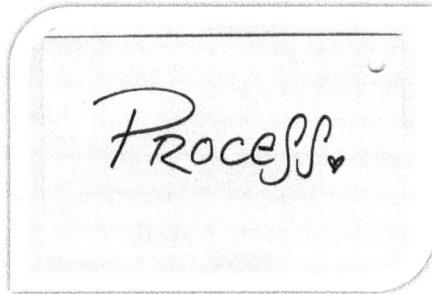

Card 11: Process: a series of actions or steps taken in order to achieve a particular end.

Absorbing Collective Consciousness

Acquiring knowledge (learning) is also a necessary component of expanding the Universe. In order for creations to be original, by definition they must not be the same as previous creations. Your Mind is adept at absorbing knowledge and storing conclusions unlike no other creature on the planet. By design, this allows human beings to absorb the collective consciousness of Humanity and build upon those creations.

The acquisition of knowledge occurs over time in a cyclical nature. As introduced in his groundbreaking book Psycho-Cybernetics, Dr. Maxwell Maltz reported observing that it took 21 days for amputees to cease feeling phantom sensations in an amputated limb (Maltz was a plastic surgeon). From further observations, he found it also took 21 days to create a new habit.

Further research has revealed that engaging in the desired habit at the same time everyday and engaging many of the senses greatly influences the habit forming function in the brain (e.g. meditating at the same time of day, while wearing the same clothes and burning the same incense). The eleven dimensions of our Universe not only govern cohesive structure and energy flow, they are also the means by which information flows between the Body, Spirit and Mind.

Absorbing knowledge from collective consciousness occurs in a similar manner. The broadcasting of collective consciousness never stops, but it is received in cycles. It is difficult to listen to this broadcast during the day when your Mind is fully in charge and your Body is performing the tasks given to it by the Mind. When you're completely still and not thinking, you're truly listening. This is why many people report breakthrough discoveries when doing routine tasks (e.g. driving, taking a shower, etc.) and during the twilight sleeping hours.

When the Mind is at rest, it is able to listen to the Spirit.

Have you ever had one of those restless nights when you couldn't stop thinking? Maybe you were working through a project at work, wondering how to build something or just going over a seemingly unsolvable problem over and over again (instead of sleeping). At times like these, you're fighting the transmission of answers from collective consciousness by thinking too much rather than sitting back and surrendering to the message.

More over, many people actually solve their problems during these inspirational sessions but can't recall the solution in the morning. They awake un-rested and bothered that they couldn't stop thinking all night long. In reality, a purposeful message came to them and became part of them, but because it didn't originate in the Mind, the egocentric Mind decided not to store the conclusion. To avoid these missed opportunities, keep a pen and notebook on your nightstand so that you can jot down your nighttime inspirations.

During those nights, you may feel like you continually revisit the same question or problem over and over again. Your Mind is thinking, "Didn't we just go over this a second ago?" The reason this sensation feels this way is due to the nature of the transmission. As the Spirit communicates with the Mind via the two dimensions of emotion and arousal, you'll feel the sensation of the message twice (once from each dimension). In the four-dimensional Mind, the messages are compiled as a single thread of information, but perceived as two different periods of time.

This two cycle experience can be visually represented as the Dual Phi Spiral:

Figure 23: Communication via 1st Dimension

Figure 24: Communication via 2nd Dimension

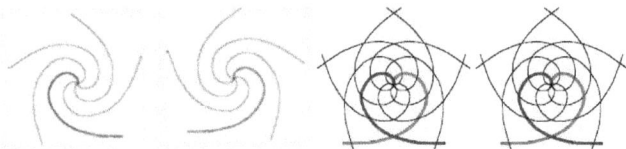

Figure 25: Communication via two emotive dimensions as perceived through singularity of a time based consciousness.

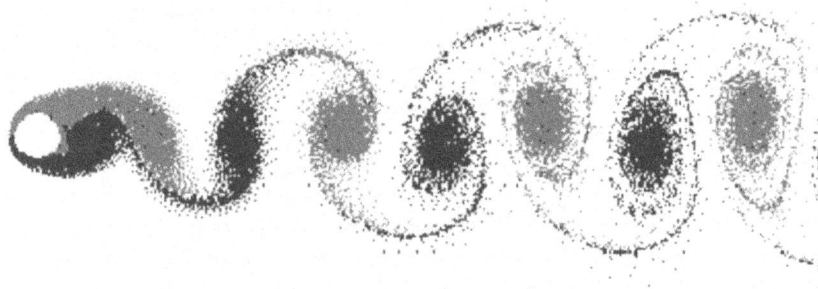

Figure 26: Each line of communication begins as a separate Phi Spiral, but when superimposed together, become a Dual Phi Spiral.

These restless nights are but one of the many indicators that you are receiving wisdom from your Spirit. In these moments, let go of the Mind and let collective consciousness flow into you. Your goal is not to disconnect and be a passive observer of this information, but rather to let it come and encourage the process. In time, your Mind will learn to play nice during these times and accept the knowledge received as conclusive thoughts. Even so, keep a pen and notebook close to your bed so you can record these messages as they arrive.

In these moments, you should embrace the process and engage your Spirit. Ask questions to which you desire answers. In this, remember that the connections between the Body, Spirit and Mind are asynchronous and thus your answers may not come immediately (e.g. similar to a back and forth conversation with another person). Rather your answers will come when they come; if you continue to listen.

Acquiring knowledge from collective consciousness is not a task with an end, but rather a repeating cycle.

In coming to an understanding of who you are, there is an awakening that you'll experience that is akin to peeling back layers of an onion. At first, there is a discovery of parts of you that you've subconsciously always been aware. The relationship between yourself and your Spirit feels more like reconnecting with a long, lost friend rather than meeting someone for the first time. But then comes an emergence of the Spiritual self that truly feels like a rebirth. Part old, part new and part Divine, the Spiritual self is the full embodiment of your full human potential.

The Cosmic Joke and Beautiful Punch line

Many religious texts and philosophical constructs refer to life as a battle that, if won, will lead to somewhere without suffering. Call it Heaven, Nirvana or the Land of Milk and Honey, we've all fallen under the spell that promises relief from this earthly prison. And in contrast to the pain, suffering and troubles that are common in our lives, it is easy to understand why we are attracted to the concept of a life without pain.

To imagine what this magical place might be like, take a closer look at any of God's creations. For example, draw your eye close to a flower and take a solitary minute to experience the flower and nothing else. Commit your Body, Spirit and Mind to experiencing the flower and nothing else for a single minute. Let your eyes take in the beautiful design, your nose smell the unique fragrance, your hands feel the subtle texture, imagine what the flower would taste like and, if the flower could emit a single sound, what would your ears hear? If the flower could convey one emotion, which one would it choose and what degree of arousal would it bring forth? Take in the full essence of the flower and give it your full attention without any distraction.

Now step back and ask yourself if you could imagine anything more perfect? Maybe you prefer a different color, find a different fragrance more pleasing or can even imagine a more perfect flower than the one in front of you. In this, you have expanded the Universe ever so slightly in one minute of your life. In this solitary, focused minute you've taken in all that is available and focused your consciousness on one of God's most perfect creations. And no matter if you're a fan of flowers or not, you've distinguished ever so softly the beauty and magnificence of a single creation.

Only now can you step back and appreciate the beauty and magnificence of both the world in which we live, but so too the vast potential of the Universe. Whereas an after life baits us with the promise of a better existence, the Spiritual existence brings the beauty and magnificence of God's creation into our present life.

The chapter you've just read explains the purpose of Humanity and seeks to help you understand your own personal relevance in this big Universe of ours. By understanding your common purpose with the rest of Humanity, you can better understand how to operate in day-to-day life and hopefully make better decisions as to what to do with your time (hint: grow).

Whereas you may have previously found life to be complicated, you now have an awareness of the simple purpose of expanding collective consciousness that you're called to fulfill. Each and every day you can keep yourself on track to achieve your purpose by asking yourself these three simple questions:

1. What have I done today to nurture and grow my Body?

2. What have I done today to nurture and grow my Spirit?

3. What have I done today to nurture and grow my Mind?

The subsequent insights in this book are designed to help you navigate your way through life using the understanding we've developed thus far. Before you turn the next page and continue reading, take a minute to let this new understanding sink into your Mind. With these types of books it is quite easy to be taken by a concept presented, but find that weeks later that we struggle to remember what we found so compelling at the time.

Understanding your role to play in life and why you're here is critical to you not only surviving in life, but also thriving in life. You now know that God desires for you to be a healthy, contributing member of the human race. As a human being, you share both a common purpose to create original ideas and an individual purpose that will provide you with a unique way to contribute to this common purpose. As such, the cards are not stacked against you and life doesn't have to be a battle; rather we all share a common purpose and God wants us to succeed in fulfilling this purpose.

Our Minds are like logical, advanced thinking computers that crave complexity. We think that understanding the interworking of the cosmos and consciousness must be complicated, mysterious and incredible. In reality, both are surprisingly simple despite our Mind's desire to make things more complicated than they need to be.

God created the Universe with the potential for life to emerge and evolve. Life evolves through the phases of physical, mental and finally spiritual. Along the way, life creates many fabulous creations that add to the collective consciousness and expand God's all knowing nature. In gratitude for fulfilling this common purpose, God provides our Universe with dark energy to power everything within the Universe including its expansion.

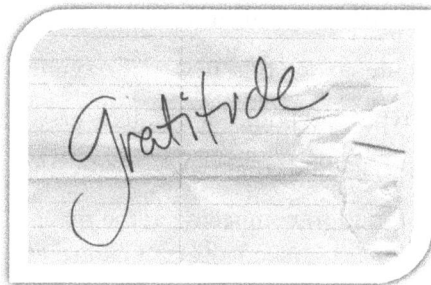

Card 12: Gratitude: the quality of being thankful; readiness to show appreciation for and to return kindness.

By awakening to the simplicity of the *how* and *why* things work the way they do in the Universe and in our lives, we can better understand how we can find peace, harmony and happiness. The union of our Body, Spirit and Mind provides us with the opportunity to bring ourselves to a place of balance. And in balance, we can nurture and grow towards becoming more complete. In this space, our consciousness expands exponentially and we are able to tap into and draw wisdom from collective consciousness.

God's influence, power and communications flow all around us and, via a Spiritual existence, we are able to connect to God. Whereas our un-evolved existence was random and chaotic, a Spiritual existence brings us to an understanding that reveals the meaning behind everything that happens in life. This revelation does not provide us with power over our enemies or blessings of God's favor. Instead this enlightenment provides us with a path that flows with God and consequently we experience less conflict, pain and problems in our life.

We attain and sustain enlightenment by nurturing our Body, Spirit and Mind into balance and pursuing our purpose. In this blissful state, we move from a passive participation to an active participation whereby we bring the eleven dimensions of our Universe into our conscious awareness. It is here that we navigate through life with ease and grace. Learning this language of enlightenment brings us into direct communication with God and it is here that all of Humanity will evolve to a Spiritual existence one person at a time.

Your Practice

A. Symbiotic Relationships Circle

Diagram below as many living things that either depend on you or that you depend on. Place living things that are highly dependent on you closer to you (e.g. a child, garden plants, etc.) and living things that are less dependent on you further away.

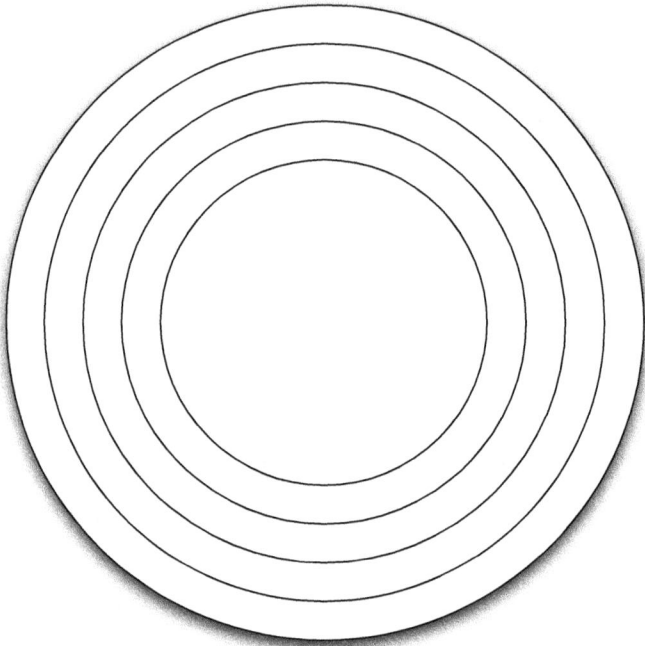

B. Original Creations

Without regard to merit, jot down the ideas that you have created in the last day, last week and last month. Ideas can be simple solutions to problems, advice you've given a friend, a work of art (even doodling), etc. Divorce yourself from your ego while you perform this exercise and refrain from judging the creations you think of.

_____

_____

_____

_____

_____

C. Symbiotic Relationships

Go back and circle every idea, creation or solution listed above that benefited another living thing. If this reminds you of living things that you forgot to list in exercise A (e.g. friends, family, coworkers, etc.) go back and add them to Exercise A.

D. Keep a Nightstand Notebook

Grab a notebook and pen to keep next to your bed for that next night where your Spirit is communicating with you. The next time you're experiencing a restless night, begin listening with intent and participate in the conversation that unfolds. As you solve problems, spark new ideas or remember something you had forgotten earlier, take a moment to write down your insights in your notebook.

E. Experience a Flower

Draw your eye close to a flower and take a solitary minute to experience the flower and nothing else. Let your eyes take in the beautiful design, your nose smell the unique fragrance, your hands feel the subtle texture, imagine what the flower would taste like and, if the flower could emit a single sound, what would your ears hear?

_____

If the flower could convey one emotion, which one would it choose and what degree of arousal would it bring forth?

_____   _____

F. My Spiritual Chessboard

Revisit the Spiritual Chessboard (p. 136) and consider moving some of the people on the board. Can you consider playing the game differently? Update your chessboard pieces below:

On My Side				Not On My Side			

INSIGHT #1

CONFLICT

When two or more people interact while their entities are in conflict (one rising, one descending), they experience conflict. How many times has someone been difficult with you and, upon asking what is wrong with them, they confide that a problem in their life is what was causing their grouchiness. In the beginning, you believed they were being a jerk, but in truth, they were experiencing a problem in their life.

Anyone that is experiencing forward descension in one or more of their entities is likely to be grouchy, depressed or even mean. However, when these people come in contact with those in forward ascension, a great deal of energy is released.

Be careful not to interpret interpersonal conflict with the ego driven, past focused, individualistic reality of your Mind. Instead look within yourself to check if your entities are rising or descending and inquire about the other person's too. More often than not, you'll find that the conflict between your colliding entities is the cause rather than any intent by either party to be difficult.

Also be weary of interpersonal conflict when you're experiencing a rise or drop in any one of your entities. When you come in contact with others that are oppositional to your motion, there will be conflict. To better equip yourself to deal with these situations, invest in activities that strengthen the Body, Spirit and Mind's ability to deal with oppositional forces (e.g. practicing yoga engages the body to push and pull at the same time and thus teaches the Body to embrace oppositional forces).

In particular, when you put each of your entities in forward ascension and experience harmony with the Universe, you will experience conflict with others. At the very moment that you are opening up and experiencing the beauty of life with vibrant enthusiasm, you too will find many of your colleagues, friends and family very difficult to deal with. Be extremely patient with them during this time in your life for it is not their fault. Their Minds will not understand the conflict between the two of you and they may deduce that there is something wrong with you.

As you become more conscious, the rising or descending of your Body, Spirit and Mind will become clearer to you. There will be periods of time in your life when any one of your entities may be knocked off course temporarily. For example, while your Body may be in forward ascension, we all catch a cold once in a while. Before you may have been aware that you were sick, but now you'll take note that your Body is temporarily descending and hopefully notice what is going on with your Spirit and Mind too. However, it is important to note that a minor illness doesn't cause the Body to change course permanently.

Similarly we shouldn't assume that when we run into someone who is having a bad day that their Spirit is in forward descension. But when someone is experiencing a true drop in one of their entities, you can be assured that there will be conflict with the people in their lives that are in forward ascension.

I recall a distinct time when I had a conflict that seemed irresolvable. We all have good and bad days at work, but I'm talking about the type of conflict that makes you want to change jobs. I had recently received the promotion of a lifetime and was throwing myself into my new job with all of my passion, energy and ideas. I found myself in the top position of one of the largest regions of a Fortune 500 company with over 300 employees to manage, over a thousand clients and one difficult boss to keep happy.

My predecessor had neglected both the employees and the workplace for so long that morale was at an all time low. What's more, the political infighting that had risen out of this region was out of control. In inheriting this region and being asked to turn it around, I faced an uphill challenge of both convincing the employees that things would get better and enlisting the management team to help me make a difference. Everyone was skeptical and at the same time eager to impress the new boss even though they weren't really on board with the changes I was recommending.

I knew that coming in and telling the employees and managers to clean up the facilities wouldn't be received well so I organized paint parties to clean up the break rooms, offices and warehouses where the employees worked. A handful of motivated managers joined me and once the others saw me cleaning their break rooms, a change started to happen with the workers. Pride of ownership began to return to the workplace and it wasn't long before our region had the cleanest and safest facilities in the company. The employees began to care for their own work areas and we introduced reward programs that incentivized everyone to maintain a level of quality in the workplace.

In short order, my region became the pride of the company and other regions started inquiring about how we turned things around. It took a lot more than a few paint parties to turn the ship around, but through these small changes the morale improved, the political infighting lessened and pride of ownership became the means by which we tackled many problems.

But then an odd thing happened. My boss and I started to disagree on many, many things. It started out with differences of opinion, but it wasn't long before we completely disagreed on important issues that drove a wedge between us. We were both reasonably intelligent people with a common vision of the business, but we seemed to always be in conflict rather than agreement. I logically came up with several different ways to resolve the conflict, but each time my efforts failed.

I learned later that my boss was going through a divorce. He wasn't someone who shared his personal life at work and very few people knew he was even married, let alone getting a divorce. In addition to the issues that he and I wrestled with, his Spirit was in forward descension while my Body, Spirit and Mind were in rapid growth mode. And even though it would make logical sense that he would be content with my performance during this time in his life, the fact remained that our entities were in opposition and this caused great friction between us.

If I knew then what I know now, I would've had empathy for him rather than contempt. At the time I was only present to the conflict between us and attempted to logically think my way out of the problems I was experiencing. Instead of trying to conquer him with logical arguments, I could've found a way to help resolve our conflict with love and compassion.

Card 13: Love in its various forms acts as a major facilitator of interpersonal relationships.

We don't often think of solving conflict with love and compassion at work. Instead we compartmentalize our lives and let love and compassion play a role in our home life, but as for our work life we let the Mind handle everything. However, instead of going through life conquering, we can let our Spirit engage in all of our relationships regardless of them being personal or professional.

In moments like these, have patience and stay the course. Refrain from attempting to convince others that their thoughts are incorrect. Enlightenment cannot occur within the domain of the Mind and thus, your Mind cannot convince their Mind that their perception of reality is incorrect. Instead, remain in forward ascension and share with them the gifts that arise from your enlightenment.

Enlightenment can only be found, it cannot be given.

Upon enlightenment, you will experience an overwhelming desire to share it with everyone in your life. Nevertheless the human Mind is quite adept at taking what it needs and discarding the information that it deems to be unnecessary. So when you share your experience, others may disregard what you have to say, because they've disregarded what they didn't agree with in your message and only agreed with what they already believed to be true. This is why when you share amazing insights, you sometimes get back, "I already knew that."

Even when you point out the breakthrough insight you've discovered through an original thought, the recipient might discard the parts of your message that their Mind doesn't want. In the *Handbook of Emotions*, this willingness for individuals to accept differing information was shown to vary by individual:

> Individuals differ not only in the categories they use to encode, interpret and manage information, but also with the ease in which they tend to preempt as opposed to assimilate data that threaten to disconfirm those constructs. This "impermeable" vs. "permeable" or "elastic" dimension of personal constructs refers to how readily an individual can incorporate new and potentially threatening (disconfirming) data into a given personal construct while still retaining it. (Lewis and Haviland-Jones 2004),

What remains is what they believed to be true prior to talking to you. Said another way, when an individual lives entirely within the consciousness of their Mind, they are unable to accept information that could potentially disconfirm a conclusion of the Mind. In communion with the Body and the Spirit, the Mind is able to accept potentially disconfirming information, because the entire being is involved in the decision making process. Therefore, when sharing your breakthroughs, share the gifts that come from your enlightenment rather than trying to share the enlightenment itself.

By sharing you unite Humanity.

Remember that by sharing, you unite Humanity. Each gift that you share with another opens up a tiny connection (e.g. a string) between their Body, Spirit and Mind. Because human beings cannot exist within a single one of their entities, any string that connects two entities actually connects all three. Thus a connection from the Mind to the Body also connects the Spirit. As such, share yourself fully with those around you and you will help bring harmony into everyone's life.

Your Practice

A. Interpersonal Conflict

Think back to the last time you experienced conflict with someone and try to remember where you were in terms of your Body, Spirit and Mind. Knowing what you know now (which hopefully is more than you did during the conflict), see if you can circle what was going on for the other person at the time in terms of their Body, Spirit and Mind on the chart below. Repeat this exercise the next time you experience interpersonal conflict.

Conflict with:					
Your Body		**Your Spirit**		**Your Mind**	
↑	↓	↑	↓	↑	↓
Rising	Falling	Rising	Falling	Rising	Falling
Their Body		**Their Spirit**		**Their Mind**	
↑	↓	↑	↓	↑	↓
Rising	Falling	Rising	Falling	Rising	Falling

Conflict with:					
Your Body		**Your Spirit**		**Your Mind**	
↑	↓	↑	↓	↑	↓
Rising	Falling	Rising	Falling	Rising	Falling
Their Body		**Their Spirit**		**Their Mind**	
↑	↓	↑	↓	↑	↓
Rising	Falling	Rising	Falling	Rising	Falling

INSIGHT #2

JUDGMENT

As much as the Mind logically loves to divide almost everything into good and bad, there is no such thing as divine and evil. We've been sold this judgmental way of living since the day we were born and this framework for understanding is reinforced with every decision we make.

Not only have we divided everything into good and bad since our early childhood, but this way of thinking has been the way human beings have lived their lives for countless generations before us. Our logical Minds divide everything into groups and from there we judge those groups according to our value system. And because everyone around us is doing the same thing, we believe this is the only way we are capable of being.

A physical existence requires this way of thinking for survival. You can imagine primitive man classifying carnivorous dinosaurs as bad and fellow human beings as good. After all, the carnivorous dinosaurs were trying to eat the human beings. In seeking a Spiritual existence, we don't ignore the dinosaurs in our lives, but instead recognize that they're not evil. They're simply non-spiritual life forms that do whatever their Minds tell them to do.

The decisions that our parents wanted to encourage were labeled as *good* and those they wanted to discourage were labeled as *bad*. From there we've grown up in a world where knowing the difference between good and bad determined how accepted we were by society. However, upon expanding our horizons to other cultures, we find that our definitions of good and bad aren't universal. For example, in Japan it is customary to slurp your soup to convey that you find it tasty. For years, American children have been taught that slurping their soup was rude and yet in Japan just the opposite is true. Is one culture right and the other wrong? Or is it possible that they're just different?

From there we extend a judgmental life to a much grander scale with the concept of divine and evil. In this context, our God is divine and any belief that opposes our belief is evil. Absolute evil is defined as the dominion of the Devil, but each society also believes that they are living a Divine existence and those that oppose them are more or less tainted with evil. In the simplest logic, we are right and they are wrong. Or is it possible that we're just different?

Our logical Minds crave absolutes and thus abandoning judgment is a very difficult adjustment to make. But by liberating ourselves from judgment, we are better able to find truth and beauty. Remember, in the domain of the Spirit, the dimensions of emotion and arousal are merely dimensions. In this domain pleasure is not good, nor is pain evil. They simply are dimensions.

Notwithstanding, one look at Humanity and it's clear that evil acts are committed all the time. Many of these evil acts are so heinous that one often concludes that evil spirits must possess the people who committed them. *Clearly, no one without evil in their hearts would be capable of such horrible crimes against Humanity.* With this view of life, one easily concludes that evildoers represent a definitive embodiment of evil.

As a result, we flock to representations of good to protect us from evil. In this, we give power to whatever is evil by saying, "If I allow evil to come near me, I will be helpless to prevent myself from becoming evil myself." Accordingly religious leaders warn of the temptations that lead an individual down the slippery slope towards evil, damnation and eternally living in Hell.

However, in our hearts, we really don't believe this. We really don't believe that it is possible that through becoming contaminated with wickedness that we will rise up and become serial killers, mass rapists or pedophiles. We surely want to instill measures that prevent others from becoming wicked, but we're fairly confidant that we (meaning you) aren't capable of such wrongdoing. Nevertheless you're not so sure about the rest of Humanity so you support rules, guidelines and laws that keep others away from evil.

In this, we separate ourselves from Humanity. We believe that our neighbors are capable of evil acts and thus we don't trust them. Once we decide that someone is a good person, we accept them into our homes and then we're shocked when we find out that they've been leading a double life. We're dismayed to learn that the preacher cheated on his taxes, an Uncle molested a child down the street and some CEO embezzled millions. Our mental concept of evil slips into every instance where the activities of seemingly good people turn out to be bad.

There is no question that there are evil acts. However, evil has more to do with a disconnected and unconscious being than it does a spiritual force that possesses your soul (or more likely the soul of your neighbor). Recall that, the way in which you were intended to operate is in balance between your Body, Spirit and Mind. In individuals with atrophied connections to their Body or Spirit, there is ample opportunity for horrible outcomes.

By design, your Body and Spirit act as counterbalances and feedback mechanisms for the Mind. The Mind, in its quest to keep you alive, is designed to evaluate countless options and ideas. Some of those ideas are good, some of them not so good and many of them are completely irrational. You may find yourself thinking random, crazy thoughts that you immediately dismiss. You may even be troubled that your Mind is even capable of thinking such thoughts. But since you immediately dismiss them and feel confidant that you would never follow through on those thoughts, you're reasonably assured that you would never actually do anything that crazy.

However, you're operating with much stronger connections between your Body, Spirit and Mind. Although your entities may be weak and the bonds between them in need of nurturing, your entities are online and functioning nonetheless. Those people that commit evil acts are operating without such strength in their connections. Their Minds are entirely in charge and, without any counterbalance and feedback from the Body and Spirit, their Minds are free to follow through on their crazy thoughts.

Gone are the days when we believed we could fend off a vampire with a crucifix. Holding a cross in front of a serial killer or pedophile doesn't prevent them from committing evil acts. And we have good reason for being suspicious of strangers before we know if they are of sound Body, Spirit and Mind. However, until we understand that it is our disconnected society that doesn't give equal emphasis to the Body, Spirit and Mind, we will continue to have more and more people lost in their crazy Minds who are truly unable to resist the irrational thoughts they generate.

Society's evolution will one day come through communion with the Body, Spirit and Mind. With the Body, Spirit and Mind rising in ascension towards balance, each individual being is receiving harmonious feedback from all three entities and guidance from God. With this, rehabilitation of evildoers is possible. With the Spirit engaged in the conversation, the being is guided towards fulfilling their purpose rather than following the logical and illogical ideas of the Mind. One's purpose is never clouded with evil acts and thus, with clarity of purpose, we bring ourselves onto the path of consciousness and living a Spiritual existence.

With the Spirit engaged in the conversation, the guiding message of God is infused into every breath we take. Our lives are embracing a path to becoming complete and this path is blessed with the flowing energy of God. By walking this path, we find ourselves seeking and finding rather than guessing and hoping.

Unfortunately, this is a personal journey towards enlightenment and one that can only be found, not given. You may be able to point out the errors in others, but in this judgmental approach, they will only listen to your words with their Minds. The Spirit must first be brought into the conversation before anyone can understand, listen and find their own way. As it will be for you, their understanding will be instantaneous when the shift to balanced harmony occurs, but it may take years before they unlock these keys to listen.

Rehabilitation of the Body, Spirit and Mind is a Universal journey. Each and every one of us requires constant nourishment and investment into our entire being. We are all children in our journey to completeness and this means that each of us is a mirror image of others that need rehabilitation. Our methods to become complete are no different than another's methods. How much we need to grow may vary but the planting of seeds and raising up of our Bodies, Spirits and Minds is identical in every human being regardless of our past.

A Life Devoid of Judgment

You may not be ready to give up believing in a reality devoid of dividing the Universe, God and Humanity into the camps of divine and evil. The world is full of awful acts committed by mankind and our belief in causal demonic possession doesn't change the reality of the Universe, God or Humanity. If there is a Devil ruling over our souls via a dominion of possessive demons, then that is our reality regardless of what we believe. Alternatively, if this is not the case, then it would be rather silly for us to run around believing it to be true. At the end of the day, the reality of the Universe, God and Humanity *is what it is* regardless of what we think.

But judgment is something that we can give up without personally weighing in on the battle between good and evil. In our everyday lives, we pass judgment on others so often that we don't even realize how much it dominates our thinking. As you begin to become aware of your labeling of people, actions and even objects as being *right* or *wrong*, you'll start to understand how much time our Minds spend judging.

From there, it is a small shift to recognize how often we judge ourselves and our loved ones. When we think of judgment, we most often think about how we assign negative labels to people, but so too are the positive labels the flip side of that same coin. When we tell a child that their behavior earned the label of *good*, we're also sending the message that when they don't exhibit the desired behavior that they are a *bad* child. And while this may have been intentional in some circumstances, often times this isn't our intent. Often times we just want to convey encouragement, rather than weighing in on the child's behavioral link to being divine or evil.

As we look at the rampant cases of depression, low self-esteem and lack of motivation in our cultures, we begin to understand the power of our words on others. All too often we recognize the power of our words when it is too late. Upon wishing we could take back what we said, we ask ourselves, "Why did I say that?"

By pursuing a life devoid of judgment, we are not seeking a life ignorant of reality. The goal is not to turn a blind eye to the actions of those in our lives, but rather to guide them without the convenient and often ignorant divisions that spring forth from judgment. It surely takes a more conscious, peaceful and connected person to live a life devoid of judgment.

But, after all, isn't that the point?

Card 14: Serenity: the state of being calm, peaceful, and untroubled.

Listen to Yourself

Living a Spiritual existence brings us to a relationship with God that reveals truth. This truth does not come from the words of man, but rather is revealed through the voice of God. For a number of reasons, mankind has concluded that a direct relationship with God is unattainable and thus not recommended. Possibly they fear that you'll develop a false relationship with your own Mind masquerading itself as the voice of God and become devout in pursuing some madness evoked by the Mind. A seeker of the truth is present to this risk and therefore considers the source of every message. Is this message a truth revealed by my Spirit or the deviations of my Mind?

So too we must actively consider religious cultures that espouse an awareness of God's intent but aren't in synch with the loving, non-judgmental God that speaks to us directly. This is not to say that religious interpretations that demonstrate an angry, judgmental God are demonstrating that their religion is false. The point is that interpreting scripture should be undertaken with an understanding of God's true nature rather than blindly based on the interpretations of others. With this you can separate interpretation and original meaning as conveyed by the prophet. And while this is a task that many will leave to religious scholars, the inherent task in considering what you know to be true in your heart is an obligation to understand God in a way that rings true with love, compassion and purpose.

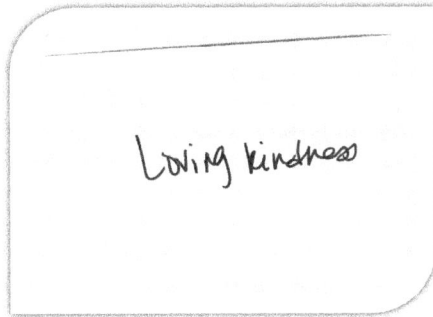

Card 15: Loving-Kindness is often associated with the Chesed Hebrew word, the Agape Greek word, and the Buddhist term Metta.

Through a direct relationship with God we are permitted to ask questions. For example, when a child questions your guidance I highly doubt that you'll condemn the child to eternal damnation for questioning you. Instead you recognize that this is a natural part of the learning process. Only when you don't have the patience to educate the child do you resort to answers like, "Because I told you so!"

Thus when we embrace a relationship with God and seek to understand our way through life, we are encouraged to question philosophies on living a Spiritual existence. When you're *told* how God wants you to live your life, it is healthy to ask yourself, "Really? Does this ring true with what I know to be true in my heart?"

Everyday people espouse to know what God was thinking when He made our Universe, envisioned what life would be like and dictated laws for our living. From there we hear ideas like, "In order to keep us from becoming too attached to earth, God allows us to feel a significant amount of discontent and dissatisfaction in life." (Warren 2002)

Really? God purposely brings suffering into my life in order to make sure I don't get attached? The same omnipotent, all-knowing God that is loving, accepting and knows no boundaries has purposely brought suffering into my life to keep me from getting attached? Does that sound like the God you know in your heart?

Or is it the Devil that brings suffering into our lives because he really seeks our demise?

Really? The same omnipotent, all-knowing God that is loving, accepting and knows no boundaries is helpless to protect me from a fallen angel? Does that sound like the God you know in your heart?

Religious pundits can run logic circles around these arguments all day long, but in the end, it is our own Spirit that empowers our relationship with God. Our relationship with God need not make sense to our Minds, nor be agreeable with our Bodies. It is the Spiritual existence that connects us to God and, in this new way of living, we find that *following* God is not quite the same as *understanding* God.

When we break free from judgment and instead seek to understand our God given purpose, we begin to develop a strong, communal relationship with God that is both fulfilling and based on love. With this new approach to living we find both value and shortcomings in the words of other human beings regardless of their stature in our social, political or religious communities. The beauty of this new way of living is that all of mankind can teach us and no member of the human race holds out the truth to which we must aspire. Our truth is God spoken and, with our newfound ability to listen, we find our way through life with purpose, clarity and love.

No longer do we give evil a role to play in our lives and instead take on life with a loving embrace. Long gone are those fearful ways that turn away from a true relationship with God. So too we find ourselves not judging others that choose to live their relationship with God through the vision of others, but instead accept them as God loving beings. In this, we find common ground and can live in harmony with all religions, different races and every other aspect of difference that makes every human being unique.

In a Spiritual existence, we find a life embraced with love and without conflict. And this is where we live in harmony. To evolve to this existence requires more than simply believing that it is possible. While believing that a Spiritual existence is impossible will surely keep you off the path, believing is but the key that unlocks the door. Walking the path to enlightenment requires a healthy Body, Spirit and Mind connection. When we retreat to the judgmental ways of our Mind, the physical existence prevails and deters us from the path.

And why wouldn't it? Our Minds have kept us alive since birth and a judgmental framework for living reinforces the Mind's grip on our lives. As much as we deplore judgment, our Mindful ways cling to the definitions of good and evil because this way of living helps make sense out of the chaotic world around us. When the world makes sense, life is a bit easier. Knowing how to not get eaten by a dinosaur surely makes walking through the valley less stressful.

In this, we want to fear God and believe that it is the Devil that brings suffering into our lives. Our parents judged us according to their personal fusion of moral and ethical values, does it not *make sense* that a loving God would also judge us according to a moral code? And while living our lives in accordance with God's laws is dutiful, it doesn't make much sense if we've misunderstood God's ways from the beginning.

With judgment serving as the foundation for living our lives, we organize the Spiritual chessboard with those that fall within our definition of good onto our side and push everyone else away. We convince ourselves that our definition of good is better, wiser and truer than all the rest. Everyone on our side of the chessboard agrees with us and, with this consensus, we convince ourselves that we must be right.

Being right carries with it great responsibility. After all, being wrong would undermine the very judgmental foundation upon which everything else is built. Elders in our community subconsciously know how interconnected judgment is in the lives we live and therefore discourage exploring alternatives that put forth a non-judgmental God. This isn't because they're unwilling to know God, but rather because their Minds have been spoon-fed judgmental living from the day they were born. And without another structured framework to replace judgment, their Minds naturally fear the unknown.

Your Mind is no different, as living in a free-will reality necessitates choosing between alternatives. There is always a choice to be made and it is natural that you will judge one option as being better than another.

But when we attach ourselves to the judgment rather than the experience of choosing, we cut ourselves off from the life that God intended us to live.

The Spiritual chessboard on which we live our lives is an illusion of the Mind's making. By driving Humanity into camps of good and evil or right and wrong, we insulate ourselves from God and become lost in an existence divorced of a connection to our own Spirit. In contrast, by living a life without judgment we connect Humanity and fulfill the aspirations of the Spirit.

Knowing that you are your Spirit, as expressed through your Body and Mind, it makes more sense to seek the aspirations of the Spirit rather than the prejudices of the Mind. Both serve a role in our lives, but by leading a Spiritual existence we experience life as it was intended by God.

Your Practice

A. Deny Evil

Letting go of the concept of good and evil takes practice because our Minds are so focused on judgment. To train your Mind, watch the evening news and take notes on every story that involves someone committing an evil act. Write down the event below and ask yourself if that person was possessed by an evil spirit or if they were out of balance with their Body, Spirit and Mind. Another way is to ask if the person(s) committing the evil act was in balance with their Body, Spirit and Mind when they committed the act. Rather than simply accepting evil and giving energy to something that doesn't exist, take this exercise seriously and see if you personally encounter evil in your life.

_____

_____

_____

_____

_____

_____

_____

B. Keep a Judgment Log

As you go through your day, write down each and every time you judge a person, an action or an object. The point is not to judge yourself in this exercise but rather to bring your awareness to how rampant judgment is in your life.

Positive Judgment	Negative Judgment

INSIGHT #3

CYCLES

There is a deep meaning in the eternal life of the Spirit, but due to the singular consciousness of our life experience, we tend to view everything from our Mind's past focused perspective. Beginning with no more than our earliest childhood memories, we stumble through life with a loose recollection of past events as charted by intense moments of holidays, life phases and the people who come in and out of our lives. In a sense, you could say that we're passively aware of the life unfolding around us.

This isn't to say that we're not intensely focused on the present moment and all that it has to offer us. We inherently know that life is fleeting and regularly cherish life's little moments and challenge ourselves to live a full life. Without an understanding of the big picture, even a full life can be a fraction of our true potential. In this, we human beings seek to understand the Universe, God and Humanity so that we can embrace life and get the most out of it.

We are each born with unique talents, interests and passions that lead us to discover who we are, what we will do with our lives and how we will make a difference in the world. In this we are all different for no two people are the same despite our striking similarities. Even identical twins have quirks, desires and aspirations that differentiate one from the other. And while twins may share the same genes, each person chooses what to do with their life.

The time that we have on this earth is finite and thus finding and pursuing our purpose is not something to be left for another day. Each day that we waste not pursuing our purpose is one less day we have to make a difference. If this were something for a few isolated individuals, we might not give this much thought. But as expanding the Universe through pursuing our purpose is what God intended for us to do with our lives, it stands to reason that we should be steadfast in finding our purpose with the few years we have on the planet.

What we, or rather our Minds, do not comprehend through the four dimensions of our Mind (length, width, depth and time) is that there is no such thing as death. There is only conception and birth. Our Spirit is eternal, existed before God created the Universe and will exist long after the end of our Universe. Thus the end of our earth bound existence seems to be an ending simply because we have no memory of life prior to this lifetime. What appears to be an ending is actually a new beginning that brings us a fresh start to once again expand God's presence in the Universe.

The question we should be asking ourselves is, "Why does life repeat like this over and over again without any recollection of our past experiences?"

After all, if we toiled through life previously and learned some lessons that proved to be wise, it would be helpful to retain this knowledge in subsequent lifetimes so that we wouldn't make the same mistakes again. However, what if our previous life was one of hardship, misery and pain? Maybe starting over with a fresh start ensures we'll have a fighting chance of attaining a Spiritual existence in each lifetime. This memory lapse from our past lives is described in the mystical Jewish tale about the Angel of Conception:

Among the angels there is one who serves as the midwife of souls. This is Lailah, the angel of conception. When the time has come for conception, Lailah seeks out a certain soul hidden in the Garden of Eden and commands it to enter seed. The soul is always reluctant, for it still remembers the pain of being born, and it prefers to remain pure. But Lailah compels the soul to obey, and that is how new life comes into being.

While the infant grows in the womb, Lailah watches over it, reading the unborn child the history of its soul. All the while a light shines upon the head of the child, by which it sees from one end of the world to the other. And Lailah shows the child the rewards of the Garden of Eden, as well as the punishments of Gehenna. But when the time has come to be born, the angel extinguishes the light and brings forth the child into the world, and as it is brought forth, it cries. Then Lailah lightly strikes the newborn above the lip, causing it to forget all it has learned. And that is the origin of this mark, which everyone bears.
(Schwartz 1994)

Without a memory of our past life constraining us, we are born with boundless opportunities to chart any course of our choosing through life. The heartache that kept us from opening up to new people and opportunities in prior lives doesn't come with us into our rebirth. And without the baggage of our previous life's Mind holding us back, the world is our oyster. Each lifetime provides us with an opportunity to reach an even greater potential than we did before. Throughout the ages we continually expand to a greater potential every time we're reborn into the Universe.

A future life beyond this earthly existence is easy for us to understand, but without a recollection of our history, we find past lives a difficult concept to accept. If your Spirit didn't exist prior to your physical birth, then why would we expect it to survive beyond your physical death? However, if one understands that our purpose is to expand God's presence, then the wisdom of a repeating role for the Spirit begins to make sense. Each time we return to an earth bound Body, we continue to achieve our purpose in a different environment but with an even greater collective consciousness to draw from. In combination, this manifests an incredible opportunity to create even more fantastic solutions to problems that previously didn't exist. In this, God expands exponentially.

Roles in Relationships

Similar to the natural separation of the Body, Spirit and Mind, we play a similar role with other people in our lives. In every relationship, you play the role of Father (Spirit), Mother (Mind) or Child (Body). With the beginning (or conception) of every relationship, there is always a Mother and Father. Do not confuse the sex of your Body with the role of Mother or Father. In your lifetime, you will play the role of Father, Mother and Child many times.

For example, before I met my wife I was involved in an unhealthy relationship that was falling apart. I was distraught over the break-up at the time, but now I know that it was time for me to emerge into a new phase of my life. In my prior relationship, I played the role of Mother as I was entirely focused on the *Past*, my girlfriend played the role of Child as she was only concerned with the *Here and Now* and my matchmaking sister played the role of Father with her intention on the *Future*. This relationship could have limped along for years, but because my girlfriend was ready to be born into a new phase of her life, it ended despite my trying to hold it together. Good thing too, because within a month I met my future wife and many years later we are happily married with three wonderful children.

At the time, I viewed this break-up as the end of a relationship. Only now can I reflect on that time and see that I was ready to be born into a new phase of my life too. In addition to my readiness for a new beginning, staying in that prior relationship wouldn't have allowed me to grow in ways that prepared me to be a Father. The path may not have been pre-ordained, but it surely manifested itself in line with what I truly needed.

As with childbirth, the process of birth is hard on all three. For the Mother, there is a great deal of energy expended and pain experienced in birthing a child. For the Child, there is a connection to this pain and energy, but no direct experience of pain. The Father, connected to both, empathizes but feels no pain nor expresses no energy in the process of childbirth. With every birth, there is an awakening of the

Child made possible through the conception of the Child by the Mother and Father.

When a relationship dissolves, do not think of it as an ending but rather a birth. The length of the relationship is directly proportionate to the development requirements of the child (gestation). Once the child's development is complete, it is natural for it to be born into the world. Similarly when relationships dissolve you are experiencing the birth of a Child.

In your most devastating relationship breakups, you will surely find fault in others. The tell tale signs of the errors of their ways will be clear as night and day. So too will your friends rally around you to reinforce that you are right and the other person is wrong. However, what you fail to realize is that you are experiencing the birth of a child.

In most relationships, you will readily identify with the role of Mother or Father. But what you might consider in the breakup is that you were actually the child in this relationship. Through the ways of the asynchronous Universe, your gestation period was complete. And even though you didn't want to leave the comfort and warmth of your Mother's womb, it was time for you to be born.

Moreover, if you stayed in the womb you would slowly die. The next phase of your life was beginning and you needed a larger environment to make your yet unknown dreams come true. Only with the passing of time, can you look back and see the wisdom in your birth.

In any relationship, it is helpful to understand your role. With any given relationship ask yourself, "Am I the Father (Spirit), Mother

(Mind) or Child (Body)?" To determine your role and that of another remember the domain of each entity:

> **CHILD**: The Executing Body lives in the domain of the present and is expressed as, "Here and Now."
>
> **FATHER**: The Master Spirit lives in the domain of the future and is expressed as, "We Are."
>
> **MOTHER**: The Thinking Mind lives in the domain of the past and is expressed as, "I am."

When new people come into your life, they will fall into one of these three roles. And when you are ready for a new phase in your life, you will meet another Father and Mother. Similarly, when others are ready for their next phase, they will seek you out as their Mother or Father. This pattern will repeat itself throughout your lifetime.

Platonic Correlations

As with the natural cycle of being human, the Universe is subject to same cycle of conception and birth. Upon collective consciousness becoming complete, all energy expended will perform no useful work because every thought that Humanity is capable of creating within their environment will have been created. With this the average density will drop to zero and the Universe will again dynamically expand through yet another Big Bang. And while this may seem like an end, so too this is the birth of the child.

With our purpose fulfilled, the Universe will be reborn and life will once again embark on expanding collective consciousness within a new environment. The Universe, suddenly exposed to a new and vibrant environment, will come alive via an abundance of energy. And in this new home, life will spring forth and once again begin creating that which had not existed before.

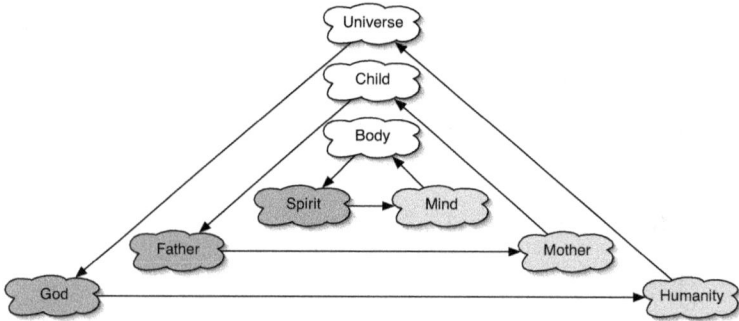

Figure 27: As shown here, the Universe is the Body of God. The Body (Universe) is the container that contains the Mind (Humanity) and enables the connection to the Spirit (God). The Spirit (God) communicates to the Mind (Humanity) and executes through the Body (Universe). As before, the Mind and the Spirit put the Body first because without the Body (Universe), the Spirit (God) cannot connect to this reality and the Mind (Humanity) cannot exist.

Understanding this universal model on a local level in order to understand the big picture is far from a new concept:

> To Plato, the complex phenomena that we observe in the Universe are not what really matters; the truly fundamental things are the underlying symmetries, and those are never changing. This view is very much in line with modern thinking about the laws of nature. For example, these laws do not change from place to place in the Universe. For this reason, we can use the same laws that we determine from laboratory experiments whether we study a hydrogen atom here on Earth or in a galaxy that is billions of light-years away. This symmetry of the laws of nature manifests itself in the fact that the quantity which we call linear momentum (equaling the product of the mass of an object and the speed, and having the direction of the motion) is conserved, namely, has the same value whether we measure it today or a year from now. Similarly, because the laws of nature do not change with the passing of time, the quantity we call energy is conserved. We cannot get energy out of nothing. Modern theories, which are based on symmetries and conservation laws, are thus truly Platonic. (Livio 2002)

The Universe, consisting of the same atoms that are the fabric of everything else in the Universe (including you), will begin to collapse if maximum entropy were ever to be reached. If collective consciousness were to become complete, every thought, idea and creation that is possible will have been created. At this point, the Universe would reach maximum entropy and collapse upon itself, including everything that exists within the Universe, because every thought contributed to collective consciousness would be unoriginal and perform no useful work.

Likewise, if collective consciousness were no longer expanding, dark energy would no longer be introduced and thus the existing life force energy in the Universe would be consumed by every living thing in the Universe. Consequently the average density of the Universe would eventually drop to zero causing the Universe to die a cold death. Conversely, if collective consciousness continues to expand, thus introducing more dark energy, the average density of the Universe will not drop outside of the its required density and the Universe will be maintained.

This model would work just fine for eternity if it weren't for the Laws of Thermodynamics. Among other things, these laws tell us that energy cannot be created or destroyed and that entropy will increase over time. In a closed system, this means that consolidated energy will dissipate over time and no longer be available to do any useful work. Thus, if our Universe is a closed system, this means that the energy present in our Universe is finite and eventually homeostasis will be attained. At that point, energy would be evenly distributed throughout the Universe and no longer be available to do any useful work.

However, our Universe is not a closed system. Similar to how our Spirit is not contained within the physical dimensions of our Bodies, so too God is not governed by the dimensions of our Universe. As such, God exists outside of the confines of our Universe. Thus our Universe as a whole is not bound by the Laws of Thermodynamics because our Universe is not a closed system. And while energy cannot be created or destroyed within our Universe, God providing dark energy in exchange for the expansion of collective consciousness explains the accelerating expansion of our Universe.

This is not to say that our Universe will never end. Once collective consciousness is complete, the Universe as we know it will come to an end. At that point, all of the energy in our Universe will be available to fuel the expansion of another Universe. In this view of competing Universes, expanding is the difference between continuing to exist or becoming the energy source for another Universe that is expanding. In this, we can think of God's entire domain as a closed system and the Laws of Thermodynamics once again applying.

We may not like the *survival of the fittest* model applying to the home in which we live. But upon recognizing that God created life for the purpose of expanding collective consciousness, one can begin to understand that not fulfilling our purpose makes our Universe look more like an energy source for another expanding Universe. However, if we do our job, our home will continue to expand and provide for us.

As with your own life, do not think of the end of our Universe as an ending, but rather as a birth. Conception (the formation of our Universe) and rebirth (the dynamic expansion of the Universe known as another Big Bang) is a cycle that has repeated itself through the history of time. So too, the dynamic expansion of the Universe (the Body) is merely the natural means by which Humanity (Mind) is reborn. The rebirth of the Universe (the Body) provides a new home for Humanity (the Mind) and a connection to God (the Spirit).

With the birth of a Child, the Father and Mother will give birth to the Child. With this birth, the Mother will expend much energy and feel great pain, the Child will experience the energy of rebirth but feel no pain and the Father will feel great empathy for both.

With the birth of a Universe, God and Humanity will give birth to the Universe. With this rebirth, Humanity will expend much energy and feel great pain, the Universe will experience the energy of rebirth but feel no pain and God will feel great empathy for both.

With the birth of a Body, the Spirit and Mind will give birth to the Body. With this rebirth, the Mind will expend much energy and feel great pain, the Body will experience the energy of rebirth but feel no pain and the Spirit will feel great empathy for both.

Collective consciousness is Humanity's gift back to God. Through the expansion of collective consciousness, dark energy is introduced by God and God's presence expands through the dynamic growth of the Universe. Accordingly, God is continually becoming all knowing through our additions to collective consciousness. If God were already all knowing[11], then there would be no purpose in Humanity. And thus, God created us in His image as unique, thinking creatures capable of birthing unimaginable, amazing and original creations.

In this, imagine God proudly looking down in awe and saying, "Wow, what will those humans come up with next?"

God specifically built a Universe that is governed by free will. Our ability to think and navigate through this constantly changing environment is what feeds the Mind and causes it to have breakthroughs. The amazing capabilities and adaptability of our brains

---

[11] Theologians and philosophers would prefer that we stop here to debate God's omnipotence and all knowing nature. I promise that this topic will be addressed herein but to discuss it now would distract us from understanding the cycle of life.

is not only central to our survival, but also at the core of our wondrous creations.

Through the regular birth and rebirth of the Universe, both God and collective consciousness are constant and do not die in the rebirth. What this means is that the creations of past Universes are also contained in collective consciousness. The opportunity for us to tap into this immense body of knowledge is beyond comprehension. Great insights into ourselves, the future and ideas that are today unthinkable are available to each and every member of the human race. All one needs to do in order to gain access to this information is learn to listen.

Your Practice

A. Know Your Role

Re-examine your closest relationships for who is playing the Child, Father and Mother role. To determine someone's role, think of the characteristics of the Body, Spirit and Mind as illustrated in this chapter and ask yourself who fits into each entity. Below are some examples but you can do this exercise with any relationship. Be careful not to place people into entity roles based on your historical relationship but rather where it is today (unless you want to compare and contrast the prior roles with today's roles).

Child	Father	Mother
Me	*Dad*	*Mom*

Child	Father	Mother

Child	Father	Mother

Child	Father	Mother

Child	Father	Mother

B. Historical Relationships

Think back to the events in your life that resulted in the dissolving of a relationship you had with someone else. This could be an old boyfriend or girlfriend, a good friendship or someone at work. In each instance, who played the roles of Child, Father or Mother?

Child	Father	Mother

Child	Father	Mother

Child	Father	Mother

Child	Father	Mother

C. Reading Collective Consciousness

Every idea that has ever been thought and shared with Humanity is contained in collective consciousness. As any question you desire answered may already exist in collective consciousness, write down below a few questions you would like answered:

1. _____?

2. _____?

3. _____?

Mark your calendar to check back within one year to see which of your questions have been answered.

INSIGHT #4

LISTENING

Every investment in your Body, Spirit or Mind brings energy into your entire being. When you turn on a light switch, energy flows through the wires and into the light bulb. Just like electricity is converted into light emanating from the light bulb, so too does energy flow into any entity in which you invest and is converted into whatever form of energy your being requires.

There are numerous ways you can invest into an entity, but to know if it is working you need only listen. By opening yourself to the energy flowing from an entity, you can determine if the investment is channeling energy. It is a rather simple cause and effect framework:

- To listen for energy flowing from the Body, you need only turn your attention to your mouth and skin. If you hear your voice and see the creations of your hands, then energy is flowing from the Body. In a wider awareness, sweat from your skin (if caused by effort, not just a hot day) indicates energy flowing from your investment.

- To listen for energy flowing from the Spirit, be mindful of your feelings. Investments in the Spirit cause emotions to flow. Be aware that in the domain of the Spirit, there are no negative or positive values associated with different emotions. The mere fact that emotions are flowing (regardless of which emotion) indicates that energy is flowing through the Spirit.

- Regarding energy flowing from the Mind... for this you need no training. You have lived in the domain of the Mind all your life. Your mind generates thoughts with the energy you invest and that voice in your head is living proof of your efforts.

When in harmony, an investment in one entity will cause energy to flow through all three. Likewise, a lack of investment in any one of the entities will cause the energy of the overall being to be drained. Thus, if you are feeling unmotivated, tired or have a "lack of energy" then take a look at which one of your entities is draining energy instead of producing energy.

Many times when we experience a problem, we want to fix it immediately by applying a solution where it hurts. For example, when our skin is cut we apply a Band Aid on the cut. However, it is the sharp object that is cutting us. Therefore, if we are to truly turn the situation around, we must avoid being cut and heal the damage caused by the sharp object. The same is the case with your Body, Spirit and Mind. Be mindful that a problem perceived in one entity, may actually be caused by a problem within one of the others.

For example, if you're experiencing a lack of energy with your Body, invest energy into the Spirit and the Mind. Subsequently when the energy begins to flow through the Spirit and the Mind, that same energy will flow into the Body. Listen to the feelings of the Spirit and thoughts of the Mind for they are tapping into the source of collective consciousness. Trust your feelings and thoughts as they express themselves to the Body. Be in action and channel the energy of the Universe.

Most importantly, as you listen to these messages make sure that you follow through on their instructions. At first you'll likely find these suggestions to be impulsive. Controlling our impulses has been how we operate in life since our parents first taught us restraint. And as we interact with others, restraint of our impulses is a necessary social skill. But it also tunes us out of the messages that are trying to get our attention.

In order to reconnect with your self, try this simple experiment:

> For 24-hours, follow through on every sensation, feeling and thought that comes into your awareness. If you want to go for a walk, go for a walk. Along the way if you feel like stopping to smell the flowers, then let yourself sit down in a bed of flowers. If you think you should call an old friend, then pick up the phone and say hello.

The point of this exercise is not to experience being impulsive, but rather to re-connect with the communications that are flowing from your Body, Spirit and Mind. You're probably afraid that if you allowed yourself to conduct this experiment that you would act so irresponsibly that you would get in trouble, offend people or even get arrested. But inherent in this restraint is the very essence that keeps you from sitting down in a bed of flowers long enough to smell them.

Some people will find themselves *blocked* and are unable to tune into the communications of one or more of their entities. If you are one of these people (or you're listening for the first time), then invest energy into your entities regardless of listening. Invest in the activities listed herein and, in time, you will develop the ability to listen. Like turning up the volume on a stereo, the more energy that flows through an entity the easier it is to hear its communications.

Full Time Listening

During the time period when I was experiencing my enlightenment, I experienced Divine communication in several ways. I can tell you that becoming enlightened doesn't shield you from the reactions you get from other people when you tell them that you've experienced enlightenment. However, I will also share with you that upon connecting directly to the Divine, the petty judgments of society doesn't really matter anymore.

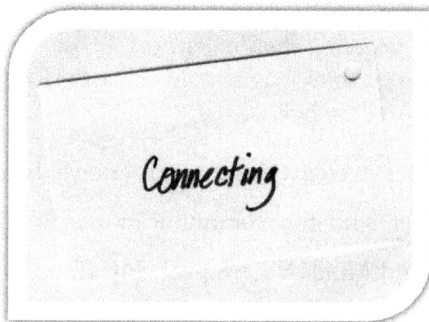

Card 16: Connecting: bring together or into contact so that a real or notional link is established.

Upon connecting with the all-knowing nature of God, many things became clear to me immediately. I instantly understood the nature of our Universe, the relationship that we have with God and how

Humanity will evolve from a physical to a Spiritual existence. And while these things are enough for any person, I had more questions. I wondered about healing, suffering in the world and why bad things happen to good people.

You might say that I had some questions that I was planning to ask God in the afterlife and upon enlightenment I decided to ask them before I died. I began asking questions and listening via the eleven dimensions that I've shared with you in Inspiration Divine. Even though my enlightenment was an amazing experience, I must admit that I was even more shocked to receive answers to my questions.

Each night as I went to bed, I would think to myself the question that I wanted answered. During the night the answer would come to me and I would often wake up my wife to share with her the insights I had been given. This experience happened so consistently that I began keeping a portable wipe board next to my bed so I could write, draw and organize the information that was flowing to me.

Each morning I would wake up and look over at the wipe board to look at the answers that I had been given. My experience was that if I didn't write down the messages upon receipt that they would be lost in slumber. As a result, mornings in my house became very busy with me running down to the office to copy down what I had written on the wipe board during the night.

On most mornings, I would wake up and find many amazing insights written on the wipe board. It isn't that I didn't remember writing the information down but rather that in the morning I enjoyed pondering over the amazing information that I had been given. However, on some mornings I would wake up to find the board empty.

I have to share with you that when the questions weren't answered in the night I was disappointed.

"Oh well," I'd say to myself. "Maybe the answer will come tomorrow."

Every morning I would start my day with a yoga class at my local yoga studio. I find this to be an excellent way to start the day and I would go to any class being offered regardless of teacher, style of yoga or degree of difficulty. Sometimes I would find myself in a beginner's class and other times I'd be struggling to keep up with a room full of advanced yogis.

And then a very interesting situation occurred. One day as I was focused on my practice, the yoga teacher walked around the room talking to the students about this and that, providing guidance on poses, explaining the history of yoga and basically keeping everyone focused on her rather than the incredibly difficult pose that we were all struggling to maintain. And then she opened her mouth and out came the answer to my question from the night before.

I couldn't believe my ears. Of course, this could've been a mere coincidence. After all, how could it be possible that a yoga teacher would be able to know my question, let alone the answer? And if this would have been an isolated experience, I would've chocked it up to chance. But over the next several weeks I experienced this amazing phenomenon time and time again with several teachers.

As I began to listen to the eleven dimensions of the Universe, my awareness expanded exponentially. I found myself seeing answers, clues and coincidences all over the place. Whereas before I was unconscious most of the time, my expanded consciousness now opened me up to an amazing threaded communication flow of which I was previously ignorant.

The point of this story is not to send you flocking into yoga studios seeking answers from the teachers or to convince you that enlightenment will provide you with a Google search engine for the Divine. The point is that we shouldn't assume that our questions aren't being answered before becoming enlightened. The answers are all around us and they can come in the oddest ways, from the most uncanny people and at completely illogical times.

As we amble through our day focused on the temperature of our latte, the traffic on the freeway and the complexities of the workplace, we should open up our listening to the amazing messages that are all around us. Listening is a proactive activity that spans the boundaries of space and time and we need only pay attention to hear the voice of God.

Your Practice

A. Listening to Feelings

Carry this book with you for the next week and jot down your feelings on the Core Effect Diagram below as they happen. For each emotion ask yourself, "What is my Spirit trying to tell me with this emotion?" You may find it beneficial to jot down the emotion when it occurs but ask about the Spirit's intention after the emotion has passed.

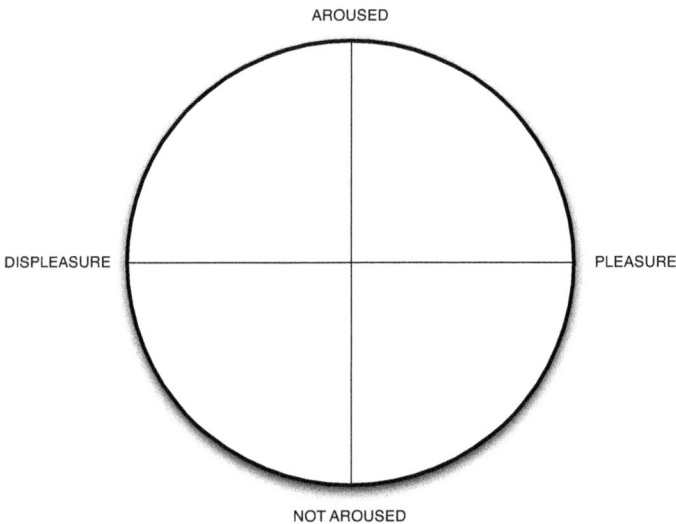

```
                    AROUSED




DISPLEASURE                              PLEASURE




                  NOT AROUSED
```

B. Journal and Index

Pick up your journal (if you don't have one, then go get one) and begin writing on the first thought that comes into your consciousness. Continue writing in a stream of consciousness with no regard to how the finished product will turn out. Assume it will be nonsense and simply focus on the process of writing. When you're finished, circle any words in your journal entry that have meaning and copy them onto a single index card. Keep this index card with you for 48 hours and reflect on the words from time to time.

C. Meditate

Take one of the words from Exercise "B" and meditate on it. Place the index card in front of you and stare intently at the word you're meditating on. Let the word become meaningful and let that be the only word that is worthy of your Mind's attention. When you're done, journal and reflect on what comes to you.

D. Savor Sensation

During your next meal, take the time to savor every bite, every flavor and every smell that you experience. Slow down the eating experience and connect with this daily ritual that we so often take for granted. Take the time to understand each sensation that comes alive within you during nourishment.

1. What did you eat? _____

2. How was your eating process different (e.g. slower)?

   _____

3. What did you notice?

   _____

4. Do you think you'll notice this difference the next time you eat this same food? How so?

   _____

5. What other foods do you think will have this same characteristic or experience?

   _____

INSIGHT #5

HAPPINESS

Like many people, maybe you have wondered, "How can I be happy?"

To become happy, one must first define happiness. Wikipedia defines happiness as, "an emotion in which one experiences feelings ranging from contentment and satisfaction to bliss and intense joy." However, this definition leaves us wanting more. Rather than constructing a more elaborate and detailed definition, I believe a simpler definition better captures the essence of what we're seeking:

Happiness is the abundance in your life of that which makes you happy.

On the surface, this definition doesn't provide much solace but inherent in this definition is the key to everlasting happiness. Unfortunately, we often choose that which doesn't last to make us happy. Thus, it isn't that we don't know what makes us happy, but rather that which makes us happy doesn't last.

This doesn't happen because we are stupid or that we are horrible people that choose the wrong things. In a sense, our unhappiness is by intelligent design.

A body that is not in motion will eventually decay. The Body requires movement, or better said, "change," in order to thrive. Thus your Mind, which needs your Body to survive, is designed to crave change. Therefore, you are predisposed to like things that don't last. Doing so keeps the Body, Spirit and Mind in motion and exposes the being to more experiences, which provides a rich field for expanding consciousness. The Universe doesn't want you to sit still.

Once you experience something for a long time you become bored with it regardless of how happy it initially made you.

If you're one of those people who doesn't like change, then you're also probably someone who experiences a lot of unhappiness in life or that finds a lot of faults in others. By fighting change, you're going against the design of being human and this brings unhappiness into your life.

In order to find happiness, you must continually be in motion to replenish that which is fleeting. Choose wisely for, if you choose that which you can never truly possess, you may again visit the state of being unhappy.

For example, if possessing nice things brings you happiness, you may choose *being rich* to make you happy. Unfortunately, as the ultra-rich will attest, someone always has a bigger or better yacht. So, despite them making you feel good, possessing *things* will never keep you happy.

There is nothing wrong with having nice things that bring you pleasure as long as you don't make them the object of your happiness.

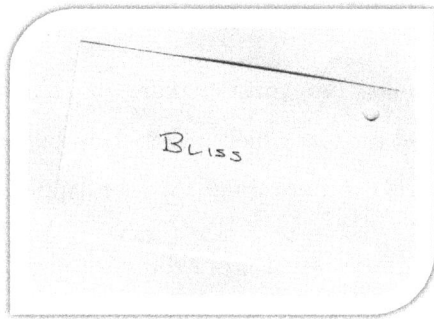

Card 17: Bliss: perfect happiness; great joy

The goal is to have abundance in your life of that which makes you happy. To accomplish this goal, you must first find out what makes you happy.

> *Is happiness a bodily function that is experienced through the five sensual dimensions of the Body?*
>
> *Is happiness a spiritual connection that is experienced through the two emotive dimensions of the Spirit?*
>
> *Is happiness a mental activity that is experienced through the four mental dimensions of the Mind?*

If you think long and hard enough about these three questions, you will eventually come to the profound conclusion, "Sometimes."

That which truly makes you happy is that which brings pleasure to your Body, Spirit and Mind.

You know what it feels like to be happy even if that feeling is fleeting. When you experience happiness, you experience energy flowing through your Body, Spirit and Mind. As human beings are governed by free will, there is no such thing as universally appealing happiness. Even universal concepts like *giving* bring about different levels of happiness in different people.

To find happiness, one must explore the human condition by continually searching for that which makes them happy. Whatever that is, the more you have, the more abundant your happiness will be.

Even so, this will only satisfy your thirst for happiness for so long. In your mountain of happiness, you will find sorrow. And, as much as you try to fill up that sorrow with more happiness, you will never fill the void.

To truly find happiness without sorrow, you must share your happiness. To be human is to be part of Humanity. The Spirit, which lives in the domain of the 'We are,' can never be fulfilled as long as others do without. Anyone that has ever experienced guilt for being happy has connected with the Spirit's desire to unite Humanity.

By giving away that which makes you happy, you bring peace to the Spirit and experience true happiness.

But to give it away, you must first be happy. Much like exchanging air from one balloon to another, if you don't create happiness, you haven't anything to share with others. To find happiness, start by discovering more of what makes you happy. With more happiness comes the opportunity to give it away.

Being happy is something that we all seek so, by definition, giving it away seems illogical. However, the path to happiness isn't followed or guided by the Mind. As much as the Mind thinks it can find happiness, you can't think your way to being happy. By recognizing our Mind's predisposition to seek happiness from that which doesn't last, we can expand our search beyond the Mind's consciousness to find happiness that does last. And when you discover lasting happiness, the Spirit becomes even more fulfilled when we share it with others.

Finding happiness and sharing it with others brings about a feeling of contentment that could never be experienced through isolated experience. This communal nature of being human is the true definition of lasting happiness. And in pursuing your purpose, your life will be so full of happiness that you'll be both fun to be around and inspiring. You may not understand the beauty of this type of existence for your life today is only partially filled with happiness. But as you grow a pool of happiness in your life, you'll find that the giving part comes much easier than you imagine.

As the cycle continues, you'll find that love and happiness are synonymous with one another.

Your Practice

A. What Makes You Happy

List below as many things that you can think of that make you happy:

B. Lasting Happiness

Circle the items above that are fleeting or won't necessarily last. A great way to manifest this exercise is to think about all the ways you try and control the item to make it last. If you're putting energy into preserving the happiness then it probably should be circled. If something exists without your nourishment then it shouldn't be circled.

C. Grouping the Joy

Combine the items above into similar groups. For example, you may have listed individual members of your family and can group them under a single category of "family."

D. Giving

Copy the happiness groups into the first row of the table below and then list under each one as many things that you can think of that either bring each group happiness or things that each group does that make other people happy. Think of all the things that make you happy that you can share, give or teach to another. The items that you write below will bring you the most joy in life when you share them with others.

INSIGHT #6

LOVE

When we imagine God, it is natural to see the Divine as perfect, without need and devoid of aspiration. Doing so makes us feel safe as it helps to believe that God's got it all figured out. But we must be careful in this conceptualization of the Divine to not fool ourselves into thinking that God is passive. Quite the opposite, God is not only active in our lives, but so too God is not casually present in the Universe. Not only has God put you here for a purpose, but also your purpose serves God and what God desires.

Your enlightenment will come by way of your Body, Spirit and Mind becoming complete. This is not to say that you do not need God in order to achieve union amongst your Body, Spirit and Mind, but instead that your work in this lifetime should continually be focused on becoming complete. By bringing your Body, Spirit and Mind into a balanced state of completion, you will connect with the Divine and experience enlightenment.

Over the course of your many lives, your being has experienced a repeating cycle relating to the completeness of your Body, Spirit and Mind. We experience this natural cycle as the ups and downs of life. In one lifetime, your Body was the pillar of health and in another it struggled with your first breath. You were fascinated with learning in one lifetime and couldn't figure out how to put food on the table in the next. With no distinction of the separateness of our Body, Spirit and Mind, the ups and downs of life can seem random, unpredictable and sometimes downright cruel.

Even when our own lives are going well, each of us know someone that has had a really rough life. We tell ourselves that we're not in their situation because we're better at the game of life. No matter if your good fortune came by way of being smarter or luckier, deep down you know how close you are to being in their same shoes. And the reason you know this deep down in your soul is that you too have been in their situation in a prior life.

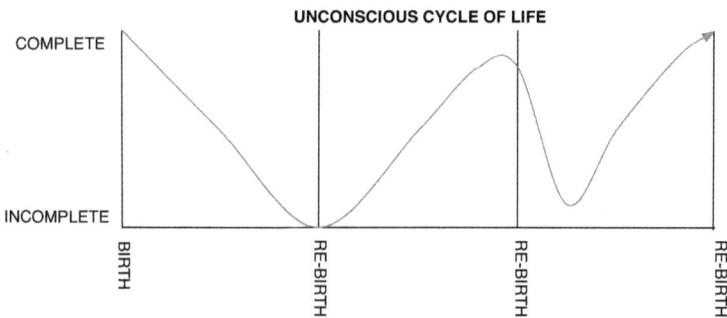

Figure 28: The natural cycle of Life.

In reality, our life is the union of the Body, Spirit and Mind but it isn't often that all three of our entities experience the same path to completeness. Sometimes the Body is sick, but the Spirit is at an all time high. Or possibly your Mind is sharp as a tack, but your Body is struggling. When we experience ourselves as a singularity of consciousness, the comingling of our Body, Spirit and Mind is difficult to understand. But when we distinguish between the three, it is easier for us to see the cycle that is playing out in our lives.

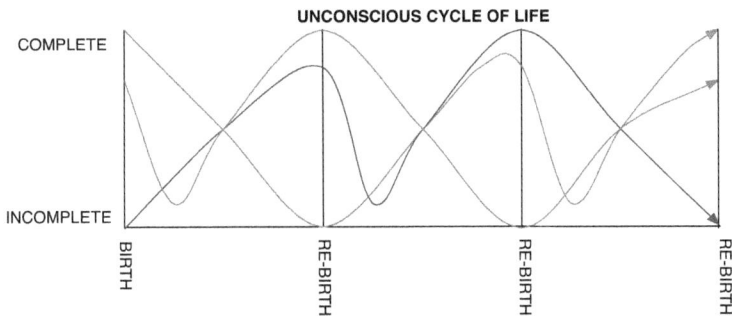

UNCONSCIOUS CYCLE OF LIFE

COMPLETE

INCOMPLETE

BIRTH   RE-BIRTH   RE-BIRTH   RE-BIRTH

Figure 29: As you review the unconscious life cycle above, can you find a life pattern between any two rebirth points that represents your current life experience (keep in mind that you've only partially completed this lifetime). Starting from birth, which line best illustrates the life experience of your Body? Did you start out healthy as a baby (top of the diagram) and slowly become less and less healthy as you progressed through life? Or did your Body start out with average health and experience a rapid decline through your life thus far? The point of this exercise isn't to find yourself in the figure above but rather to distinguish your Body, Spirit and Mind's cycle beyond your current lifetime.

With the goal to grow the Body, Spirit and Mind into balanced union towards completion, life would be so much easier to manage if our three entities were in perfect synchronicity. However, for most of us, the Spirit may be rising, but the Body is dropping and the Mind is flat-lining. Or the Body is rock solid, but we're Spiritually bankrupt and the Mind has never experienced the nurturing it craves. With the three out of synch, our efforts to make our lives better never seems to garner the impact we expect.

As a result, is it any wonder that we hear stories everyday about perfectly healthy people dropping dead from a heart attack? Or being dismayed to find out that someone committed suicide when they appeared to have it all together? With our three entities not operating as a team, our efforts to nurture one of them in isolation is a futile exercise that often ends without achieving the results we desire.

If this cycle were unbreakable, then life would have very little meaning. Without the ability to change the course of our lives, we could do little more than hang on and wait for our next lifetime and hope that it is better. But this cycle is not only breakable, but breaking this cycle is instrumental in both you and God attaining enlightenment.

Whoa? God attaining enlightenment? You're probably asking yourself how that would even be possible with God being God? Isn't God already enlightened? When we envision enlightenment, we tend to think of this experience connecting us to the Divine. God is *all knowing* and by way of us connecting to God, our enlightenment will bring with it an understanding that is Divine. So if that is the case, then how could God possibly not already be enlightened?

To understand, consider that before there was a Universe or Humanity there was only God. In this state, God was complete, all knowing and perfect. In this singular state, God's love was less than it could be. With only God and no other, love could not be shared and thus was not the full embodiment of love. And so God created the Universe and brought forth life. To do this, God took part of himself to make what we now experience as the Universe and Life.

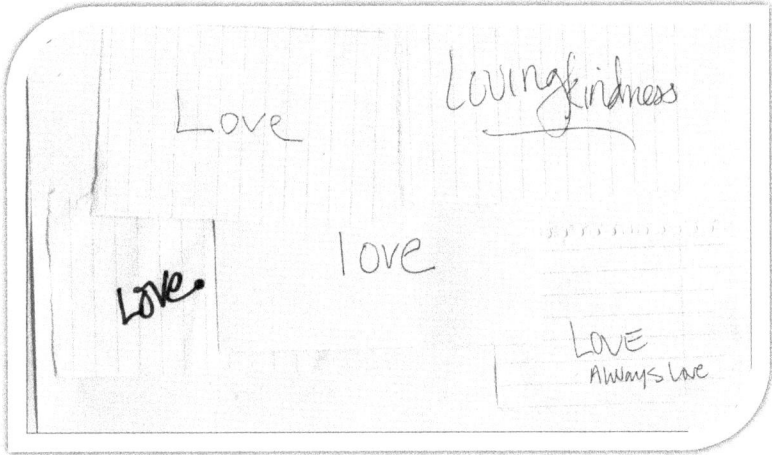

Card 18: Love: Usually refers to a deep, ineffable feeling of tenderly caring for another person. Even this limited conception of love, encompasses a wealth of different feelings, from the passionate desire and intimacy of romantic love to the nonsexual emotional closeness of familial and platonic love to the profound oneness or devotion of religious love.

In this selfless act, God allowed himself to be less than complete in order to expand love. By bringing forth life capable of loving and embracing God's love, God sacrificed his completeness for us. He created a Universe that sustains life so that we could exponentially bring more and more love into the world. In return, we provide God with original creations that expand collective consciousness and fascinate his all-knowing nature.

However, we should not think of God as being satisfied with his creation. His bringing forth of the Universe and Life is the means by which love grows, but our purpose is tied to his original intention. God's hope for us is that we will become complete so that he too can return to completion.

Hope

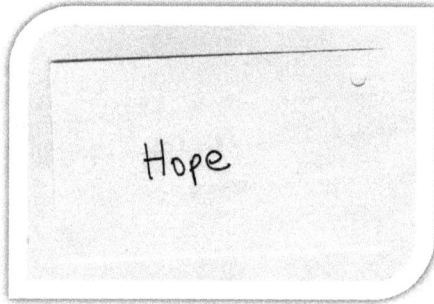

Card 19: Hope: a feeling of expectation and desire for a certain thing to happen.

He loved us enough to give away his enlightened state in order to bring forth life into existence. Take a minute to think about how much God loves you in that he allowed himself to become less than complete in order for you to live. In this, the singular God became three in one: Universe, God and Humanity.

Accordingly God brought forth free-will with the absolute greatest potential for love to grow. With free will giving each person the choice to love or hate, God gave each of us the option to connect with his loving nature and choose to love. However, choosing to love is not universal and thus Humanity has not yet fulfilled its purpose to make God complete once again.

Repeating many cycles throughout the history of time, numerous Universes have come forth with life having the choice to live a physical or Spiritual existence. Each time, the balance between love and hate has trended towards hate. Time and time again, Humanity has failed to become complete and the Universe so too has progressed towards becoming incomplete. With each failed attempt of Humanity achieving its purpose, the Universe was reborn with a new beginning. And every single time this cosmic reset button brings with it an opportunity for God to once again attain completeness.

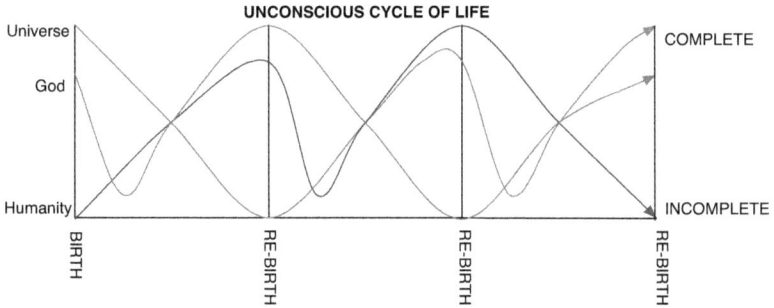

Figure 30: Repeating itself over an over again throughout time, each cycle provides Humanity with an opportunity to achieve its purpose to do its part to help God once again become complete.

We should remember that God exists outside of our Universe and is thus not governed by the eleven dimensions including time. While this is a difficult concept for us to grasp, this means that God is both complete and incomplete. In the reality in which we live, he is incomplete because he gave part of himself to create the Universe and Humanity. Outside of our Universe, he is complete because he was complete before creation and, presumably, Humanity will one day do its part and God will once again become complete in our reality too. Without the dimension of time, both of these states are true. Consequently we shouldn't consider God as being less than his potential and at the same time we should understand the purpose that he calls us to fulfill.

We are at an inflection point in the current cycle of our Universe. The path that Humanity has taken to get to this point has been an unconscious path, but we stand on the doorstep of the future of Humanity's new path. Before us exists the opportunity to fulfill our purpose and bring God to enlightenment. In this new enlightenment, he will be more complete than he was. The reason for this is love.

When God was singular, his love was less than it could be. By bringing forth the Universe and Life, God expanded his love and gave

Humanity life. The love that we bring into the world did not exist prior to our lifetime and therefore we do our part in expanding God's love. So too when God returns to his state of completeness, by way of Humanity becoming complete, he will be both complete and in the presence of beings that choose love over hate. And this is God's enlightenment.

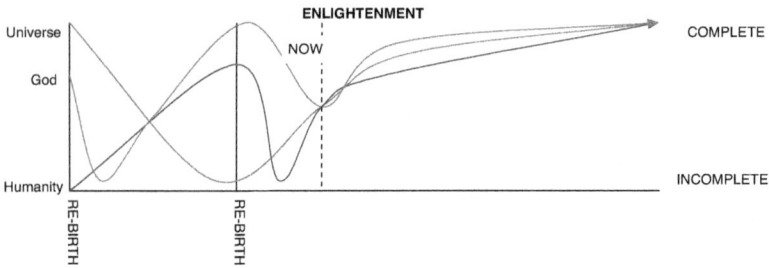

Figure 31: We are at an inflection point where our choice to love or hate will determine if God will attain enlightenment in this cycle of the Universe.

Much like we cannot escape the random chaos of life if we do not bring our Body, Spirit and Mind into union, the Universe, God and Humanity must be brought into union towards completeness in order for God to attain enlightenment. When we see ourselves as disconnected beings with no purpose, we cannot fathom that God would depend on us to attain his own enlightenment. However, when we accept that God created us with a purpose, we can begin to understand that our purpose benefits God. We are called to fulfill our purpose as our very existence was brought forth in order to fulfill God's intention to increase love.

Every day we are faced with hundreds, if not thousands, of opportunities to choose love or hate. With a physical existence, we can forget God's intention for us to fulfill our purpose and fool ourselves into believing that our choice doesn't matter. Or we can believe that

God will punish us for not making the correct choice. Alternatively, we can live a Spiritual existence and make choosing love our only choice.

One by one, soul by soul, each and everyday more and more people choose to live a Spiritual existence. In choosing love over hate, they invite more loving energy into their lives and find that life is miraculously better. By listening to their Spirit, they allow God's love to guide their path through life. Listening and loving, they navigate through the trials and tribulations of life with an understanding that their purpose is Divinely inspired.

Do those who live a Spiritual existence have magical, mystical powers? Do they have immune systems capable of beating any illness? Are they able to walk on fire? Most certainly not, for a Spiritual existence is not a physical existence and does not elevate us beyond the eleven dimensions of this Universe.

However, there is one distinct advantage of a Spiritual existence that is worth noting. When you live a physical existence, you're on your own with no reason for God's healing energy to flow through and into you. When you live a Spiritual existence, your purpose fulfilling actions draw God's healing life force energy into and through you.

It can't get simpler than this. God desires to become complete and return to his enlightened state with us by his side. In fulfilling our purpose to expand collective consciousness and choose love, we do our part in making Humanity complete. Doing so brings the Universe, God and Humanity into union towards becoming complete. When we do our part in bringing about this Divine transformation, God's healing life force energy draws near to aid us in fulfilling our purpose.

Your Practice

A. Transform Your Symbiotic Relationship Circle

Go back to your Symbiotic Relationships Circle (p. 172) and the contents of your Spiritual Chessboard (p. 136 or p. 174). Are there any groups on the Spiritual Chessboard that you can move onto one of the rungs of your Symbiotic Relationships Circle? Ask yourself if it is possible to engage each of these groups with love instead of hate. For each group that you find a way to love, move them onto your Symbiotic Relationship Circle.

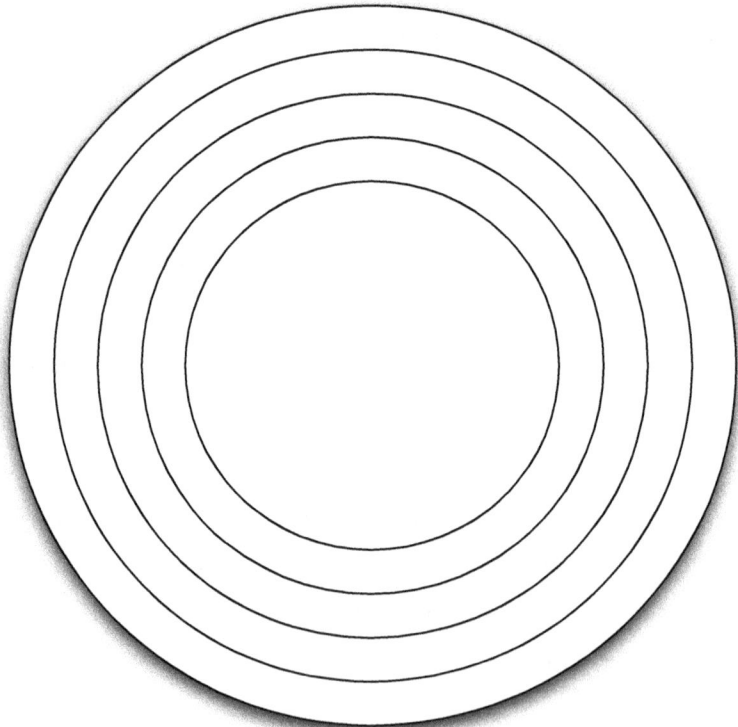

B. Update Your Spiritual Chessboard

If you were able to move any groups onto your Symbiotic Relationships Circle, update your Spiritual Chessboard to reflect which groups have moved from "Not On My Side" into a relationship of love. If you were not able to move any groups, then copy the contents of your Spiritual Chessboard "as-is" onto the one below:

On My Side   Not On My Side

Is there anyone or any group that didn't get moved? These are the very groups that can't be conquered and must be approached with love in order for Humanity to evolve to a Spiritual existence. Moving them on this piece of paper won't change the world, but living a Spiritual existence that includes everyone (in action and in words) is the key to Humanity's enlightenment.

INSIGHT #7

HEALING

The marvels of modern medicine have brought us so many blessings that it is tough to even imagine how difficult it must've been to be healthy one hundred, a thousand or several thousand years ago. Even today we don't take our health for granted and seek every advantage to cheat death out of a few more years. We take vitamins, exercise, eat right and live stress free lives to ensure that we are providing the Body everything it requires to be healthy.

Oh wait, those are more intentions than actions aren't they? One of the oddest aspects of being human is that we know what it takes to be healthier and yet few people actually live a healthy lifestyle. We know better, but for some reason, we fail to act upon the Mind's prescription for health. As a result, we spend more time doing what feels good rather than what is good for us.

And then illness strikes. From the common cold to a deadly cancer, nothing gets the attention of the Body, Spirit and Mind like an illness does. Fulfilling our purpose in life becomes a secondary priority when our Bodies are fighting an illness. This seemingly necessary diversion from the path unfortunately pulls us away from the very life force energy that keeps us alive and healthy. Pulling this energy back into our lives is possible and in this insight I'll explain how.

Channeling Energy

Many people suffer from a malnourished or sick Body, Spirit or Mind. In truth, the mere fact that you're alive conveys that all three are not unhealthy. Thus, if you're under the impression that your Body, Spirit and Mind are all sick then your Mind is being too hard on your being. Take stock in the fact that in order to be alive, life force energy must be flowing through you and thus your being is healthier than you might believe.

In order to heal one of your entities, you must channel this life force energy that flows through you into the ailing entity. If you're having trouble *believing* there is a life force energy flowing through you, then consider the relationship between the Body and the Mind through the five sensual dimensions. To you, the world around you is filled with sights, sounds, smells, tastes and feelings (touch). In reality, around you is only energy in the form of waves and particles.

Ibn al-Haytham (960-1040) was the first to argue that vision is the result of light from objects entering the eye and that vision occurs in the brain rather than in the eye itself. Known as the pioneer of modern scientific method, he developed extensive experiments in order to prove that vision is the result of light particles traveling to the eye and that personal experience has an effect on what people see and how they see.

These energies are subsequently interpreted into the sensations you experience in your brain. If you were to record sound levels inside your brain during a concert you would only hear silence. Packed away snugly inside your skull, the brain never hears sounds, sees light or directly experiences any of the sensations of the Body. It is your ears that convert the energy of sound into what you *hear*. Likewise there is a life force energy of the Universe that flows through your Body, Spirit and Mind that scientists are only now starting to develop methods sensitive enough to measure.

This same energy powers the Universe and everything (including you) within the Universe. Moreover, the Universe has a symbiotic relationship with Humanity. Without Humanity expanding the Universe, through the creation of original ideas that are the catalyst for dark energy, the Universe will eventually collapse. So too, if the Universe collapses, the Universe and everything contained herein will die. Thus as much as you were made possible by means of the Universe, similarly the Universe needs you to survive. And dark energy, abundantly present in our Universe, is the life force energy that sustains all life in the Universe.

As such, God wants you to be healthy. God needs you to be at your fullest potential so that His Body, the Universe, will continue to expand. Therefore, the life force energy of the Universe is readily available to help you heal your Body, Spirit and Mind.

God wants you to be at your fullest potential so that He will continue to grow.

To heal one of your entities, you must channel more energy into it. Much like more balloon volume is not created by exchanging air from one balloon to another, in order to heal an entity you must bring in more energy than was present before. Thus by channeling energy, you will bring the healing life force of the Universe into your ailing entity[12].

In order to channel energy for healing into one of your entities, you must first bring peace the other two entities. Thus to heal the Spirit, you must bring peace to the Body and the Mind. An example of how to do this would be through meditation as no movement and very little to no thought occurs during meditation. The premise of meditation is to quiet both the Body and the Mind.

Similarly to heal the Mind, you must bring peace to the Body and the Spirit. An example of how to do this would be through learning and teaching. By reading a book, your Body is still and your intentions are focused on the contents of the book. By teaching, you bring the Spirit into peace by sharing with others. We all have something to learn and every one of us has something that we can teach to someone else.

To heal the Body, you must bring peace to the Spirit and the Mind. This can only be achieved in concert with others. The Mind, in isolation, is not capable of turning-off and the Spirit, in isolation,

---

[12] Please note that we human beings, or any other form of life, do not have the ability to heal ourselves or others. We are capable of channeling the healing life force energy of God for healing purposes but it is the life force energy of God that is responsible for the healing. Some may be more capable of doing this than others.

suffers like a drowning child gasping for air. In isolation, these two entities become engaged and begin to fight for survival. Thus to bring peace to the Spirit and the Mind you must connect with Humanity. In sharing and helping others in line with your passions, you'll find the Mind and the Spirit return to a state of peace.

As you can see, precisely at the moment when you are at your weakest point is precisely when you need to connect and share with Humanity the most. If you are reading this at a time in your life when your Body is healthy, recognize that you can live a longer life by connecting with Humanity today so that you can be healed tomorrow. And if you are reading this with a Body that needs healing, know that you can still connect with Humanity in small ways that are within your means. Give an encouraging word to those that are sicker than you, read a book to a child or write a loving letter to a friend. One way or another, connect with others and share with them your gifts.

Bringing peace to the competing entities, prepares you to channel the healing life force energy of the Universe into the ailing entity. In concert with two peaceful partners, the ailing entity will begin to thrive like a neglected child being taken to Disneyland. By investing in your ailing entity, with the other two entities in silent support, your ailing entity will blossom and begin again to heal.

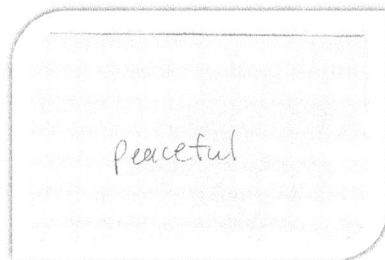

peaceful

Card 20: Peaceful: free from disturbance; tranquil.

As we've previously discussed, activities that quiet the child of the parent will nourish the parent. Can you imagine working out or meditating next to your crying child? When a parent experiences their child at peace, they can focus on their own nourishment. Thus to heal the Body, perform activities that quiet the Spirit. To heal the Spirit, perform activities that quiet the Mind. And to heal the Mind, perform activities that quiet the Body.

Healing the Body

When your Body is the focus of the healing process, you will direct God's healing life force energy to the location in the Body that you want to heal. You will be manifesting this flow of energy through the thoughts of your Mind and the feelings of your Spirit, but the Body's language of sensation is the means by which you will govern the flow of energy. In concert, your three entities will work together to channel the healing, life force energy of God to the part of your Body that requires healing.

For the Body to participate in the healing process, it should be directed to tune into its five sensual dimensions and express energy with its voice (sound) and actions (touch via the skin). Said another way, the Body must accept the energy and communication in order to channel the life force healing energy. Do not worry if, by the means of your sickness, that one or more of your dimensions is unable to listen or express energy. Your Body is quite adept at adjusting with greater intensity through the remaining dimensions.

If possible, the Body should express energy through sound and touch. Employ the voice and hands to release energy in any way possible. For example, when you channel energy into the Body, you are washing away the built-up energy that is sustaining the illness that has taken up residency. We don't want to build up even more energy, so express energy with your hands and mouth during and after the healing process. You can do this by singing or chanting with your voice and creating, in any number of ways, with your hands (e.g. writing, painting, sculpting or even pretending you're a musical conductor)[13].

It matters not what is expressed, but rather to let the cycle of energy flowing through your Body, Spirit and Mind be complete. If you, or the patient, are unable to express energy in the form of sound and touch then employ a healer to help (discussed later in this chapter).

Engage the Spirit in Healing

A healthy Spirit will listen to its child the Body, draw wisdom and energy from the collective consciousness of Humanity and direct the Mind. The Spirit, with its boundless connections to God and Humanity, operates beyond the four mental dimensions of the Mind. As a result, energy from the Spirit will be received via both the Mind (remember that the Spirit communicates and governs its child the Mind) and the other people that come into our lives[14].

With the Spirit being able to tap into collective consciousness, you have the healing power of the Universe at your disposal. Every healing idea that has ever been expressed and every treatment that has ever

---

[13] You don't have to do this during the healing experience per se, but when you're focused on healing the expression of energy should be part of your daily routine.

[14] Too often we think that God's words will only come to us in moments of solitude. God speaks to us all the time through our Spirit, but when we don't or can't listen, the message comes through the voice of others. As such, always be listening!

been created is available. In this, the healing procedures of mankind are equally represented with the mystical healing powers that are beyond our medical community's consciousness. In collective consciousness, everything is available and this means that whatever you require for healing is available to you.

Because of these vast possibilities for healing, it is important that your Mind doesn't get in the way of your healing. In the pursuit of healing the Body, your Mind will convince you that one method of treatment is correct and others are incorrect. In as much as this is an interpretation of your Spirit's communication, this is acceptable. However, all too often our Minds get in the way and attempt to think our way through the healing process. When you are pursuing healing, you should be particularly aware of the methods of healing that present themselves to you by way of people coming into your life. If someone suggests an alternative approach, you might want to listen[15].

Your Spirit will direct God's healing life force energy to your Body and will also bring healers as well as healing techniques into your awareness. These may manifest via your local family doctor or through a stranger you meet at random. In pursuing these paths to healing, be careful not to give into the Mind's desire for absolute truths. There is more than one path to healing and choosing one shouldn't necessarily require rejecting others. If your Spirit advises chemotherapy, then receive chemotherapy treatment. If your Spirit advises acupuncture,

---

[15] It is important that you do not interpret this as a call to not listen to your doctor. Instead be open minded and consider more than one path to healing.

then receive acupuncture treatment. And if your Spirit advises both, then do both.

Speak to the Spirit in present tense to convey the healed state in the future. For example, "I am cancer free and completing my first marathon race." The Spirit desires you to be a full and active contributor to the Universe's expansion, so tell it what it wants to hear. The Spirit (who lives in the domain of the future) will express to the Mind (who truly doesn't know any better because it lives in the domain of the past and doesn't get messages directly from the Body) that the healing is working. As a result, healing that is *not possible* suddenly becomes *possible*.

Because the Body lives in the present, healing the Body takes time. If you are always healing the Body *now*, then the Body will heal faster. So too, whenever you're *not healing* the Body in the present moment, the Body is *not being healed*. Thus healing the Body requires perseverance, regular investment and time.

Like you, when I first discovered this lesson I was both optimistic and skeptical. I very much wanted to be able to heal my Body, but mentally healing the Body by telling it that healing had already occurred seemed too good to be true. However, the next time that I was injured I decided to give it a try.

On the way down to the park to play catch with my kids, my five-year-old son handed me his water bottle and told me he didn't want to bring it. Since the park was around the corner and we had only ventured halfway down the block, I decided to throw the water bottle back into our front yard. Being past my prime and not warmed up, this proved to be a painful mistake. I tossed the water bottle, threw my shoulder out and wound up with a severely injured shoulder.

I decided to give self-healing a try and began imagining myself doing all kinds of things that one would do with a healthy shoulder. I imagined playing catch with my son in the front yard, working out at the gym and shocking my friends with my amazing recovery. Not only did I imagine these healthy activities, but I also refused to engage in any internal dialogue about my shoulder being injured, being in pain or not getting better. As those types of thoughts entered my Mind, I simply let them be and moved onto imagining myself doing wonderful activities with my healthy shoulder. Much to my own surprise, within 48-hours my shoulder was healed.

A month later I was helping out at my daughter's softball practice and strained my hamstring while running after fly balls in the outfield. I'd pulled my hamstring during college and knew that it would take months for it to heal completely. However, by applying this same technique, my hamstring was healed within a week. Even without really knowing what I was doing, I was able to heal myself in ways that I previously thought to be impossible.

Through my own personal experience I knew that much more was possible, but I lacked an awareness of the communal power of healing. When I told my friends and family about my experiences, they responded that I must have become a *healer*. I conveyed to them that everyone is capable of healing in this manner, but they instead convinced themselves that somehow I had tapped into a healing ability that wasn't be available to them.

I knew there wasn't anything special about my experience, other than my willingness to believe I could be healed. My injuries were minor, but something deep within my soul told me that the healing power of God is available to all of us. I soon discovered that not only is healing available to everyone, but that we each have a responsibility to heal ourselves and others.

During the time when I was editing Inspiration Divine, I got one of those phone calls that a husband never wants to get from his wife. Through tears and cries of pain, my wife told me how she was in so much agony that she couldn't get up off the floor. While visiting a girlfriend, she threw her back out and was stricken with so much pain that she couldn't move. The kids managed to put her into the baby stroller and were slowly pushing her back home. I can imagine this was quite a site to behold with the children pushing Mom home in a stroller.

I was in downtown San Francisco at the time and unable to immediately help beyond coordinating how we could get her medical treatment. By the time I made it home, a friend had managed to drive her to a local chiropractor and she was up on the examination table crying out in pain anytime he put his hand anywhere near her injured back. The chiropractor told us that he wasn't sure what had happened, but right now she was experiencing the worst back spasm (a painful and involuntary muscular contraction) he had ever seen in his twenty-years of practicing. He sent us home and asked her to return in the morning to see if the spasm had subsided enough for him to treat her.

That evening my wife and I worked to heal her back. We agreed that we would go back to the chiropractor's office in the morning and, if he wasn't able to help, she would go see our primary care physician. Using the techniques described in Inspiration Divine, I placed my hands on her back and tried to connect with her injury.

As I consciously moved my hands over her lower back, I detected the location of her injury and could feel tension radiating away from this spot of concentrated energy. As I began to lightly drift my hands over her skin, I visualized her injury in my Mind and imagined it being pulled from her Body. Due to her sensitivity, I knew that I couldn't massage or put any pressure on her at all. She was like a raw, exposed nerve.

"Do you feel that heat?" she asked me. "Your hands feel like they're on fire."

Indeed I did feel the heat she was referring to and continued moving my hands to and fro to pull this excess energy from her Body. For reasons that only she can know, she had stored excess energy in her lower back and this put her into a vulnerable position for injury. Now that the injury had occurred, we worked on removing this excess energy in order for her to be able to be healed.

While moving my hands over her injury and visualizing the energy leaving her Body, we talked about what her finish-time was going to be in an upcoming ½ marathon race. She could barely walk and yet we only spoke of the amazing accomplishments she would be achieving in the near future. We also chuckled about how the chiropractor was going to be blown away when we walked into his office in the morning completely healed and pain free. Our thoughts and words were entirely focused on the only outcome that we accepted.

It was a long night with lots of healing, praying and alternating heat and ice (recommendation from the chiropractor). In the morning, she rose from bed and went downstairs to make breakfast for the kids. Her back was still sore, but she was walking upright and going about her day.

We kept that morning appointment and loved hearing the chiropractor say, "It's a miracle, I can't believe how much better you're doing." Not only was she able to recover from an intense injury in record time, but she also knew that she had tapped into the healing power of God.

I don't want you to think that this was some sort of miracle cure or that the healing work we focused on was the sole cause of her recovery. Surely the heat, ice and time helped as well. However, I will offer to you that my wife opened up to the healing power of God and expressed to her Spirit the healed and vibrant state in which she was going to take on the world. She kept her thoughts focused on *herself already being healed* rather than focusing on the pain, spending the night on the couch commiserating with her girlfriends on the phone about her injury and believing that her recovery would be long and painful.

Engaging the Mind to Heal

As a result of the means by which the Spirit operates, the Mind must be open and accepting of the emotions, creations and people that *want* as well as *feel* compelled to help us heal. When we're healthy, it is easy to visualize being open to accepting whatever healing path is put before us. But when we are sick, the choices become much more important and we tend to abandon the Spirit in favor of the Mind's logical decision-making approach. In healing as well as in life, a balance between the Body, Spirit and Mind is best.

We focus healing energy by bringing an awareness of the sickness into our Minds. To do this, we imagine the sickness and then direct energy to flush it away from our Body. When you are visualizing the expulsion of the sickness from your Body, imagine the sickness according to the five sensual dimensions of the Body:

> **Vision** - What does the illness look like? What color is it? Does it move or is it still? Is it pretty or ugly?
>
> **Taste** - If you were to place the illness in your mouth what would it taste like? Would it be sweet, salt, sour, bitter or umami[16].
>
> **Sound** - As you pull the illness out of your Body what will it sound like when it detaches from you? Will it scream in pain or roar like a lion?
>
> **Smell** - What does the illness smell like? Is it sweet and pungent or does it stink like rotting garbage?
>
> **Touch** - If you were to hold the illness in your hands what would it feel like? Is it slimy like a snake or rough like a horny toad?

By imagining the sickness via the five sensual dimensions of the Body, you actually put the sickness into a four dimensional space. As these are the mental dimensions of the Mind, you now have two of your entities focusing on the expulsion of the sickness. With two

---

[16] Umami (旨味) is a proposed addition to the currently accepted four basic tastes sensed by specialized receptor cells present in the human tongue. The same taste is also known as xiānwèi (鲜味 鮮味) in Chinese cooking. Umami is a Japanese word meaning savory, a "deliciousness" factor deriving specifically strong detection of the natural amino acid, glutamic acid, or glutamates common in meats, cheese, broth, stock, and other protein-heavy foods. Taste experts say that Doritos and Cheetos are an example of Umami. *Umami*, http://en.wikipedia.org/wiki/Umami (accessed February 23, 2009).

entities working to heal, you can both push (from your Body), pull (from your Mind) to flush the sickness away. And as the Spirit wants nothing more than you to be healthy, you have now created a powerful bond between the three to keep the sickness away.

Your sickness may be quite fond of its home within you and be resistant to leaving. Your Mind's constant reinforcement that you're sick and your Body's continual reaction to its presence, feeds it with energy to keep it alive. Do not be deterred if results are not immediate. The Body lives in the present and thus the process of healing must continually be applied in the present. When we're sick, we desire immediate results. Instead, know that your entire being aligned with the intentions of God is an incredibly powerful force capable of causing miracles to occur. And this is much more powerful than your previous mindset, which allowed the sickness to reside within you.

Know that when you invest in any one of your three entities that a connection (string) is opened up between all three. If it is difficult to work with one entity, you can still invest energy into it by driving energy into the other two. In time, the life force energy that flows through the Body, Spirit and Mind will bring healing powers to the ailing entity.

Remember that only the Body and Mind have limits imposed by a four dimensional reality. By investing in the Spirit, the healing energy of God can transcend both space (distance) and time. Consequently, the prayers and energy of others are directly beneficial to one's recovery. Every prayer is a container of energy transmitted to and through the Spirit. As with happiness, healing is defined as the abundance in your life of that which will make you healthy. Know that the healing power of God is consequently magnified in direct proportion to the focused energy of those praying for you.

Healing Others

For the healer, there is a different role to play. As one of the people tasked with helping the patient heal, your job is to channel the healing energy into and out of the patient. The patient, due to their ailment, may not be able to physically or mentally invest in themselves. Thus your job, as healer, is to help channel energy on their behalf.

In a balanced and complete human being, energy is transmitted from the Spirit via the language of the Mind (Parent) to the Body (Child) as expressed through the Mind's four mental dimensions. As such, to channel energy into the patient, you must emulate the Mind of the patient and communicate to their Spirit through their Body.

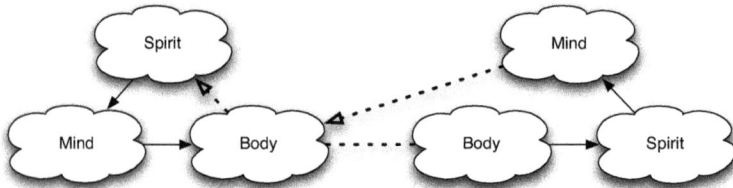

Figure 32: By placing your skin to the patient's skin and emulating the Mind of the patient, your thoughts go to their Body and Spirit and back through to their Mind to complete the circuit.

To do this is easier than it sounds. As we've already learned, the Body listens to its parent's four mental dimensions (reception), but communicates to the Spirit via the two sensual dimensions that are capable of receiving and expressing energy:

Sound ~ the mouth

Touch ~ the skin and hands

Consequently, as healer, you must express energy to the Spirit through *your voice and your touch*. With this approach to healing, you are connecting with the patient through touch so that you may connect to their illness. Just like the patient would imagine the sensational descriptions of the illness, your job is to connect with the patient so that your Mind can describe the illness like the patient would. It doesn't matter if your interpretation of the sensational aspects of the illness differ from the patient's description, for you're interpreting their illness with your Body.

The physical connection between healer and patient is best if the healer may place his or her hands directly over the area of the Body where the illness resides. Skin to skin is best, but if this is not possible or appropriate, the next best approach would be to hold both hands (patient and healer holding each other's hands). The point here is to connect healer to patient and if either is uncomfortable with how this is done then it won't work. In this situation, it is advised to find a new healer for the patient until a connection is made.

Healing via the voice can come in many forms, but heals regardless if you're talking, singing, chanting or humming. What's important is that you're communicating to the Spirit. What to communicate is surprisingly simple. To heal the patient, tell the Spirit what it wants to hear. Remember that the Spirit exists in the domain of *We Are* and this first requires the Body to be *Here and Now*. As such, the Spirit wants the Body to be alive and healthy in the present moment. And so you should tell the Spirit that its Body is healed rather than it needs healing.

Refrain from asking the Spirit to do something because to *do something* requires the Mind and the Body. In essence, when you ask the

Spirit to do something (e.g. heal the patient), you're talking to the wrong entity. So instead of saying, "Please heal," say, "This person is healed." Describe to the Spirit the vibrant, healed Body that will be active in the Universe birthing original creations (expanding God's presence). In return, the Spirit will transmit more, not less, life force energy to the patient.

When you express these thoughts to the Spirit, touch your skin to theirs. Place your hands on the patient (skin to skin) and let the energy flowing through your being flow into them. Express your healing words through your external voice rather than the internal voice that is trapped in your head.

In your Mind, visualize your healthy, life affirming energy flowing through your skin and into their Body. Similarly visualize their sickness being drawn out of them through your hands.

Remember that the definition of healing is the abundance in your life of that which makes you healthy. As such, in order to heal, you need an abundance within you of that which heals in order to heal others. Invest today to infuse your being with the healing power of God so that when you or your loved ones become ill you can heal them.

The Healer's Predicament

Even when you learn how to heal the sick, you may find yourself not engaging to heal. "Absurd," you say. "If I knew how to heal the sick, I would do nothing other than heal everyone I could."

While the Spirit, living in the domain of *We Are* desires to heal everyone, the Mind, living in the domain of *I Am*, puts the survival of the Body at the top of its priorities. Your Mind, in its pursuit to avoid entropy, is highly efficient at conserving energy. Every bit of energy that your Mind can conserve represents energy that can be used to heal your Body. Therefore, even when you're not sick, the Mind will put up mental roadblocks to healing those around you.

Be mindful of your Mind in these moments because limiting healing is to deny yourself of a full human potential. God wants an army of human beings loving one another and generating countless original creations. And, as you know from those times when you've caught the flu or the common cold, when you're sick the last thing you think about is creating. Thus to heal is not only part of being human, but it is also your obligation as a member of the human race.

Like the Universe, in order for you to expand, you need more energy than was present before. Remember, if you simply take air from one balloon and put it into another you have not expanded the balloon's volume. So too, if you simply transfer the healing energy from yourself to another, you have not expanded the Universe. To do so would put your Body at risk and the Spirit will never allow you to heal another while putting your Body into a potentially unhealthy state. For God, one less human being, is one less human being capable of contributing to collective consciousness and loving one another.

Thus God is not a fan of sacrificing one life for another, regardless of which human being is being saved. God wants you both to live, so if you try to deplete even a little bit of healing energy from you for another at your own expense, the Spirit will not allow the healing to take place. Therefore only with an abundance of energy flowing to, through and from your entire being, will you have ample energy to heal others. Like all things in the Universe, balance is required.

Maintaining Health

When we think of healing or staying healthy, we tend to consider our Bodies as being perfect specimens that have been invaded by a foreign organism. We get bacterial infections, attacked by viruses, overwhelmed by the flu bug and defeated by cancerous cells. And this is precisely how we should think of ourselves: perfectly healthy until we are invaded by that which is not healthy. By dispelling the illness, our Bodies return to a state of wellness and we are once again healthy.

But what we fail to understand is why we got sick in the first place. Sure we know what is causing the illness (e.g. bacterial staph infection) but as to why we got sick and the person next to us didn't remains a mystery. However, in our quest to understand the healing power of God, we come face to face with the one thing that every form of life requires to survive: energy.

Every living thing requires energy to exist and so too where you find energy you'll find the potential for life. Without food, you would wither away until you succumbed to starvation and thus we human beings tend to populate areas where we can sustain a food supply. Without an ample amount of food, we would fail to thrive and this is also the same with the life forms that invade our Bodies and make us sick.

While energy is abundant in the Universe, it tends to collect in clumps as is evident in stars and collections of solar systems. These clumps of energy build up mass as they get bigger and eventually become large enough to gravitationally dominate their environment.

Where this gravitational force is greater than its surrounding matter, we find the formation of solar systems and galaxies. As you can imagine, a comet flying too close to our sun would be pulled into orbit around the sun or be pulled directly into the sun. However, if the comet in our example were to be replaced with a parasitical life form (e.g. an illness) and instead of the Universe we consider your Body, the path that we can imagine wanting to avoid is one where the illness comes into contact with a build-up of excess energy within your Body.

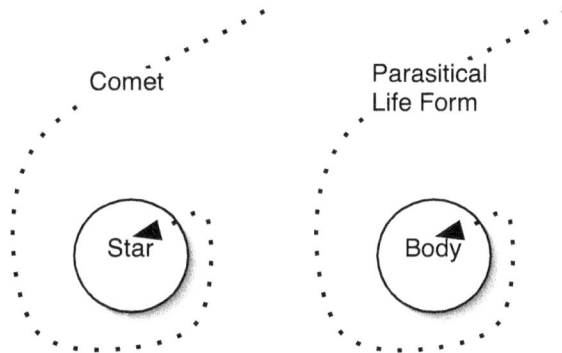

Figure 33: Like a comet drifting too close to the larger mass of a star, as an illness comes in contact with our Bodies, it is attracted to any excess energy built-up in the Body.

The build-up of excess energy is what both attracts and sustains illness in our Bodies. It is the illness that makes us sick, but it is the excess energy that dwells within us that enables the sickness in the first place. Without the presence of excess energy, the illness wouldn't find our Bodies to be a hospitable home. And without a hospitable home, the illness will leave our Bodies and not return.

Western medicine has demonstrated one way to remove illness from the Body by attacking the illness. Through pills, scalpels and radiation, we attack the illness until it dies or gives up. Our survival instinct surely prefers effortless healing procedures and therefore we've put a lot of our healthcare hopes into the Western approach. And with good reason as the benefits of Western medicine came about through the fulfillment of mankind's purpose and access to the knowledge available from collective consciousness.

But this has also shielded us from the root enabler of illness. Our cause and effect Minds love the idea of an invading parasitical life form without the responsibility of personally providing the excess energy that brought the illness to our Bodies in the first place. However, by awakening to this paradigm, we can not only unlock the keys to healing but also prevent sickness in the future.

In this insight, we've discussed how to remove illness through an understanding of the Body, Spirit and Mind. However, we must be mindful of why we were storing excess energy within a particular part of the Body to begin with. If we don't channel this energy elsewhere, we run the risk of replenishing the very energy that we just removed from the Body. Herein lies the key to staying healthy for the rest of our lives.

Non-Judgmental Healing

It is important to note that there is no such thing as good or bad energy. Energy simply is part of our reality. The entire notion of good and bad energy is born from mankind's judgmental ways and leads us down a path that will not bring us closer to health. Energy is part of our reality and all life is attracted to energy because without energy life will cease to exist. Thus we can find fault in our illness, but we should avoid believing that somehow there is a bad or evil energy that lives within us or somehow caused the illness to manifest.

Once we let go of demonizing energy we can begin to understand that just like life, balance is key in managing energy. Without enough energy we cannot function and with too much energy we store more than we need. One look at our modern lives and it is easy to see how we consume more energy than we need. We eat too much, we drive too much and we waste too much. Criminals are more likely to rob banks full of cash and illness is more likely to be attracted to Bodies that have more energy stored up than they need.

As you begin to understand how you can heal yourself and others, take time to discover why energy is built-up where the illness lives within the Body. You can surely remove the illness through a variety of Western, Eastern or Energy Healing techniques, but if you don't curb the building up of excess energy, the illness will return. Thus to attain and maintain health, one must become in tune with their Body and learn to detect excess amounts of energy.

Awareness of Healing

We've grown up in a society that regularly tells us that we're not good enough and that we can't have that which we seek. Be it financial success, happiness or health, the message is continually reinforced that we are missing something essential. Subsequently we convince ourselves that obtaining the missing piece will bring us to that which we seek. As a result of this line of *thinking*, we want to believe others who tell us that they know how we can obtain what is missing. Thus the world is full of get-rich schemes, happiness prescriptions and miracle cures.

What is truly missing is the awareness that we already possess everything we need to obtain that which we seek. God is perfect and a perfect God is surely capable of producing perfect life. You are the result of that perfection and possess everything you need. Discovering the tools that are already within you is all that is needed to realize your potential in this life. With this, you already have within yourself the path to healing for yourself and others. Following this path only requires that you open up to your true self.

Your Practice

A. Visualize Sickness

Somewhere in your life find illness that can be used in this exercise. If you're not sick then interview someone that is sick and ask them to answer these questions about their sickness:

Vision - What does the sickness look like? What color is it? Does it move or is it still? Is it pretty or ugly?

_____

Taste - If you were to place the sickness in your mouth what would it taste like? Would it be sweet, salt, sour, bitter or umami?

_____

Sound - As you pull the sickness out of your Body what will it sound like when it detaches from you?

_____

Smell - What does the sickness smell like?

_____

Touch (feel) - If you were to hold the sickness in your hands what would it feel like?

_____

B. Bring Peace to the Parent

Activities that bring peace to the parent, put the parent entity at peace and enables the healing life force energy to flow to the child. Below are a few activities that bring peace to each entity. Pick a few and practice them so that when you need healing you'll know what to do:

> **Body** (parent of the Spirit): meditating, massage, warm bath, working out (if you're already in shape), walking…
>
> **Spirit** (parent of the Mind): forgiveness, charity, devotion, volunteering, donation (time or money), praying (especially for others)…
>
> **Mind** (parent of the Body): meditating, writing/reading poetry, yoga, tai chi, listening to music, watching a sunset or sunrise, smelling flowers.

C. Connect with Healing

The next time you encounter someone that is sick put your hands on them. Your goal is to connect with and feel their sickness. At this point, you're not trying to pull the sickness from their Body but rather just feeling its presence. If you don't know the person that well, you can simply hold their hands. Ask yourself the questions from Exercise "A" above. To compare and contrast with your own experience, ask the person who is sick the same questions and see if you come up with similar or different answers.

D. Become Convicted

The next time your commitment is tested to invest in your Body, Spirit or Mind, remind yourself that you're investing in yourself so that you'll be able to heal your loved ones in the future. Identify with every meal as an opportunity to invest in the health of your Body and you'll find your eating habits improve immediately.

9

MOVING ENERGY

The healing process we've discussed is a method for moving energy into and out of the Body. For a variety of reasons, excess energy builds up in the Body, attracts illness and is unable to transition out of the Body on its own. In turn, more energy builds up and the Body becomes overwhelmed until it can no longer sustain normal cell production. Our Western medical practices treat the symptoms that result from the buildup of excess energy, but fail to address the actual enabler of the illness.

Long before we Westerners became focused on bacterial infections, cancerous cells and diseases, Eastern medicine had been treating illness by managing energy within the Body for thousands of years. For example in Traditional Chinese Medicine, vital energy within the Body called qi (氣) runs through twelve defined channels called meridians (經絡). Disruptions of energy-flow along these meridians can cause discomfort, disease, and even death according to Traditional Chinese Medicine practitioners. Their teachings have been accumulated over thousands of years of meticulous observation of nature, the cosmos, and the Body.

Whereas techniques such as acupuncture manage the flow of energy within the Body, we must also bring the healing life force energy of the cosmos into our Bodies and remove the buildup of excess energy from the Body. As you can imagine, this might make some people wonder if this eliminates the need for healthcare services such as acupuncture, acupressure and qigong. Quite the opposite, as they are all methods for managing energy and so all are complimentary to one another.

The healing energy force of the Universe is much more than a prescription for removing sickness from the Body. The very same energy that brings you to optimal health is the same force that expands the Universe, powers all living things, and keeps everything in order. By understanding your relationship and dependency on this life force energy, you will begin to develop an awareness of how this energy force is part of you. The Universe as a whole is nearly two thirds dark energy[17] and we are just beginning to understand the incredible role it plays in the cohesion of our Universe. So too are we at the forefront of learning how to manage this energy as it flows into, through and around us.

---

[17] I tend to resist using this term because of the negative, "evil" connotations that our society associates with the word "dark." Dark energy is merely a technical term that physicists have created to describe this energy that neither produces or reflects light.

The internal skeptic tells us that this is not possible and that we cannot understand, let along manage, this energy force. But just like we harvest and manage energy from fossil fuels to power our vehicles, you also can harvest and channel dark energy for healing purposes. By channel, I mean that you can direct energy to where it needs to go rather than letting it flow without guiding it.

Before embarking on a path to channel the energy force of the Universe, know that the result will not provide you with super powers, magical abilities or control over others. There is nothing mystical, supernatural or exotic about the life force energy of our Universe. Dark energy is simply the life force energy of our Universe and it will always expand, power and serve all life within the Universe. You, as member of the human race, have been placed on Earth to fulfill your purpose of expanding the Body of God (the Universe). As such, dark energy is available to you in ways that will enable you to fulfill your purpose. And, in that quest, this life force energy is healing energy for your Body, Spirit and Mind.

The ego driven Mind desires to understand what dark energy is and how we can control it. We tell ourselves that if we cannot take something apart and put it back together, then we really don't understand it. And with this line of thinking, we limit our reality to those experiences that fall within the domain of knowledge and commonly held belief systems. However, visionaries that have break-through discoveries know that in order to harness the power of discovery, one must break from the domain of existing knowledge into the domain of that which we cannot control.

The life force energy that powers everything within the Universe is available to you despite our inability to control it. While you may not be able to control or possess dark energy, it is possible to channel and direct it. The subtle difference between controlling and channeling energy contains an understanding of the ways of the Universe that are beyond the egotistical ways of the Mind. In order to direct energy, one must employ the ways of the Spirit in a way that benefits and expands the Universe itself. If your intentions are in line with the health of our Universe, your life will be much more enjoyable, fruitful and long lasting.

To channel energy, first consider where you desire to direct the energy, for what purpose, and when the energy needs to be there. For example, if I desire to heal a sprained ankle, I would direct energy to the ankle injury within my Body, for the purpose of healing, and in the present moment. As you can see from this simple example, the Mind is employed to channel the energy of the Universe because, as human beings, we *think* using our Minds. And because we direct energy using our Mind (intention), we must use the language, or rather dimensions, of the Mind to channel the energy.

Don't confuse the dimensions of the Mind with the possibilities available from channeling energy. Through the three-dimensional space and time constraints of the Mind, you will form an intention for channeling energy but the energy itself is not constrained by these dimensions. As such, it is possible to channel energy into both the future or the past depending on the entity you desire to work with. For example, the Spirit exists within the domain of the future and thus you can channel energy to the Spirit in the future. So too the Mind exists within the domain of the past and thus you can channel energy into the past for the Mind. However the Body, which exists within the present, must have energy channeled to it within the present moment. That is why healing the Body can take time, because one must continually channel energy to the Body in the present (which is always now).

As our conscious existence comes through our Mind's perception, our ability to imagine healing occurring in the past or future is difficult for us to understand. In our Minds, the past is done and the future hasn't happened yet so affecting either seems impossible. To understand, consider what occurs in the Mind when you forgive someone. When a person wronged you in the past, your Mind stored that memory so you wouldn't make the same mistake again. However, by harboring this memory in your Mind, you're perpetuating the memory into the present and subsequently into your future.

When we forgive someone, we let go of the memory from our past and consequently we are freed from the constraints of this memory in the present as well as the future. By submitting to the power of forgiveness, we are actually fusing life force energy into the past, present and future. So too, there are many healing ways that transcend both space and time.

Also you shouldn't confuse energy with growth. For example, the Mind grows through new and unique experiences so channeling energy into the Mind alone will not necessarily stimulate it to grow. There may be an inconclusive memory that is preventing the Mind from growing and channeling energy to break free from this constraint is certainly the catalyst to get the Mind to grow. However, the growth itself comes from nurturing and investing in the Mind. Therefore channeling energy into your Body to become physically fit will only be beneficial if the Body is engaged in growth activities as well.

Riding the Efficient Frontier

When you think of channeling energy for yourself or another, first consider which entity will receive the energy. Each entity (Body, Spirit or Mind) has an optimal existence that corresponds to an efficient utilization of energy. Too little energy and the entity starves and too much energy causes the entity to suffer. For example when someone whispers in your ear, the right amount of energy comes into your ear for listening. However, when someone screams in your ear, the Body is overwhelmed with too much energy and consequently reacts by pulling away from the source of energy (i.e. whoever is screaming at you).

This balance between *too much* and *not enough* was eloquently described as *flow* by Mihaly Csikszentmihalyi in his seminal work 'Flow: The Psychology of Optimal Experience'. Csikszentmihalyi described flow as a state of concentration or complete absorption with an activity. Accordingly, flow occurs when a balance is struck between the challenge of the task and the skill of the performer. If the task is too easy or too difficult, flow cannot occur. If skill level and challenge level are equally matched we experience flow; if skill and challenge are not matched, we experience apathy. (Csikszentmihalyi 1990)

In an interview with Wired magazine, Csíkszentmihályi described flow as "being completely involved in an activity for its own sake. The ego falls away. Time flies. Every action, movement, and thought follows inevitably from the previous one, like playing jazz. Your whole being is involved, and you're using your skills to the utmost." (Geirland 1996)

A similar framework for optimizing energy can be demonstrated as an Efficient Frontier. Originally proposed by Nobel laureate Harry Markowitz, an Efficient Frontier is the set of all financial portfolios that will give the highest expected return for each given level of risk. That's a fancy way of saying that your portfolio would be perfectly balanced between risk and financial benefit. In the context of energy, instead of a financial return we measure the utilization of energy and rather than risk we measure the flow of information from an entity.

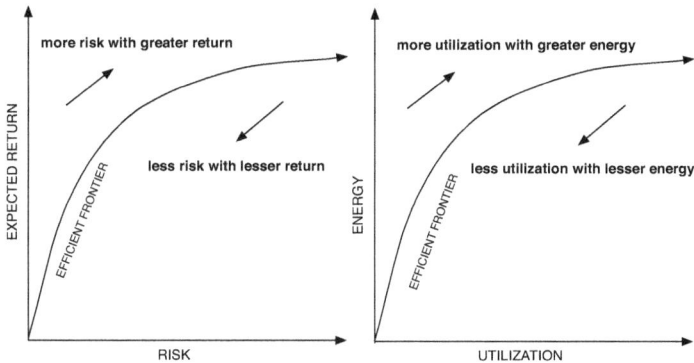

Figure 34: The Markowitz Efficient Frontier graphically represents the relationship between two related forces such as return vs. risk or energy vs. flow of energy.

As depicted in the Markowitz chart, an efficient frontier represents the optimal balance between two forces along an x and y axis. In financial terms, this demonstrates an optimized path providing the best balance between financial return and risk. If you don't take enough risk with your investments, you're not likely to have any gains. Conversely if you take too much risk, you might lose everything. However, by managing your investments along an efficient frontier, your investments would be perfectly balanced to get the maximum amount of financial gain without taking too much risk. Thus by following the efficient frontier, the investor would achieve an optimized return on investment according to the risks present in the investment.

With energy, the efficient frontier represents the optimal balance between energy and utilization of energy. One way to understand this relationship is by the elasticity of one's muscles. If you push a muscle too far by applying force it will tear. Conversely by not applying enough force to the muscle it will fail to fully contract. Thus by following the efficient frontier of energy and muscle elasticity, you can demonstrate how much force one can apply to a muscle to achieve maximum output without causing injury.

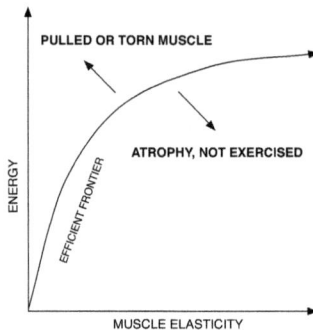

Figure 35: By comparing force to muscle elasticity, the Efficient Frontier diagram represents the optimized force that can be applied to a muscle to achieve optimal performance.

As we've discussed, you are the collective consciousness of your Body, Spirit and Mind. Because the life force energy of the Universe powers everything contained within our Universe, your three entities are powered, managed, and even governed by the management of this same energy. And while you can't necessarily control this energy force, you are able to channel and throttle it in order to help as well as heal yourself and others, bring opportunity to your doorstep and achieve your hopes and dreams.

Therefore, in order to manage your life, channeling and throttling energy to one or more of your entities can help you balance and optimize your utilization of energy. Your entire life has been a game of balancing energy without an awareness of where this energy was coming from or how to manage it. You have simply tried to cope by adjusting via the tools that were made available to you. When problems occurred, you adjusted the best you could and learned to avoid the source of the problem in the future. But the free will reality in which we live brings with it so many possibilities for problems that coping and adjusting can only take you so far. The problem with this approach is that you've been playing the game without an awareness of the rules or knowledge of how to play the game. Now that you're learning how to play the game, your ability to survive and thrive in life will clearly be enhanced.

Optimizing Energy within the Body

The Body is quite adept at managing energy through natural body processes. Our Bodies are very intelligent as is evident by the thousands of decisions that are made each and every day to keep you alive. The human Body takes over 17,000 breaths a day, pumps 1,584 gallons of blood each day via 100,000 heartbeats and blinks over 27,000 times a day. Thus your Body has been optimizing your management of energy since day one but doesn't have the ability, on its own, to direct more energy to itself. But by channeling energy to your Body, you can aid the Body's ability to heal itself, improve its physical condition, and enhance its strength. Before doing this, you must first understand what can result from too little or too much energy being directed into the Body.

Too much energy in the Body is not an unfamiliar experience. Most commonly we experience too much energy in our Body as pain. As illustrated previously, too much force being applied to a muscle can cause it to tear and too much energy can also cause other parts of your Body to have problems as well. We most often experience this as pain, discomfort, injury or simply becoming overweight. But illness can also result from too much energy concentrating in one part of our Body. Conversely too little energy in the Body manifests itself as a lack of energy.

It is important to remember that there is no such thing as good or bad energy. The life force energy available to you is simply energy and has no intention on its own to help or hinder you. However, all living things are drawn to this energy and thus a build-up of too much energy within you can attract parasitical life forms (e.g. bacteria, viruses, cancer, etc.) that believe your Body to be an ideal host.

Medical practices (both Eastern and Western) seek to remove the parasitical life forms from your Body and clearly possess effective methods for doing so. But it is the build-up of excess energy within the Body that attracts these invasive life forms into the Body in the first place and sustains their residence.

Thus the fundamental enabler of energy healers is their ability to flush out the built-up energy within the patient by channeling a flow of energy within the Body. An amusing side note of this is that many energy healers don't even realize this is what they're doing. And as you can now see, one doesn't need to understand how energy healing works in order to channel energy for healing.

So too, because it is the build-up of excess energy that attracts parasitical life, healing another person by channeling the flow of energy and drawing out the parasitical life form doesn't necessarily put the healer at risk of becoming the new host for the illness. If you don't have excess energy built up in you, then the illness won't be attracted to you. However, if you have an excessive amount of energy built up in your heart, your Spirit is not likely to allow you to help someone with heart problems.

Keeping the Body alive is the top priority of the Spirit and Mind. Because of this primary objective, your ability to heal another person or to be healed by another is directly tied to the overall health, balance and the presence of built-up energy within the healer. Thus you don't run the risk of becoming infected with the illness of the patient through healing if you don't have a similar build-up of excessive energy. The Spirit simply won't allow the energy to flow through healer to patient because it would put the healer at risk. However, if the energy requirements of the parasitical life form are so low that it can survive on very little or occasional amounts of energy, then the healer runs the risk of infection. This is one of the reasons why we are so susceptible to viruses but can't be infected by interacting with someone that has cancer.

We determine how to channel energy to the Body by remembering which entity governs the Body. The Body is the child of the Mind and thus we channel energy to the Body via the dimensions of the Mind (i.e. height, width, depth and time). Thus the location of energy (x) can be expressed as:

$$e(x) = h, w, d, t$$

Equation 1: e = energy, x = location, h = height, w = width, d = depth, t = time.

For every part of the Body, we can plot an efficient frontier representing the optimal utilization of energy as an expression of the sensation (sensual dimensions) of the Body. Energy is consumed as it flows through an entity and thus if energy is not flowing into the Body, the result will be a lack of energy.

Conversely if energy is flowing into the Body, but not being expended or expressed back out, there will be a buildup of energy which we immediately experience as pain and discomfort. You have been a passive observer of this relationship your entire life but now you can actively engage.

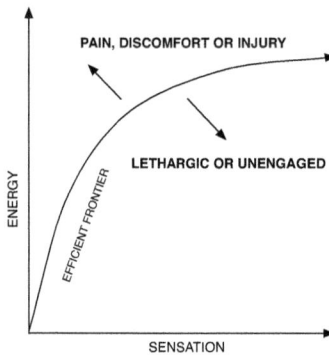

Figure 36: Along the efficient frontier there is a perfect middle ground between not applying enough energy and applying too much.

Thus to channel energy into the Body, you must first visualize your intention via the four dimensions of the Mind (height, width, depth and time). This is simply visualizing energy flowing into a particular area of the Body in the present moment (remember that the Body exists within the domain of the present). By forming an intention in your Mind, you channel the energy flowing into your Mind directly into a particular part of the Body. By flooding the ailing Body part with life force energy, you provide it with everything necessary for it to heal.

However, you must also be able to throttle the flow of energy in order to avoid the buildup of too much energy. Otherwise the life force energy that is flooding into the healing entity can actually cause damage. Thus to bleed off energy, one must express energy via the two dimensions of the Body that express as well as absorb energy (i.e. skin/touch and mouth/voice). So too if you're experiencing pain or discomfort in your Body, you can bleed off the excess of energy by expressing energy via these two dimensions[18].

Conversely if you're not getting enough energy into an ailing Body part, by bringing peace to the Body as a whole, one can direct more energy to one part of the Body, rather than throughout the entire Body. We bring peace to the Body through stillness activities such as meditation. As a result of these techniques, you can direct energy into one part of the Body and optimize the utilization of energy along the Efficient Frontier by bleeding off or channeling energy within the Body.

Optimizing Energy within the Spirit

Just like your Body, your Spirit and Mind require nurturing, maintenance and even repair. Even though you may be able to identify with your Spirituality, you may have trouble envisioning the Spirit as being something that is capable of being anything less than healthy. However, consider a human being that has never experienced their Spirituality throughout their lifetime and you can imagine that their neglected Spirit not being as strong as the Spirit of someone that has nurtured their Spirit since birth. Thus your Spirit has the capacity for growth and therefore also requires investment and nourishment.

---

[18] This is why martial arts teachers have you shout when you strike a blow.

Inherently we know that our Spirit can never die. When we envision our Spirit needing nourishment, it is all-together a different situation than when the Body needs nourishment. We can certainly conceptualize our Spirit being less than its full potential, but it is hard to imagine it atrophying like a muscle does when it isn't used. And while lack of nourishment certainly is disappointing to the Spirit, it is comforting to know that you really can't destroy it from lack of use. No matter what life throws at us, our eternal Spirit is always capable of bouncing back.

So what troubles and harms the Spirit? The answer comes from understanding the domain in which it lives. If you recall, the Spirit lives within the domain of *We are*. Whereas the Body lives within the domain of *Hear and Now* and the Mind lives within the domain of *I am*, the Spirit is all about the human collective rather than the individual. Thus when relationships break down and people do harm to one another, the Spirit is weakened and saddened. We experience this as the language of the Spirit flowing through the emotive dimensions of emotion and arousal. We feel sad, disappointed and sullen when events happen that trouble the Spirit.

Even though the Spirit will always bounce back from disappointment, we may not be interested in experiencing prolonged sadness during the recovery period. Moreover, in order to heal ourselves and others, the life force energy that flows through the Universe comes to us via our Spirit. As such, keeping the Spirit strong is as important as keeping a healthy Body.

Just like energy flows optimally through the Body along its Efficient Frontier, so too does energy flow along the Efficient Frontier of the Spirit. With too much energy flowing to the Spirit we find unfounded emotions of anger, disappointment and despair. And with not enough energy flowing we experience unexplained sadness, uncontrollable self-judgment and depression. Although these are merely the language of the Spirit, it is hard for us not to attribute values and judgment to these emotive dimensions. However just like a muscle expresses pain when it is nearing its breaking point, so too the Spirit provides us with feedback when we're nearing trouble.

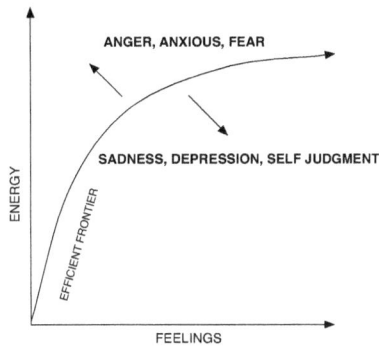

Figure 37: The efficient frontier for the emotive dimensions of the Spirit.

To channel energy to the Spirit, remember the flow of information that goes from the Body to the Spirit via the sensual dimensions. As such, energy flows *into* all five sensual dimensions, but only *out* via the two dimensions of touch (skin) and voice (mouth). You will recall that through these two dimensions, our original ideas and creations are released into collective consciousness for all of mankind's benefit. So too, these two sensual dimensions are the vehicles through which energy flows to the Spirit.

We begin by forming an intention in our Mind to let energy flow to our Spirit. We do this because, without first forming this intention, the energy that flows through our Mind will be distributed to our Body.

Our intention is to move energy to the Spirit and thus we want to shut down our Body and Mind as much as possible in order to conserve energy. As the Spirit needs the Body in order to connect to this world and the Mind needs the Body in order to survive, the Body will always be given all of the energy that it requires. Thus to enable this energy to flow through the Body to the Spirit, we must become still and at peace.

Managing energy is sometimes required during transition times in our lives. There are times when our Body, Spirit or Mind need more energy than usual to support an event in our life. After the event has concluded, our system sometimes doesn't re-balance as quickly as we would like. As a result, we experience the outcome of too little or too much energy flowing into one of our entities.

For example, the owner of my local yoga studio tells a story of how she began her yoga practice after her first child was born. She was suffering from post-partum depression and upon taking her first yoga class she noticed that her depression went away. For the previous nine months, her Body needed more energy than usual to enable her pregnancy. However, upon giving birth, her system didn't re-balance and the result was a feeling of depression (indicative of a lack of Spiritual energy). Yoga, which unites the Body, Spirit and Mind in balance, enabled her to direct more energy to her Spirit instead of her Body. And, as a result, her Spirit was able to return to its own efficient frontier and the depression disappeared.

From that one event in her life, her purpose emerged and several years later she is running a very successful yoga studio. Each and everyday her studio is full of people pursuing their own yoga practice as a result of her awakening. Because she was conscious, she noticed the change that occurred within her when she took that first yoga class. She could've treated her post-partum depression through a variety of techniques, but by noticing the change within herself and pursuing that change as a practice, she found her purpose.

It isn't that she was destined to own a yoga studio or even that this is her purpose. The yoga studio is the means by which she achieves her purpose, like this book is one of the means by which I pursue my purpose. By awakening to the communications of our Body, Spirit and Mind, we can tune into the Divine message that is trying to break into our consciousness. Thus we don't think our way to discovering our purpose, but instead open up to listen for the communications that are all around us.

Listening requires both the *intention* to listen as well as the *ability* to listen. You are already capable of listening, as the eleven dimensions of the Universe are uniquely human. Being *able* to listen requires turning down the volume of noise in your life so that the communication can be heard. We do this by listening to one of the three entities and quieting the other two.

A great way to still the Body and the Mind is through meditation. There are many forms of meditation and they each will bring the Body and Mind sufficiently to a state of rest in order for energy to flow freely to the Spirit. In time, you will find a type of meditation that brings your Body and Mind to its most restful state. However, for now, any form of meditation will suffice.

Placing energy within the Spirit is not something that is done within the domain of the Mind. Therefore, the mental dimensions of the Mind will not enable us to direct energy like we do with the Body.

Whereas the location of energy is important for the Body, for the Spirit we need only concentrate the flow of energy to the Spirit through the skin and mouth. The formula for channeling energy to the Spirit can be expressed as:

$$e(x) = (v, h, o, t^1, t^2) * (v^2, t^3)$$

Equation 2: e = energy, x = location, v = vision, h = hearing, o = olfaction, t1 = taste, t2 = touching, t3 = touch, v2 = voice.

As you can see from the formula above, channeling energy to the Spirit is a bit more complex than the Body. This isn't to say that it is harder or more difficult, but rather that it requires a bit more focus. The method is simple and can be performed in small pieces or in a dedicated session. Either is fine and you should trust what works for you. Remember, this is *your Spirit* that you're nurturing, so trust yourself to find a path that works for you.

The most basic method is to choose one of the sensual dimensions and stimulate it with a favorite sensation. For example, by placing a chocolate chip on your tongue and allowing it to melt you are stimulating the sensation of taste. Doing this while meditating or in a restful posture will still the Body and allow the energy that is created from this stimulation to flow to your Spirit. While the chocolate chip melts softly hum to yourself. In combination, the sensation of taste combined with the energy flowing from your mouth allows the energy to flow directly to your Spirit.

You can do this with any of the sensual dimensions and, with practice, via the skin as well. For example, experienced yogis (people who practice yoga) can find a place of rest within a posture. The sensation doesn't necessarily need to be a favorite or even pleasant, but should always bring forth a sense of stimulation and energy. Similarly you can meditate by staring at a beautiful flower, playing a favorite song, smelling the petals of a rose or rubbing the ears of your pet (the sensation is your feeling of touch). You don't need to make an event out of this practice, but rather every time you experience a stimulating sensation you can pause, form an intention and let the sensation flow to your Spirit via the sound of your voice.

The full embodiment of this gesture is to combine all of the senses with a meditating chant. To do the full version, select five foods that contain the five flavors (sweet, salt, sour, bitter and umami) and place each one of them on your tongue throughout your meditation. As each flavor stimulates your taste buds, let a harmonious ohm[19] sound resonate from the back of your throat. You can do this same practice with each of the sensual dimensions.

With the flood of energy that we direct to the Spirit, we must be mindful of the feedback that is returned. Like a muscle receiving too much force, we should listen for the emotive dimensions that come back from the Spirit. If emotions of anger, anxiety and fear are returned then we're applying too much energy. If we feel sadness, depression or self-loathing then our Spirit needs more energy.

Whereas the Body warns us when too much energy runs the risk of damaging the Body, the Spirit can't be damaged by too much energy, but rather provides feedback in order to provide you with guidance. The Spirit takes what nourishment it needs and returns any excess

---

[19] Some adherents of Eastern religions believe that amen shares roots with the Sanskrit aum (ohm) which invariably emphasizes God's singularity.

energy to the Universe. In the domain of the Spirit, recycling is a way of life.

Remember that the Spirit doesn't live within the confines of the mental dimensions and thus it is not constrained by the dimension of time. Thus the feedback from your channeling energy to your Spirit may be instantaneous or return sometime in the future. There is no reason why the emotional feedback would take an extraordinary amount of time. However, there is no reason why it would not take a long time either. But when the emotional feedback comes, be mindful of the source and take note of what your Spirit is trying to tell you.

If the emotional feedback tells you to throttle back the energy flowing to the Spirit, you will do so by performing activities that bring peace to the Spirit:

- Meditation
- Sharing
- Helping Others
- Forgiving
- Praying
- Loving

In time, you will learn to listen to your Spirit and govern the energy that flows to it in order to sustain your own personal efficient frontier. The harmony that will result from nurturing your Spirit in this way will be nothing short of amazing and your path to a Spiritual existence will pave the way for others. But first, you'll need to overcome the hardest challenge of them all: *getting your Mind to let go of the ego and follow its own efficient frontier.*

Optimizing Energy within the Mind

Of all the entities, channeling energy to the Mind is the most difficult. This is because the Mind is both required to begin the process of channeling energy to itself and the Mind always puts the Body first. Without the Body, the Mind cannot exist and thus all energy that is channeled to the Mind will be funneled to the Body.

As such, there is no logical way to convince the Mind to accept more energy than it thinks it needs to thrive regardless of the reason why the Mind needs the energy. You can come up with every possible argument but you'll never win because the Mind will *over think* every situation. And even if you're successful in convincing the Mind, it will lie to you if it means insuring what it believes to be in the Body's best interest. In the end, you'll conclude that it is impossible to channel energy to the Mind.

But you'll try endlessly until you come to this conclusion. Until your Mind gives up and accepts the Body and the Spirit as co-managers of you, the Mind will rule your existence. Our Minds have become overly developed through years of evolution devoid of a Spiritual balance. We've spent so much time and energy developing our Minds, that we even find the concept of *self* to by synonymous with our Mind. Consciousness is too often a vacation from the reality of everyday life, but when reality hits, we quickly push the Spirit aside and vault the Mind to center stage. We do this because we truly don't know our Spirit and we don't really trust God.

Not trusting God is such a horrible thing to say that few would utter the phrase. For years we've bought into the concept of a judgmental God and, as much as this may not ring true in our hearts, it is difficult to let go of judgment. Our entire life is filled with judgment, ranging from performance reviews at work to social clicks in our neighborhoods. Judgment is so much a part of being human that a life without it seems like a fantasy. With this comes a hang-up about God judging us and this is what keeps us from admitting, or at least verbalizing, how we really feel about God. And thus when trouble hits our lives, we unconsciously turn to our Minds to solve our problems.

Now this isn't to say that we don't turn to God as well. But we turn to Him asking for help rather than trusting that His ways are Divine. We ask for reality to be different and for outcomes to sway in our favor. When the plane is crashing, we ask God to save us and when someone is going to lose their job, we pray that we're not the one getting axed. Praying often turns into a request line for assistance rather than a communal connection with the Creator. The human way is to pray with the Mind, manage with the Mind and trust in the Mind.

Right now, as you read these words, you may even be saying to yourself how this isn't true. You may be thinking that others may not trust God, but as for you...*trusting in God shouldn't even be questioned.* Or maybe you don't believe in God anyway and thus you're agreeing that you don't trust God. You learned long ago that the only person you can trust is yourself. Either way, none of what you're thinking matters. For these are the logical and illogical thoughts of the Mind. And if you were nothing more than your Mind, then these thoughts might actually matter. But you're not simply a Mind. Nor are you a Mind attached to a Body. You are the collective consciousness of your Body, Spirit and Mind.

You are not those logical thoughts that put so much value in right, wrong, judgment, faith, commitment... the list goes on and on. Those thoughts are just thoughts and nothing more. They are the ways of the Mind. The thoughts of the Mind are endless and, by design, will always lead to a conclusion that it wanted to arrive at anyway. If you are a person that believes in God, then your Mind will find every possible argument to conclude that there is a God and that you're a true believer. And if you're a person that doesn't believe in God, then your Mind will do just the opposite. The Mind doesn't want to be proven wrong and it surely doesn't want to be made out to be a fool. For there is too much at stake for the Mind to be anything less than fully competent and in charge.

A Spiritual existence is one that accepts the Mind for what it is and empowers the Spirit to take its rightful place as governor of you. Once the shift of power transfers from the Mind to the Spirit, you will come into balance and achieve ever-lasting harmony. In this blissful state, the Mind will continue to operate in the same fashion that it always has functioned. There will be no clearing, no ah-ha moment, or transcendental shift that turns the Mind off. The Mind will not understand this transition, for understanding requires the logical ways of the Mind.

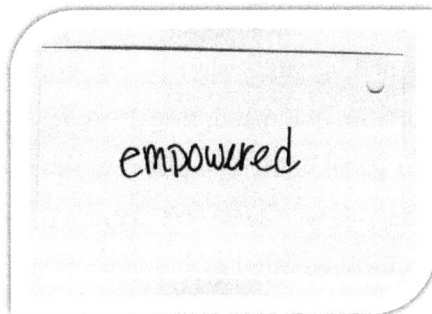

Card 21: Empowered: the authority or power to do something

The shift to a Spiritual existence is triggered by the Mind surrendering to the Spirit. Surrendering is not synonymous with being conquered. To conquer the Mind, it would have to be convinced that it is wrong. The endless logical thoughts that put the Mind through countless loops of analysis would need to ultimately resolve a conclusive answer. But that is not surrendering. On the contrary, surrendering is acceptance. Once the Mind accepts the Spirit as rightful heir to you, the Mind will assume its more suitable role as co-pilot in concert with the Body.

The Spirit, in contrast, doesn't believe or not believe in God. Judgment doesn't enter into the equation. The Spirit is part of God and something that is part of God needn't question the validity of its own integrity. Faith in God is replaced with God. Trusting in God is unnecessary, for the Spirit need not trust that which it knows to be true. Prayer becomes a means to connect with God and our lives become fulfilled in achieving our God given purpose. We, in turn, find our purpose in God for there is no other way for the Spirit.

And so we are left with the dilemma, "How does one's Mind surrender to the Spirit?"

As we've discussed, we will never be able to reason our way to surrender. Nor can we simply put our faith in God to make this happen because God designed us this way. If He wanted our Minds to surrender to the Spirit on command, then He surely would've designed us with the ability to do so in the first place. As much as we try to push the Mind to surrender, we will always fail because we are using the ways of the Mind to convince the Mind to surrender. This is akin to fighting for gun control by shooting people with guns.

The only way to empower the Mind to surrender is to channel more energy to the Mind. This healing life force energy is the essence of God and through this beautiful presence the Mind will transcend itself to surrender. Abundantly present in our Universe, the dark energy of God not only shapes and binds everything, but is here to bring forth the Spiritual evolution of mankind.

Just as the Body is akin to the Universe, so too is the Mind akin to Humanity. As we are helplessly governed by our Minds, so too is the Universe hopelessly governed by Humanity. Our inability to conquer the Mind, despite the promise of harmony with the Body and Spirit, is merely a mirror of Humanity refusing to surrender to God. Our Minds must surrender to our Spirit before Humanity will surrender to God. And just like one cannot conquer the Mind to bring about this Spiritual shift, so too can we not expect to conquer Humanity into submission.

To bring energy to the Mind, for the purpose of enlightening the Mind, one must take the Mind offline. If the Mind is engaged in a fight for survival, it will deflect all energy to the Body for it knows that the Body ensures survival. The challenge we all face in this quest is that our Minds never turn off. They're forever in charge and, even when we're sleeping, they're never really offline. But through calming exercises, we can encourage the Mind to move to a nearly offline state. We do this by bringing the Mind to a state of peace. When the Mind is calm, restful and safe it will embrace the life force energy from the Spirit for its own benefit.

Calming the Body and Spirit is a piece of cake compared to the Mind. Even when we're meditating, dreaming or relaxing in a hot tub, our Minds are busy working on something. That little voice in your head is good at everything but being quiet. However, we can bring our Minds to this desirable state of peace by managing the energy of the Mind. If we could do nothing more than meditate all day this might be something that we could cause to occur, but that isn't an option for most of Humanity. For those of us that can't find the way to a life of meditation, we must find the Efficient Frontier of our own Mind.

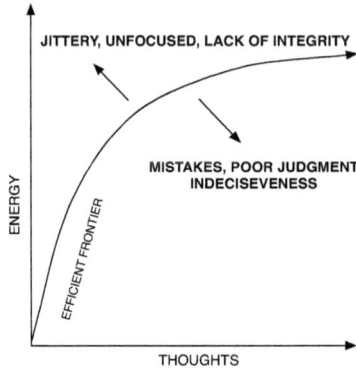

[Figure: graph with vertical axis labeled ENERGY and horizontal axis labeled THOUGHTS. A curved line labeled EFFICIENT FRONTIER rises from the lower left. Text near the top reads "JITTERY, UNFOCUSED, LACK OF INTEGRITY" and middle text reads "MISTAKES, POOR JUDGMENT INDECISEVENESS" with arrows pointing to the curve.]

Figure 38: The efficient frontier of the Mind balances between not applying enough thinking, in which you'll fail to make good decisions and over-thinking, in which you'll make no better decisions but you'll drive yourself into a state of high-stress.

As we monitor the ways of our Mind, we will see that as too much energy flows into the Mind we become jittery, unfocused and fail to complete what we set out to do (lack of integrity). So too, these conditions give rise to stress in the Body because the Mind funnels this excess energy directly into the Body. This isn't to say that if you have stress in your life that you already have abundant life force energy flowing into your Mind, but rather that your Mind is simply transferring energy to your Body. To allow the Mind to accept this energy, one must bring the Mind to a state of peace. And this is precisely where calming activities come into play.

If you're feeling stressed, then you need to incorporate calming activities into your daily life. These activities can range from meditation to cross country running, as they will vary by individual. What brings you to a state of peace is not the same thing that will bring your neighbor there. With these calming activities in place, your Mind will open up to the energy coming to it. With the Body, Spirit and Mind at peace, the Mind will allow the energy to flow into itself and become nourished.

We channel energy to the Mind through the language of the Spirit. Through the dimensions of emotion and arousal, energy flows from the Spirit into the Mind. Thus to bring life force energy into your Mind, find your favorite emotion and bring it into existence through those activities that bring the emotion out in you. By actively bringing up emotions, the energy of your Spirit will channel into your Mind where it will reside if the Mind is at peace. As you can see, channeling energy into the Mind is more than simply forming an intention and wishing it to occur. With the Mind, we must both give and prepare ourselves to receive.

If your favorite emotion is happiness, select a photograph of a memory that makes you happy. Skip past the photos of people that *should* make you happy and find that one photograph of a wonderful moment in your life where your life was full of happiness. Sit in a comfortable position and focus your gaze on this photograph for a solitary minute. Let your eyes wander around the photograph and take in everything that was happening when the camera lens captured this moment. What you've done by taking a minute out of your day to be happy is accept the energy flowing from your Spirit. In this moment the

Mind is accepting and, with the Body at a state of peace, this energy will nourish the Mind.

If your life is filled with poor judgment (logical thought rather than judging others), mistakes and failures then your Mind is lacking energy. You can meditate until the cows come home, but without energy flowing into your Mind, it won't make a difference. To heal the Mind, you'll need to bring a constant flow of energy into the Mind. If this is your issue, you'll need to first invest in strengthening your three entities by nurturing them and the connective bonds between them (covered in earlier chapters). Once the entities are stronger, the energy will begin to flow and you'll find yourself experiencing fewer mistakes in your life. Then you can begin to find ways to calm your Mind so it can be receptive to this energy.

A Path to Integrity

Earlier I put forth the question, "Can a person ever become entirely complete?" As you can see in this chapter, the management of energy requires effort when we are not in harmony. Too much energy into the Body causes injury, not enough energy into the Spirit causes depression, and without proper preparation, all energy funneled into the Mind will be transferred into the Body where it can cause stress and illness. In total, this is a lot to manage. Unfortunately, the management or mis-management of energy isn't an optional choice for it is happening within you whether you attempt to balance it or not.

As each of your entities move towards becoming complete and harmonize, the Spiritual self will emerge and energy will begin to balance effortlessly. Similarly as the Universe and Humanity harmonize with God, life as we know it will become Heaven on earth.

Card 22: Blessing: the infusion of something with holiness, divine will, or one's hopes.

With strong connecting bonds between the Body, Spirit and Mind, energy will naturally flow from one entity to another. With this, a person can become complete through fulfilling their purpose of loving one another and expanding God's presence in the Universe.

The same model applies with the Universe, God and Humanity. With strong connecting bonds between the Universe, God and Humanity, energy will naturally flow from one to another. With this, collective consciousness will become complete, Humanity will have fulfilled its purpose, and the next chapter in God's plan will emerge.

A Spiritual Existence has its own efficient frontier that manifests itself as a harmonization of the Body, Spirit and Mind. As the energy flows through each entity, the entire being becomes energized and one with God. Our purpose in serving God continues in this perfect state and we will thus witness Humanity surrendering to God through acceptance rather through being conquered. So too the Universe, God and Humanity will harmonize and God will become complete. The cycle will finally be complete as God trusted and intended it to be.

Your Practice

1. Energy Ball Meditation

Often we struggle with meditation because we believe that our Minds are to be silent. That silly voice in our head won't shut-up and thus we conclude that meditation is really hard. Instead imagine your meditation as a technique that enables you to connect to your Spirit by bringing peace to the Body and Mind. In this context, the Body and Mind are not expected to be silent, but are instead paying homage to their companion the Spirit.

In this meditation, you'll visualize a ball of energy that drifts through your Body. As this ball flows through you, it collects any pent up energy that you've stored in your Body and takes with it the energy source of any illness that has decided to take up residence in your Body. Focusing on both prevention and cure, this ball of energy can draw out of you everything that you don't need.

To begin, sit in a comfortable position of your choosing. If you're new to meditation, prop yourself up against the wall with cushions or pillows. Remember, the goal is to bring the Body and Mind to peace so forget about looking like your meditating and instead get comfortable. Close your eyes and continue visualizing the room around you. Even though your eyes are closed, keep the focal point of your attention focused on that area just beyond your eyelids. In your Mind, visualize the room you're in and little details such as colors, lighting and the textures all around you.

Continue by taking a deep breath through your nose and notice any smells or odors that you detect. Then take notice of your mouth and bring any flavors that you notice to the surface. You may be in a room with no smells and have no flavors in your mouth or you might notice subtle sensations.

Bring your awareness back behind your eyes and focus your attention into a tight ball of energy. Slowly draw the ball back through your head and let any thoughts that are in your head become attached to this ball of energy. As the ball pulls back through your head, let it come to rest at the base of your skull and then slowly lower it through the center of your neck. The ball of energy will pass through your throat and be drawn to any tension in the upper back.

Let the ball come to a resting position wherever you experience the most tension in your upper back and, as you breathe, let the stored energy in your back be pulled into the ball with every out-breath. As you breathe in, the ball expands and reaches out into the fibers of your muscles and, as you breathe out, the ball pulls back in and combs all of the pent up energy stored in the muscles into the ball.

Take four or five breaths in this way and then move the ball to your spine. Slowly let the ball lower through the center of your back. You will find that the ball will find its own pace and take longer to pass through areas of your Body with lots of stored energy. Let the ball take its time, knowing that every second that the ball chooses to remain in your Body is time well-spent clearing energy from you.

Let the ball drift down to the lowest part of your Body and then, after pausing, bring it back up. As you pull back up through your Body, let any remaining energy become attached to the ball and pull away from your Body. The ball will rise back into your head and forward to the front of your awareness. With this energy now collected into a singularity, release it from your Body by chanting or singing with a long breath. As your vocal chords resonate with sound, the marooned energy of your Body escapes back into the Universe where it can do great work.

Open your eyes and smile for you are healed. That which would've been attracted to feed off of this energy will need to find another home in the Universe. In this, you are one step closer to rising towards integrity.

10

SPIRITUAL EVOLUTION

In 1859, Charles Darwin published his book Origin of Species and initiated a chasm between science and God that has never healed. The ensuing debate has divided Humanity into God loving theists and scientific thinking atheists even though your average human being hardly relates to the extremities of either camp. As a result, otherwise intelligent people often bury their heads in the sand when it comes to the topics of evolution and natural selection because they fundamentally believe these scientific constructs seek to demonstrate a Godless reality.

At the end of this philosophical or scientific debate you're still left with the fundamental question, "Is there a God?" In truth, no amount of scientific discourse or religious proselytizing can unequivocally convince the Mind that God does or does not exist. However, underlying these logical debates is an assumption that presupposes to understand God. When theologians attempt to understand God, they rely on religious texts and mental constructs that can never really convincingly be sourced beyond the hand and Mind of man. At the end of the day, some human being wrote down the words that he or she believed to be the word of God. Unfortunately, this line of reasoning will never convince the scientific Mind that God exists.

So too, the scientific Darwinian thinking that traces the lineage of mankind back to the simplest of life forms will never convince those that believe in God that He doesn't exist. No amount of proselytizing or logical debating will ultimately convince either camp to change their position. As a result, we retreat to our respective camps and resolve that religion is yet another topic not to be brought up in polite conversation. Unfortunately, this leaves the topic unresolved and leaves each camp to a meaningless accumulation of reasons why they are right and the other party is wrong.

From the Darwinian perspective, modern scientific discoveries involving genes and DNA have unequivocally demonstrated that evolution is a fact of life. You can bury your head in the sand if you want, but the results are in with DNA and gene mutation now well established. And clearly adaptation has been in play since life first appeared on our planet.

Recently Time Magazine ran a series of articles updating Darwin's theory with current scientific discoveries:

> Darwin proposed that natural selection could gradually transform a species. Scientists have observed thousands of cases of natural selection in action. They've documented that beaks of finches on the Galápagos Islands have gotten thicker when droughts forced the birds to crack tough seeds to

survive. They've observed bacteria developing resistance to drugs that were believed to be invincible. (Zimmer 2009)

Has this scientific discovery dissuaded the millions of followers of Jesus Christ? Are the mosques in Mecca empty or have the synagogues in Jerusalem become nothing more than historical artifacts? Clearly the evidence of how we got here hasn't had the fundamental impact that all of the anti Darwinian extremists feared would occur.

Our lineage back to the simplest form of life may be scientifically plausible, but the simple fact remains that the scientific community has failed to demonstrate how life can spring forth from no life. And before you fire up your petri dish to show how life can spring forth from bacteria combining with the crystal forming properties of primordial clay, let me short circuit your argument by stating, "It won't matter anyway."

The truth of the matter is that you can't scientifically demonstrate the existence or non-existence of God. The argument that our Universe is too complex to exist without a Creator doesn't impress the scientific community. For every complex system you say could only be constructed by God, they'll show you a complex system that operates without the hand of God. On the flip side, demonstrating how all life on our planet (algae, plants, insects, animals, human beings, etc.) sprang forth from the first dividing cell, won't explain why God didn't cause the cell to divide in the first place. You can't convince either side that they're wrong. So why even try?

God's Intent

With the aid of modern science, evolutionists have a very convincing argument demonstrating how all life on the planet evolved from a single life form. You can disagree if you so choose, but upon intellectually considering the evidence, you'll eventually come to the conclusion that this argument isn't worth debating. The facts are in and we are at the top of the tree of life and there is only one way down[20]. Our ancestors won out over their neighbors and we're the beneficiaries of their superiority (or luck). But this is where our egoic Minds get in the way.

We human beings assume that we're the only possible outcome of the evolutionary process. We actually believe that if we dropped the building blocks for life onto a neighboring planet and waited a few hundred billion years, that we would find human beings crawling all over the place. It is akin to replacing the human centric Adam and Eve story with a similarly self-centered perspective that evolution will always result in cohabitating humans with 2.3 children, a sport utility vehicle in the garage and a nine-to-five workweek.

Why we do this is easy to understand. We want to be special and loved by God. If God made us in His image, then we're His favored creation and entitled to His glory and blessings. In our Minds, we always position ourselves as the ultimate benefactors of God's love. The alternative, we incorrectly assume, is that God doesn't love us and that life is without meaning. Or, at the very least, God won't protect us from evil, the Devil and other things that might harm us. In our Minds, if we're not at the top of the food chain then we're nothing more than prey.

---

[20] The latest thinking on the tree of life suggests there might be multiple ways down the tree, but historically speaking there is only one way up (the way that resulted in "us").

The Darwinian thinking scientist would have you believe that evolution is a natural occurring algorithm so incredibly complex that to require God to initiate the beginning is illogical. They would ask you, "How does it makes sense that I can trace the evolution of life back hundreds of millions of years to the most simplest life form, only to conclude that only God could provide the initial building blocks of life?" So too the scripture-quoting theologian would have you believe that only through God's omnipotent power that it is possible for our Universe to exist the way it does and for human beings to be here.

Is there a common ground? Is there a marriage between science and God where both co-exist without strife? For far too many years, the faith filled and the logically oriented have failed to come together in a common understanding of why we're here, how we got here and the existence of God. And neither camp has thus far been optimistic that there even is a common ground. In the judgmental world in which we live, the men of God and the men of science seem to have resolved that one group is ultimately going to be crowned the winner.

As boldly illustrated by Daniel C. Dennett in *Darwin's Dangerous Idea*:

> I know it passes in polite company to let people have it both ways, and under most circumstances I wholeheartedly cooperate with this benign arrangement. But we're seriously trying to get at the truth here, and if you think that this common but unspoken understanding about faith is anything better than socially useful obfuscation to avoid mutual embarrassment and loss of face, you have either seen much more deeply into this issue than any philosopher ever has (for none come up with a good defense of this) or you are kidding yourself. (Dennett 1996)

Obviously Dennett doesn't get invited to speak at many church picnics. But he brings up the excellent point that our current understanding of our relationship with God doesn't make any sense in light of our understanding of science. And with this not so subtle framing of the situation, we can take a look at our fundamental assumptions in a new light. The basic question, "Why am I here?" deserves an answer and in this answer we will find the common ground between God and science.

Embedded in the answer to the *why are we here* question is both an explanation of mankind's purpose and the common ground we seek. Our purpose is to love one another and expand God's presence through the creation and expression of our original creations. In freeing our original creations from our earth bound Bodies, we release knowledge into collective consciousness. In return, God provides our Universe with dark energy which, in turn, expands the Universe in which we live, breathes life into our Bodies and heals us so that we can continue fulfilling our purpose. Our symbiotic relationship with God brings with it a parental love that beams when we fulfill our purpose. And while this doesn't necessarily tie us to the offspring of Adam and Eve, it doesn't take away from how special and loved we are by God.

In stark opposition to the Darwinian premise that God the Creator makes no sense in lieu of the complex evolutionary algorithms that resulted in human beings, I offer that God's thirst for unique knowledge is all the more satisfied in a reality that springs forth from the random and uncharted evolution of life. If all possible knowledge were constrained to the possibilities from an Adam and Eve lineage, then the total potential knowledge would be rather small. Alternatively, if life were to evolve naturally, the resulting life forms and possibilities from their creations would be incomprehensibly vast.

To better understand this line of reasoning, imagine that God created multiple Universes capable of originating life. In providing the constructs that governed their existence, each Universe is allowed to independently evolve and bring forth life (or not). Hundreds of billions of years later, God checks on each Universe's collective consciousness. When He finds knowledge in a Universe's collective consciousness, that Universe is provided with dark energy to fuel its continued existence. However when a Universe doesn't generate knowledge, God doesn't provide it with dark energy and eventually it succumbs to entropy and collapses. Presumably this process would repeat itself over and over again until a species emerged that evolved beyond its physical existence and into a Spiritual existence.

In due course, we will discuss why God desires knowledge derived in this manner. But for now recognize that in this reality, God created you for a purpose and loves you for fulfilling your purpose. In creating, you are doing what God intended you to do and He was able to do this without sending down a lightning bolt to get your attention. God didn't have you in mind when he created the Universe, but He knew that where life is possible, life will spring forth. And where life springs forth, life will evolve. In time, life will evolve into forms that have both Bodies and Minds. The thinking creature will provide a host for the immortal Spirit, which will guide and protect the individual life form.

In this, God and science are once again reunited in holy matrimony. The rules, laws and properties that govern the Universe in which we live were provided by God and, at the same time, the life forms that evolved in our Universe were inspired by God but left to their own devices to manifest into what we today see in the mirror. God purposely doesn't control life because that would limit the fantastic creations that are generated by life. We should not confuse this with God not being accessible or God's presence not being influential in our lives. In fulfilling our purpose, God's will manifests itself as omnipotent energy capable of miraculous power.

To free your Mind from the mental constructs that limit your consciousness, consider a different planet with all together different conditions under which life could evolve. On this imaginary planet covered entirely in a soupy mud, light would only touch the outer, unstable surface of the planet. Life on this planet would largely be confined to a sub-surface existence. And while we find this to be an inhospitable environment, intelligent life could just as well evolve under these conditions. In this environment, would the intelligent creatures' evolution necessitate eyes to see? Possibly, on this planet, the most intelligent life forms would develop an alternative way to *see* similar to sonar used by bats.

Would these creatures develop the iPhone, high definition television and laser technologies? Probably not, for their environment wouldn't benefit from such creations. Alternatively, they would create other fantastic creations that suited and benefited them in their environment. And thus when God peeked in on this species' creations, He would find an all-together different and unique set of creations than if He would've dropped Adam and Eve onto the mud planet. You may find this to be science fiction, but the fact remains that with the possibility of *any* life form winning the evolutionary race up the tree of life, comes an unpredictable outcome as it relates to the creations that would result.

Why Does God Want an iPhone?

Our society's monotheistic understanding of God is framed around Him being omnipotent and all knowing. Not all religions subscribe to this theory, but I hope to demonstrate that Inspiration Divine doesn't invalidate the concept of an omnipotent and all knowing God. In truth, we can only hope to better understand God through a relationship with God, so too we should accept that we might never fully understand God during our earth bound existence. Thus we will really never know why God desires knowledge created by us fulfilling our purpose. Surely it is not because He is incapable of deriving this knowledge on His own. But as to why He has made the creation of knowledge our purpose may never be known.

Assuming there is a Mind of God, surely God could know anything that is possible to be known. Theologists debate if an all-knowing God must think in order to know or if He simply knows everything. Again, no man or woman on our planet is uniquely equipped to answer this question. But as God exists outside of the confines of our Universe, it is logical to deduce that God is not governed by the dimensions of our Universe. Thus without being governed by the dimension of time, it is feasible that God would not know something until it was created and also already know it once it is created. Being time-governed creatures, it is difficult for us to wrap our Minds around this concept, but within this model exists the potential for us to create knowledge for God's consumption and be present to an all-knowing God.

So too, an omnipotent God surely is capable of creating the world described in the Bible or also capable of creating a world that springs forth life without his causal hand infusing life into the Universe. Simply creating a Universe capable of springing forth life is enough. With God knowing that life will happen, but not specifying when or where, we find ourselves in a loving relationship with God in which we are the prodigal offspring. You can imagine God's amusement when he peeks in on our Universe and say's, "Wow, those are really interesting creatures. I can't wait to see what they'll dream up!"

We have to be careful when envisioning God to not confuse what God *chooses* to do with what God *can* do. When you began reading this book, you could've skipped to the last chapter to read how it ends. You were certainly capable of doing this. And while we have all done this in the past, most people find this to be an unfulfilling experience. As a result, even though we can skip to the end and know the conclusion, we rarely do so. So too it is possible that God desires to be surprised and amused by the outcome of our creations even though He is capable of knowing everything.

On the flip side, would you say that God is incapable of not knowing all? To say so would postulate an omnipotent God that is incapable of not knowing everything. And thus He really wouldn't be omnipotent then would He? Thus we must not interpret our purpose as providing something that God is incapable of doing on His own but rather, for reasons we may never know, our purpose is fulfilling God's wishes.

Spiritual Evolution

When we revisit evolution and recognize that we are but one possible outcome up the tree of life, we begin to understand that our evolution is not a state of entitlement. As human beings, we don't universally get to evolve, but rather some human beings will evolve. And some human beings will not evolve. On our path to a Spiritual evolution, we should not assume that there is a switch that will magically shift the entire human race to connect with their Spirit and embrace this new chapter in life.

The awakening that is taking place around the world is an early signal of this Spiritual evolution. Many have evolved and many more evolve each and every day. However unlike the natural selection of physical evolution, we have a participatory role to play in our Spiritual evolution. The ability to listen to God and bring one's Body, Spirit and Mind into balance is the means by which human beings can evolve. And as much as we would like to share the grace and beauty of this transcendence, a Spiritual evolution is one that must be initiated by the individual. You simply can't make someone evolve if they're not ready.

Upon enlightenment, you'll find peace, happiness and a profound understanding of the Universe as well as everything in it. The outcome is not the goal and this is, unfortunately, something that you'll have to come to understand. Your Spiritual evolution can be brought forth if you're ready to begin the journey. Whereas this journey cannot be forced on another, it is available to all who seek the path.

We begin, together, by living the wisdom that comes from a deep relationship with God. In shedding judgment and replacing it with love, you'll find yourself called to a new place that brings forth your growth. In this calling, you'll hear the familiar voice of God speaking to you. In an instant, you'll recognize that the voice has always called to you, but somehow it was previously difficult to listen. And once you're there, you'll begin a new lease on life, because you'll become causal in the future of the Universe, God and Humanity.

Your Practice

By connecting to emotion, sensation and thought around an exercise, you will find that the flow of information from your Spirit to be less encumbered.

1. Practice a Body Immersion

First focus for one minute on a memento (e.g. photograph) that brings about an emotion within you (any emotion). After focusing, begin a repetitive exercise routine (e.g. yoga flow, tai chi or even running on a treadmill) for ten minutes to get yourself out of your Mind and into your Body. During this time, let your sensations, emotions and thoughts flow without restriction or too much intention. Once the 10-minute workout is complete, rest for one minute, then place a flavor in your mouth (e.g. sweet, sour, etc.) and begin journaling. Write without regard to composure, grammar or even making sense. When you've journaled for three minutes, take your pen and circle any words that speak to you. Copy those words onto an index card and review them from time to time. These words are direct communication from your Spirit. Be mindful of these words and then let them go. This 15-minute immersion is easy to do and can become part of a regular practice.

2. Practice a Spirit Immersion

Instead of the 10-minute Body workout, meditate for 10 minutes to nurture your Spirit. Experiment with different starting emotions to learn this language.

3. Practice a Mind Immersion

Repeat the immersion process, but this time nurture your Mind by taking one of the words from your index card and learning something new about it. Type the word into Google and instead of clicking 'Google Search' click 'I'm feeling lucky.' Printout whatever website loads and focus your Mind on learning its contents for 10 minutes.

11

YOUR PURPOSE

In ancient Rome, Marcus Tullius Cicero (January 3, 106 BC – December 7, 43 BC) coined the term afflatus to indicate a Divine communication of knowledge. The term roughly refers to *inspiration* which meant, at the time, "to be blown into" by a Divine wind. Whereas inspiration may bring forth any idea, an afflatus refers to the sudden and stunning blow of a new idea. Only a few visionaries will think up great ideas, but everyone can be stopped in their tracks by an afflatus.

The book you're reading is just such a revelation. Beginning on July 3rd 2008, my afflatus came to me while I was on vacation with my family in central Wyoming. As I relaxed reading a book with a warm summer breeze blowing across my Father's porch, I began to write down ideas that began streaming into my consciousness. I submitted to this stream of consciousness as these ideas branched into a completely new dialogue on a distinct, unique and previously unknown subject matter.

Ideas turned into diagrams, diagrams turned into sentences and strings of sentences became chapters. I immediately felt compelled to write down this message and the flow of information came to me as if it were being dictated. Each concept tied elegantly to another and subsequently supported the next inconceivable revelation. Even though I had no previous experience with this subject matter, the information entered my Mind with the same clarity that comes from years of study.

One chapter became two, two chapters became three and, in a short period of time, Inspiration Divine was written. From start to finish, this entire book was received and written in twenty-one days. At every stage along the way, despite my not being qualified or trained to understand this information, the details fell into perfect order without any effort on my part.

Along the way I had questions. Much of the information that I received, brought forth questions on related topics and I found myself asking for answers to come to me. Much to my surprise, the answers came. But when they came, they came with more information than I had requested. Despite the diverse subject matter, everything I was given tied elegantly into the other messages.

After twenty-one days, the messages concluded in a collective body of information. I didn't ask for the information to stop, but knew the body of work was complete. My questions had been answered and the logic of the content appeared to be without any loose ends. Not being an author by trade, the process of self-editing came next with a great deal of grammar corrections, background supportive research and sharing this message with anyone who would listen.

I knew from the very first message that these were messages from God. But something within the message communicated that this message wasn't intended solely for me. This message has been broadcast since the dawn of time for all life forms to hear. Although this message manifests itself through Divine inspiration, I am no more a prophet than you are. The message contained in Inspiration Divine is for all of us.

Sri Aurobindo

After the editing was nearly complete, I began searching for related bodies of work that proposed the same conclusions as the message that I had been given. My personal opinion was that this was an afflatus (I didn't know the term at the time) and that surely there had been other authors who had received similar messages. And although I didn't find other authors extolling their books having been written via Divine inspiration, I did stumble across Sri Aurobindo (August 15, 1872– December 5, 1950).

You will note that Aurobindo is referenced in this book and that is because, upon reading his writing, I became mystified at the paradoxically amazing similarities in our messages. Subsequently I went back and inserted references to his eloquent writing. Despite Sri Aurobindo being born nearly 100 years before my birth and passing from this earth before I was born, his perspective on modern physics, the ways of the Universe, Humanity's role and God are incredibly in synchronicity with my afflatus.

How could this be true? How could two authors separated by time, distance, religion and culture be so beautifully espousing the same perspective on being human?

The answer is Divine. The afflatus of both of our messages is being broadcast to all of Humanity. Sri Aurobindo and I were both listening. Not only did we listen, but we put pen to paper and shared our insights with those around us. In doing so, we helped expand the Universe and I hope to inspire as many inspirational thinkers as this man did in India some sixty years ago (parts of *The Life Divine* were published in 1914 and the book in whole was first published in 1939).

I have studied and since met other people who have received an afflatus. There are commonalities and differences between each experience, but they all bring forth an understanding of our role in life. Each afflatus is subject to the interpretation of the biased human Mind and thus no afflatus is perfect or absolute. Each will contain truths delivered from the Spirit and untruths inserted by the Mind. However in comparison, they will reveal common messages that bring forth God's message to mankind.

Throughout history there are many examples of messages from God and inspirations from unknown origins. As most human beings are ignorant of the distinction between their Body, Spirit and Mind, we herald those that have received an afflatus as privileged, special or even chosen. We also categorize those people that receive the words of God as mystical or crazy because we don't believe that it is possible to be in direct communication with God. However, every week billions of people attend religious services based on communications received from God by everyday human beings. We believe in God, but not ourselves.

Each and everyday God speaks to us through our Spirit regardless of our ability or inability to listen. God knows that we will one day awaken with the ability to listen and understand our purpose, our role to play and our individual path. Once that awakening begins, you will no longer be able to *not listen*. Born with the potential for harmony, once you attain harmonious communications with your Spirit you will learn to listen, ask questions and receive answers.

Be in Communication

In distinguishing the Body, Spirit and Mind from the singularity of a mental conscious experience, you're able to expand beyond everyday existence. Whereas everyday life may be overwhelming, tiring or just plain hard, a life in balance with your Body, Spirit and Mind is filled with joy, happiness, and peace. However, instead of this being an achieved state of nirvana, this balance is a journey that continues.

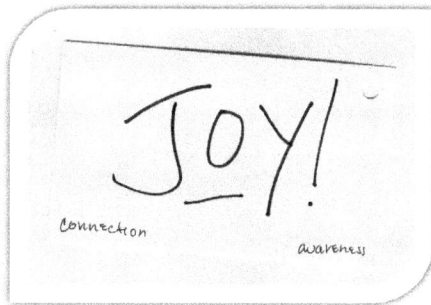

Card 23: Joy: a feeling of great pleasure and happiness

Try and accept that your Spirit has existed outside of your Body, prior to your birth, despite your not being aware of it. The communications between your Body, Spirit and Mind have been flowing from the moment you were born, but you have thus far only been a passive observer. As interpreted by your Mind, these communications become one in our singular experience of consciousness. With singular consciousness, many of these communications are not understood, considered or even heard. For example, many emotions aren't enjoyable and thus are avoided rather than understood as a communication from the Spirit.

Recently at a yoga class, one of the students gave a warning to new people in the class to be prepared for the rush of emotions that could result from practicing yoga. She described this rush of emotion as something that needed to be defended against. Rather than defending yourself from emotion, accept that emotion is how the Spirit communicates with the Mind. And if you're opening up the lines of communication for the first time, please don't prepare yourself but rather immerse yourself in this connection and all of the emotive energy that flows between your Spirit and Mind.

Communications between God and mankind occur within the balance of the Body, Spirit and Mind. Our waking life is primarily engaged in *thinking* rather than *being* in harmony. We power our way through the day by encountering situations, solving problems and seeking pleasure. However you have probably had insightful thoughts in the downtime moments of your day such as during twilight sleep, driving, showering or, for those that have begun their practice, meditation. It is during these times when we submit and let go, that information flows effortlessly between the Body, Spirit and Mind. In a sense, as soon as you let your Mind's guard down, the information begins to flow.

In today's society, we avoid such moments of tranquility by filling our lives up with activity. When we get into the car, we turn on the radio and when we climb into bed, we read a book. Rather than simply being with ourselves, we focus our Minds on an activity. But when our Minds disengage, there is no activity and the information begins to flow. You may not realize it, but this occurs each and everyday when you sleep.

During those twilight moments between when you're awake and when you're fully asleep, there is a narrow window where the Mind can be in conscious communication with the Spirit. During these times, the Mind is only able to receive information due to the order in which the three entities communicate with one another (e.g. the Spirit communicates with the Mind, the Mind communicates with the Body). As such, questions that the Mind has asked earlier may be answered by the Spirit during these tranquil moments of clarity. The asynchronous communication pattern manifests itself by the Mind perceiving information flowing into it based on questions that have been asked previously in one's life.

It is important to note that only the Mind operates within the boundaries of the dimensions of the Mind. As such, remember that the Spirit is always broadcasting answers to your questions irrespective of the dimension of time. Thus it is impossible to miss the answer. However, you can *not be listening*. Whereas listening with your ears only requires functional hearing, listening to God requires that you be in tune with your Body, Spirit and Mind. When you don't hear the answers to your questions, don't assume that they haven't been answered. Instead, recognize that you may be out of harmony and should invest in activities that will bring you back into harmony.

When you come to these realizations, refrain from retreating into the logical ways of the Mind to try and discover what you need to do in order to get back into harmony. The Mind will attempt to think its way into harmonization and this is a fatal flaw. Harmonization can only be brought about by your three entities being in close proximity of completeness and in forward ascension. And while you can't bring about completeness overnight, putting your entities into forward ascension is well within your control. Thus put your Body to work, connect with your Spirit and expand the horizons of your Mind.

Regardless of the questions that you may or may not have asked, your Spirit is always in communication with you. The base message of God calling us to our purpose in life is always flowing through our Spirit to us. By first unlocking the awareness of our purpose in life and becoming able to listen, we are then able to be in harmony. Without this purposeful message, we would toil endlessly on the Earth without resolve.

With communication comes the flow of information. Your Spirit broadcasts information outside the dimension of time and thus there is no window of time to catch or receive this information. Rather your Spirit broadcasts in overlapping sequences as discrete packages. Contained in one package is not only the message itself, but the key to unlock the next message. Similar to frequencies, each message is preceded by underlying frameworks that must be understood before the next message can be understood.

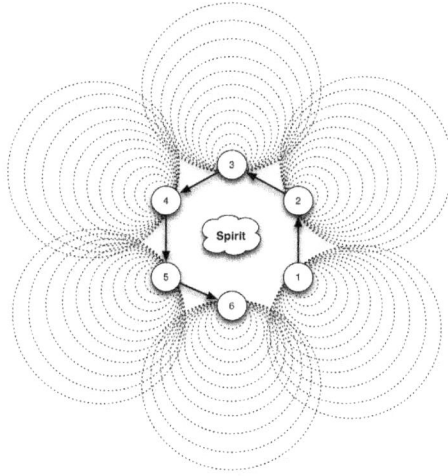

Figure 39: Communication from the Spirit is not sequential but appears that way in our temporal based reality.

With your connection to your Spirit and God, you may be tempted to ask big picture questions such as, "Why is there suffering?" If you ask these questions, you certainly will be provided with an answer. However, the answer may be preceded by other messages that must first be understood before your question's answer can be understood. As a result, when your Spirit calls to you, it is important that you listen and be in action when called to act.

Communication Channels

The most elemental form of communication is between God and mankind. And while God is certainly capable of communicating with us in any form, the flow of information through your Spirit is a method through which every human being can and is obliged to hear God. However, your Spirit empowers you to do so much more than simply ask God questions. Through your Spirit comes the means by which you will change the world.

If you visualize a communication pattern flowing from your Mind to your Body and through to your Spirit, the circle from point to point would complete. However, this would also indicate a closed loop communication path. In this communication path, information would flow within the system of *you* but no information would flow in or out of this system. In your own life, you know that information is not closed, but rather flows in and out of every human being. Through this exchange of information, ideas are shared around the world.

So too is the case with the flow of information through your Spirit. As information flows through your Spirit, there are countless connections made with God, collective consciousness and the Spirits of other enlightened beings. Remember that you are your Spirit as expressed through your Body and Mind. Thus don't think of your Spirit as a ghostly entity that floats around in space. Your Spirit is an entity that is not restricted by the four mental dimensions of the Mind or the five sensual dimensions of the Body. Thus the Spirit's ability to be in communication with other Spirits is not limited by the boundaries of time, space or bodily means of communication.

When you ask questions, the answers do not *only* come through a connection with your Spirit. The flow of information that brings you an answer may very well come through other people that you encounter in your life. The key is to be mindful of the flow of information that surrounds you at all times, for the answer you seek may be coming from the very people you would never expect to answer your question.

When I first began asking questions I got into the habit of waking up in the morning and asking myself if the answers had come to me during the night. I kept a notebook next to my bed and often jotted down insights that came to me in line with my questions. Sometimes my questions would be answered in the night and other times not. I could never predict when the answers would come and I learned not to be disappointed when my questions remained unanswered.

I then noticed the strange phenomenon referenced earlier. I was going to a yoga class after breakfast and one day my teacher answered one of my questions. She didn't walk up to me and tell me the answer, but rather as she was teaching the class she discussed many topics and one of them included an answer to my question. I began listening and received many answers through her during the coming weeks. After a while, I began asking more questions and looking forward with amusement to see if she would blurt out the answer in class.

When I finally told her this was happening she wasn't surprised in the slightest. "Oh yeah," she said calmly. "My students tell me that all the time."

How often are our questions answered by people in our lives but we weren't paying attention? Is it possible that the solution to many challenges in our lives are being provided to us but we've been too caught up in our own lives to notice? Indeed these answers are all around us, but we too often fail to listen.

Evolution of Humanity

Your Body, Spirit and Mind are a reflection of the Universe, God and Humanity. So too is the Universe, God and Humanity a reflection of your Body, Spirit and Mind. This reflection is more than a symbolic representation. Before there was a Universe, there was only God. Thus when God made the Universe, He made it from Himself for there was nothing other than God. This is why the Universe is the Body of God. From that initial moment of singularity, everything in the Universe burst outward to become what we know to be. We are included in this totality of creation and thus we too are part of God.

It is a bit unsettling to discover that we are part of God since we consider ourselves to be imperfect. Try to avoid the mental trap of this indicating that God is imperfect. The error in that line of logic begins with the premise that we are anything less than perfect.

We've been handed a world that tells us that perfection is without flaws, devoid of evil, and without ignorance. We've never experienced anything that is perfect, but we believe that God embodies ultimate perfection. And thus when we find ourselves to be less than this idealized perfection, we judge ourselves as being flawed. However, within the context of real life problem solving and devoid of the constant guiding hand of God, imperfections are merely differences that bring forth entirely fresh and new solutions.

A delay in reporting a fatality fire in Britain was the genesis of the 999 emergency network (the predecessor to the 911 system in America). A failure to formulate a strong adhesive resulted in the creation of a weak glue, which made Post-It Notes possible. Inserting the wrong type of resistor into an invention to record heart beats instead resulted in the pacemaker. In every perceived flaw, we instead are presented with an opportunity to create and expand the Universe.

Inspiration Divine reveals a new understanding of our reality in which flaws, evil, and ignorance simply do not exist. The exploration of knowledge for the purpose of expanding the Body of God brings forth an experience that isn't without strife, but we now know that this struggle is the means by which collective consciousness truly expands. Thus if an experience results in the expansion of the Body of God, then it cannot be flawed, evil or ignorant. It simply is.

When we judge ourselves, we limit the expansion of God's presence. Instead of investing our energy to expand God's presence, we expend energy to tear ourselves down. With this experience, we focus on decay rather than growth. When we remove judgment from our reality and focus on the expansion of God's presence, we bring ourselves into harmony with God.

As our Minds are a reflection of Humanity, so too when Humanity removes judgment from its reality and focuses on the expansion of God's presence, Humanity will be brought into harmony with God. By purging our thoughts of judgment, complaints, and expectation we align ourselves with our Spirit's intention for us to fulfill our purpose of expanding God. With the Mind free of judgment, an alignment with the Spirit and the Body brings forth a powerful force of change that makes a difference every moment of the day.

Imagine every bit of energy you consume judging, instead being focused on the expansion of God's presence.

Imagine every bit of energy Humanity consumes judging, instead focused on the expansion of God's presence.

Even though you've gone through life without being in conscious communication with your Spirit, you can develop this ability. Resist your Mind's inclination to judge everything in your life including being in communication with your Spirit. Remember that the Mind has been in charge of your survival for such a long time that it will initially resist any attempt to share control of *you* with the Body and the Spirit. Even though this is how you have evolved to live, your Mind will resist the growth of the Body and Spirit for fear they will be irresponsible or incapable in their co-management of you.

Instead focus on a path of growth regardless of the thoughts and judgments of your Mind. When judgment enters your Mind, do not judge yourself for being judgmental, but simply accept judgment as a weakness of the egocentric Mind. Have empathy for your Mind, like you would for a dear friend that couldn't resist being anything other than the way they've always been. Let the judgment be untrue and it will disappear. And, in time, your Mind will let go of judging everything in life.

On a path of growth, you will notice areas of your Body, Spirit and Mind that need nourishing, require more investment or are flourishing. Invest in growing each without judgment of the outcome. By growing your Body, Spirit and Mind, the being will come into balance. And, in balance, everything is possible.

In balance, you will find yourself asking questions and receiving answers directly and through the people that come into your life. So too will you find people coming into your life that need your presence. Through your Spirit, you will answer their questions. You will be called to action in ways that you previously avoided. When in balance, energy flows through you and takes you to a place of wisdom.

Enlightenment starts with a question

To begin, start by asking questions. Before you fall asleep each night, ask a question of your Spirit. Know that your Spirit is connected to God, collective consciousness and other enlightened Spirits. Keep asking questions and be mindful of the answers that come to you even if they are not the answers you were expecting or even if they are answers to questions you didn't ask. Your path to wisdom may require an understanding that you presently do not possess. Accept this path and let it unfold.

As important as asking, make sure that when you receive your answer that you share it with others. As a member of the human race, your purpose is to expand God's presence and you cannot do this in isolation. Take your answers and share them with your friends, family, colleagues, strangers on the street or the invisible individuals on the Internet. Your answers will inspire others and may be answers to the questions they have been asking. If information is flowing from your hands or your mouth, you know that you are creating and, in doing so, expanding the Universe.

Your Purpose

The path you are beginning is continual and will never end. A life fulfilled is heaven. Your life has purpose beyond what you have been taught and fulfilling your purpose will bring you happiness, joy and peace. Your happiness, joy and peace will never be fleeting for you now know how to maintain this path and bring more happiness, joy and peace into the world through your connection to Humanity. With this, the life force energy that powers everything in the Universe will flow through and be powered by you. With this energy, you will change the world, heal the sick, and expand God's presence.

Discovering your individual purpose can only come from your Spirit. By learning the languages of the Body (sensations), Spirit (feelings) and Mind (thoughts), you now can listen where before you were only a deaf observer. With this newfound ability to listen, the voice of your Spirit will ring true with clarity. Your purpose will be revealed in a message that will not come as a surprise to you. This calling has been broadcast to you since time began, but you've only heard a whisper up until now. The voice will now be raised and you will be unable to not listen ever again.

Waste not in achieving your purpose. Follow the path that is brought before you and trust that investing in your Body, Spirit and Mind along this path will bring you to your hopes, dreams and highest aspirations. Know that judgment deters you from your purpose and the path will be filled with opportunities to grow disguised as problems, roadblocks, heartache and pain. This is merely part of the human condition, which provides you with the opportunity for expanding God's presence.

Know that you have survived every challenge that has been placed at your feet and you have done this without the strongest connection amongst your Body, Spirit and Mind. With your path now in forward ascension, you have more strength, wisdom and power than before. You're more than you were when you began this journey and, in this transition, you are now ready to contribute to Humanity like never before.

No matter how complete you are today, the path you are now on is one of growth. With the growth of a single seed, an entire forest will emerge.

If the chamber's door is even a little ajar,

What then can hinder God from stealing in

Or who forbid his kiss on the sleeping soul?

Already God is near, the Truth is close...

(Aurobindo, Savitri -- A Legend and a Symbol 1997)

You are your Spirit as expressed through your Body and Mind. Unite the three in harmony on your new path to enlightenment. Along the way you will help, heal and inspire others to follow in your footsteps. Guided by God in the journey, you are never alone. What you have always known to be true in your heart, you now know how to put into action.

Our common purpose has been revealed and now you're not only able to help Humanity achieve its purpose, but your efforts will actually bring about Humanity's Spiritual evolution. With this understanding comes an obligation to achieve your purpose. Whereas you previously could hide in the crowd, you have now emerged to lead those around you on the path. Guided towards a harmonious balance between your Body, Spirit and Mind, you are now the embodiment of the beautiful Spirit you always knew lived within you.

Meeting your Spirit brings you closer to God and helps you avoid the path of the unconscious. Strengthening the connective bonds between your Body, Spirit and Mind puts you in a position of strength and wisdom beyond your earthly existence. Understanding your purpose brings every decision in your life to the elemental simplicity of the Spirit:

Which choice before you expands the Universe, God and/or Humanity?

By asking this simple question, every choice you make in life becomes simple. The strength and beauty of an enlightened soul is something that most people only envision experiencing in heaven. You now truly know how to bring heaven to your earthly existence. Go forth and achieve your purpose and share your experience with everyone.

Begin Anew

To chart a course to nirvana, begin by wasting no time in putting your Body, Spirit and Mind into forward ascension. In time, you will take stock of the completeness of each entity in order to balance your investment, but without each in forward ascension, harmony cannot be sustained. Thus begin with a balanced investment in each.

Each and every day of your life brings with it an opportunity to become aware of your Body, Spirit and Mind. With every meal comes an opportunity to help the Body. With every experience comes an opportunity to feed the Mind. And with every connection to another living being comes an opportunity to grow the Spirit.

The Western Mind wants immediate satisfaction and, without such quick results, it will often employ brute force. The world is certainly full of individuals who have achieved their hopes and dreams through force by way of their determination, talent, skills and knowledge. And while this individually powered approach is available to us all (the favored approach of the Mind), through harmonization of the Body, Spirit and Mind, you can instead achieve your goals faster, more effectively and in harmony with God.

In this, do not feel compelled to propel your Body, Spirit and Mind into forward ascension with brute force. Bringing your being into harmony does not necessarily involve a lot of work. Nirvana does not necessitate effort but rather motion. The motion of your Body, Spirit and Mind rising in ascension puts you on a path to harmony with God.

Once you are in harmony with God, you will be in a position for the energy and power of the Universe to propel you to greatness. Much like riding a wave, once the surfboard is picked up by the wave, the energy of the wave will propel you to your hopes and dreams awaiting you on the beach.

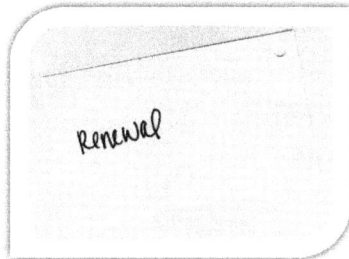

Card 24: Renewal: an instance of resuming an activity or state after an interruption.

To begin, start with baby steps. Putting each entity into forward ascension simply requires it to be growing rather than decaying. By investing regularly in each (e.g. daily stretching (Body), meditation (Spirit), and reading (Mind)) you bring all three into forward ascension. With all three in forward ascension, they will be pulled towards becoming more complete. As each entity becomes more complete, your consciousness exponentially expands and the resulting energy further propels each entity into a more complete state.

Much like other aspects of life, the hardest step is the first.

Becoming aware of your three entities and investing in their development is paramount to your success. Begin now and make today the first day of your new conscious life.

Closing Thoughts

In reading Inspiration Divine you've encountered a new way of understanding yourself as well as the Universe, God and Humanity. Whereas a physical existence makes us feel like life happens *to us* without any ability for us to navigate, a Spiritual existence provides us with the ability to listen and understand the events that unfold in our lives. Our ever expanding consciousness is not only indicative of the growth of collective consciousness, but also a rich field of information from which we can draw upon to better manage our health, happiness and enlightenment.

Understanding your sensations, feelings and thoughts is now more than just an awareness of being alive. Your connection to these languages of the Body, Spirit and Mind are the keys to unlocking your own enlightenment for they contain messages from the Divine that are trying to get through to you. By becoming in-tune with your Body, Spirit and Mind, you will now be able to determine when these messages are simply the intercommunications of your Body and Mind, as opposed to those times when they indicate a message being conveyed by your Spirit.

Modern metaphysical philosophers would have us believe that by simply turning-off the negative thoughts of our Mind, we can tap into the possibility of health, happiness and our own enlightenment. And backing up their claims, the scientific community is now beginning to understand the power that emotions have over our health:

> On the spectrum of "bad" emotions, depression and loneliness appear especially damaging. Depression affects cortisol levels and has been shown to worsen outcomes in people with cancer and heart disease. As for loneliness, "being isolated is as bad for your health as smoking and high serum-cholesterol levels, " say's Spiegel (David Spiegel, M.D., medical director at the Stanford School of Medicine). Loneliness and social isolation, in fact, have been linked to weakened immune systems, high blood pressure, and even a faster progression of Alzheimer's disease. John Caccioppo, Ph.D., found that lonely people tend to have more "micro-awakenings" during the night rather than getting a full night of sound, health-replenishing sleep.

> And now for the good news. Just as negative emotions spell trouble for your health, positive ones can improve it – dramatically. Recent studies suggest that feeling uplifted can potentially help fend off cardiovascular disease. Other findings indicate people who tend to experience feelings like relaxation and hope have lower rates of high blood pressure, diabetes, and viral infections like the common cold. And those with HIV/AIDS who experience positive emotions appear to live longer than their counterparts who don't. Again, it's about chemistry. Positive emotions help the brain release progesterone, oxytocin, and dopamine, which help the body buffer the effects of stress. (Lefkowitz 2009)

On the surface, we could interpret this new scientific link between emotions and health to indicate that we should force ourselves to walk around everyday with smiles on our faces. But in understanding feelings to be the language of the Spirit, we can connect the positive health benefits of listening to our Spirit's communications to the natural state of health that would result from listening. In combination, we can interpret the negative feelings of depression, guilt and anger as indicating we're going in the wrong direction. So too feelings of happiness, joy and love indicate that we're on the right track.

So too we can better understand our health conditions by connecting with the build-up of excess energy in our Body. Once the damage is done, we must embark on the sometimes lengthy journey of healing, but before this day arrives we can become present to the changes that occur within us on a daily basis. Becoming in-tune with one's Body opens up powerful methods for preventing illness from entering into our lives. When you notice pain, anxiety or distress in your Body, you now can engage your Body, Spirit and Mind to diagnose what brought about that change.

In discovering one's purpose, these messages from the Divine are but gentle nudges to stay on track. Unconscious to these messages, the messages get louder and louder in an attempt to get our attention. And, in time, this build up of excess energy causes damage in many ways. In listening and acting upon these messages, we can instead chart a new course to understanding, pursuing and achieving our purpose. And in this purpose, enlightenment awaits each and every one of us (including you).

Your Practice

A. Keep a Spiritual Notebook

Go out today and buy yourself a very special notebook for journaling your Spiritual journey. Pick out a notebook that is beautiful to you and one that you'll be able to keep by your side. As you encounter miracles, breakthroughs and ideas, be sure to write them down in your notebook. There is something magical and empowering in the writing process so make sure that you write down your experiences rather than just thinking about them.

B. Share This Book

You've read this book and are now ready to progress to the next stage in human evolution. By investing in bringing your Body, Spirit and Mind into harmony you have everything you need to become complete. Give this book away to another so that they too can experience the joy and happiness of expanding God. Everything you need to know is available to you from your Spirit. By reading this book you have unlocked the keys to living a Spiritual existence. The keys themselves are no longer of any value to you, but they surely can unlock the door for others.

BCID

Register and release this copy of Inspiration Divine at **www.bookcrossing.com** so you can see where it goes as it gets handed from person to person around the world.

C. Plan for Tomorrow

Regardless of your schedule tomorrow, list below one thing that you'll do to invest in your Body, Spirit and Mind:

Body: _____   **Spirit:** _____   **Mind:** _____

The Dream Twilight of the Earthly Real

If in the meaningless Void creation rose,

If from a bodiless Force Matter was born,

If Life could climb in the unconscious tree,

If green delight break into emerald leaves,

And its laughter of beauty blossom in the flower,

If sense could wake in tissue, nerve and cell,

And thought seize the grey matter of the brain,

And soul peep from its secrecy through the flesh,

How shall the nameless light not leap on men,

And unknown powers emerge from Nature's sleep?

Even now hints of a luminous Truth like stars

Arise in the mind-mooned splendor of Ignorance;

Even now the deathless Lover's touch we feel:

If the chamber's door is even a little ajar,

What then can hinder God from stealing in

Or who forbid his kiss on the sleeping soul?

Already God is near, the Truth is close...

(Aurobindo, Savitri -- A Legend and a Symbol 1997)

APPENDIX A

INSPIRATION PRACTICE

The path to enlightenment is unique for every person that begins the journey. Some people stumble upon the path and others focus their intentions on completing the journey. For me, the path was the stumbling sort, but in becoming enlightened I became present to the language of enlightenment, the purpose that we are each called to fulfill and my unique purpose to help others (that would be you) find their purpose.

I recognize that there is more than one path to enlightenment. Those that choose to meditate in a cave for a decade have my utmost respect and admiration. However, I must point out that true enlightenment requires that we engage in life rather than retreat from it. The enlightenment one gleans from detachment is truly an aspect of enlightenment, but it is fleeting and not sustainable unless one remains in the cave.

For the rest of us, life is not something that we can or choose to turn-off because we've decided to seek enlightenment. I can imagine that a Mother that leaves her family behind to become enlightened would receive this message upon connecting with the Divine: "Go take care of your family!"

As such, it would be strange if enlightenment were only accessible to those who didn't engage in life. And because enlightenment seems unattainable, we decide that it is too difficult and conclude that we shouldn't even try. From there, we conclude that it probably isn't possible for anyone else either. After all, if we're not able to become enlightened, then it probably isn't possible anyway. From there, you can imagine the judgmental thoughts that pop-up into our Minds when we encounter an enlightened being.

The truth of the matter is that enlightenment is only truly sustainable through pursuing one's purpose. The purpose that God calls us to fulfill is fueled by enlightenment and so too we must understand that, without our purpose, there is no need for enlightenment. In this context, enlightenment isn't a key to unlock the secrets of the Universe, but rather a means by which we will achieve our purpose.

If you return to the premise that enlightenment is difficult, takes a lot of time and is impossible, you can appreciate that all these are true if you're trying to become enlightened without first knowing your purpose. You can go into a cave for ten years and still not become enlightened, if there is no reason for you to become enlightened. Think about it, why would God give the keys to understanding everything to people who meditate in caves? Does that makes sense on any level?

Instead we should recognize that the life we live was intended by God and the fabric by which we interact in the Universe is the very means by which we experience and connect with God. In this relationship, we discover our purpose and, in fulfilling our purpose, become enlightened. With this conclusion, we're left with the single question we're all asking, "What is my purpose?"

30 Day Inspiration Practice

It is a bit insulting to those that have dedicated their lives to becoming enlightened to propose that enlightenment can be obtained via a prescribed method in about a month's time. So let me be clear that the 30-Day Inspiration Practice will not necessarily result in your personal enlightenment. The concept behind this practice is to bring you into connection with your Spirit by experiencing the language of enlightenment. If you follow this practice and engage your entire being in the conversation, your purpose will be revealed to you via this method. And through your purpose you will attain enlightenment.

It should be noted that I'm purposely using the word "attain" instead of other destination words such as obtain, achieve or become. The subtle difference here is that enlightenment is not something that we achieve but rather something we attain by nurturing our Body, Spirit and Mind. We don't "get there" and then sit back and enjoy the enlightenment. Instead we strive to attain this state of bliss and continue to invest in the practices that help us continue this beautiful state throughout our lives.

The Inspiration Practice is one part method and two parts experience. The exercises are designed to not only teach you the language of enlightenment, but also to re-train your brain to experience life differently. In this, there is no judgment in how your brain works today, but rather the goal is to break free of the thought patterns that have become engrained in your life.

For example, you have developed an attention span over the years that those around you clearly recognize. Your friends and family clearly know how much information you can process and thus control the amount that they expect you to consume in a single setting. If you're attention span is low, those around you have learned through trial and error that you need to be fed bite size chunks of information. Attempts to give you too much information will only result in you shutting down and probably not processing the information that they intended you to obtain.

Conversely if you have a deep attention span, those around you have figured out that they need to manage the information they feed you because of your propensity to digest information; while they're still telling you the problem, you've started formulating an answer. Either way, you've developed an attention span that has become a habit in your life. By breaking free from this pattern, the elasticity of your brain is stretched and this opens you up to new learning opportunities.

The exercises in the Inspiration Practice are not difficult but they must be followed consistently if you expect to get results. Like with weight loss, if we expect results, we need to follow the diet. It is only 30-days, so set aside some time each day to commit to your practice and make discovering your purpose as important as the other activities of your day.

The Inspiration Practice is both a healing practice and a method for putting yourself on the path to growth in pursuit of enlightenment. If you believe that enlightenment is possible but wonder how to begin, then the Inspiration Practice is the first step in bringing you onto the path of enlightenment.

Before beginning this journey, recognize the dichotomy of enlightenment. Attaining enlightenment requires no effort, necessitates no change and has no relationship to time. The instantaneous properties of enlightenment are represented symbolically in the ancient vajra or dorje symbol[21]. Conveying the thunderbolt of enlightenment, a dorje symbolizes the abrupt change in human consciousness that is recognized by most religions as a timeless transformation in the lives of mystics and saints:

> *The Bell and Dorje, or thunderbolt, are inseparable ritual objects in Tibetan Buddhism. They are always used in combination during religious ceremonies. The Bell held in the left hand, representing the female aspect as wisdom; the Dorje, or male held in the right hand, aspect as method. Together, they represent union of wisdom and method, or the attainment of Enlightenment.*

---

[21] I do not mean to convey alignment with one religion or another through sharing this passage, but rather to illuminate the instantaneous transformation that is recognized by different religions around the world.

The transformative enlightenment experience is recounted in various religions. In the Christian tradition, the conversion of Saul of Tarsus is a well-known example and that of Mohammed on the mountain is fundamental to Moslem belief. For Buddhists, it is what occurred to the historical Buddha and to all those who experience kensho-satori, the dropping away of 'self'. The Tibetans call this "the Great Death" to distinguish it from that physical one which will be the experience of us all. (Cited n.d.)

So too your path to enlightenment may come through great effort, substantial change and over a long period time. The path to enlightenment should be viewed as an unfolding. In order to have an understanding revealed to you, there may be several insights that you must understand before enlightenment will occur. As such, your path is a journey of learning that may come in an instant or reveal itself to you throughout one or many lifetimes. In this, all you can do is stay the course without expectation of outcome.

Your path to enlightenment started many years ago and the messages that you're being called to understand are circling all around you. Through a sudden Divine breath, these messages have passed through your consciousness on the wings of your thoughts, through the people that have come and gone in your life, as well as a long series of coincidences. As such, you should not expect your first understanding to be dramatically shocking. More likely, you'll find an answer that you've seen many times over. But now, you can recognize that these answers are keys to a greater understanding.

Beginning the Inspiration Practice

The Inspiration Practice is designed to be adopted over a thirty-day period, but is intended to be employed throughout your lifetime. In time, you'll customize the practice to make it your own; but I caution you to not deviate from the prescribed method during the first thirty days. The first nine days of the practice are educational sessions that are designed to engrain you in the practice so that during the last 21-days you'll be able to follow the practice without exception.

For these first nine days, you'll be adding a new component of the practice each day so that you can become familiar with the component. For example, on the third day you'll add music to your practice. As such, for the first two days you experienced the practice without music and therefore on the third day you'll notice the difference that music brings to the practice. If you were to begin on day one with all of the components of the practice, they would likely comingle into a singular experience. Our goal, in contrast, is to bring the eleven dimensions of the Universe to the surface of your consciousness, so that you can actively experience them as communication channels rather than passive sensations, feelings, and thoughts.

Inspiration Practice Materials

To engage in the Inspiration Practice, you'll need the following materials:

☐ **Comfortable Clothes** – choose comfortable clothes that can be washed regularly for you should wear the same clothes every time you do your first Inspiration Practice. Most people find loose fitting, workout clothes to be the most comfortable.

☐ **Yoga Mat** – the Inspiration Practice incorporates basic yoga postures and most people find a yoga mat more comfortable than the hard floor. There is no need to purchase an expensive yoga mat but simply to have something stable and padded beneath you.

☐ **Journal** – any writing journal will do, but choose one that can stay open easily so you can write comfortably.

☐ **Index Cards** – a basic pack of 100 blank index cards.

☐ **Writing Pen & Thick Marker** – choose a writing pen that flows smoothly in your hand as you write. The thick marker is a separate writing device that you'll use with the index cards.

☐ **Essential Oil(s)** - An oil is "essential" in the sense that it carries a distinctive scent, or essence, of a plant. You can purchase essential oils from your local health food store or online. You can choose a favorite scent or a few different options, but you'll only use one essential oil during the first Inspiration Practice. If you can't find any essential oils, try and choose a food (below) that is aromatic.

☐ **Food** – any food will do but fresh, organic fruits provide a strong burst of flavor (e.g. blueberries, strawberries, orange wedges, etc.).

☐ **Music** – your choice, pick your favorite. But make it something you really love because you'll be listening to the same music every time you engage in your first Inspiration Practice.

☐ **Fresh Flower** – pick a beautiful flower that has a distinctive or interesting petal structure.

☐ **Emotional Photos** – go through your photo albums and pull out one photo that brings out a positive emotion (e.g. joy, happiness, bliss, etc.) and one photo that brings out a negative emotion (e.g. sadness, longing, pain, etc.). Choose photos that truly bring out these emotions in you rather than photos that *should* make you feel one way or another. For some people, their photo of choice is personal in nature and, for others, it is more symbolic in nature (e.g. illustration of Jesus Christ). The point is to choose a photo that strongly connects *you* to *your feelings*.

☐ **Three Candles** – each candle represents your Body, Spirit or Mind. As you light each candle, form an intention as to which candle represents one of your entities.

The preceding list of materials for the Inspiration Practice is a basic setup that you can modify over time. For your first Inspiration Practice, the setup should be identical every time except for the order in which the materials are introduced. Once you've completed your first Inspiration Practice, you can change out the oils, foods, music and movements that help you get the most out of your practice.

Inspiration Practice Components

Each component of the Inspiration Practice brings out a different communication channel of the eleven dimensions of our Universe. By bringing these dimensions into your consciousness, you'll learn how to listen and interpret the messages from God and your Spirit as they travel along each dimension:

Sensual Dimensions

SIGHT ✿ the environment you choose to setup your Inspiration Practice will provide you with the dimension of light/vision.

SOUND ♪ your musical choice will provide you with the dimension of sound/hearing.

TASTE ● By placing a food in your mouth during the Inspiration Practice, you'll awaken the dimension of taste/flavor.

SMELL 〰 The best way to experience the dimension of smell/odor during the Inspiration Practice is to rub a drop of your favorite essential oil into your hands. As you go through your practice you will catch whiffs of your chosen scent.

| TOUCH | **T** The motion of your activity will bring the dimension of touch to the surface as you will feel not only the texture of the mat beneath you, but also the feeling of your Body through the air. |

| YOGA | **Y** The recommended activity for your first Inspiration Practice is yoga, but subsequently you can swap out yoga for other movements such as Tai Chi, dance or other movement based exercises. |

Emotive Dimensions

| **PHOTOS** | Your positive and negative photos will bring forth both an **emotion** and a degree of **arousal** depending on the photos that you choose. |

Mental Dimensions

| **JOURNAL** | When journaling during the Inspiration Practice, write down the thoughts that enter your consciousness as they appear without regard for composition, grammatical errors or even making sense. No one is going to read your journal and the journaling process is not designed to creatively or analytically compose your thoughts. Instead just let the words flow into your Mind and onto the page. |

| **FLOWER** | Your brain has developed an attention span over the years and the consistency of your attention has developed rigid structures in your mental patterns. By intensely focusing on a flower for a longer or shorter period of time than usual, you expand the elasticity of your brain and open up new pathways for learning. |

| **CARDS** | At the end of your journaling process, go through what you've written and circle any and all words that have meaning to you. After you've circled all of your important words, copy |

each word onto a separate index card using your thick marker.

MEDITATION M At the end of every Inspiration Practice, conclude your practice by performing the Energy Ball Meditation described in the Moving Energy chapter.

Yoga Postures

The postures below are simple yoga postures that are intended to be performed in sequence as a repeatable series during each practice. You will perform the series three times during each of your first 30-day Inspiration Practice sessions.

If you've never performed yoga, you should consult with a medical professional before beginning. You don't have to perform the postures with perfect yogic form to get a benefit from the Inspiration Practice; but you want to make sure that doing the postures won't cause you injury. If you stop by a yoga studio or health club that offers yoga, most yoga teachers would be happy to show you the proper form for performing these postures.

1. Start standing and raise your hands up from your side.

2. Clasp your hands together .

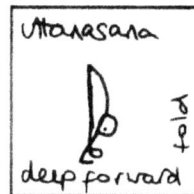

3. "Swan Dive" your arms forward into a forward bend.

ardha uttanasana

½ forward fold

4. Put your hands on your shins and look up and forward.

dynamic half to full

uttanasana

5. Return to a forward bend.

ardha virabhadrasana

half warrior 1

6. Put your hands on the floor, slide your right foot back and raise your hands over your head.

kumbhakasana

plank pose

7. Return your hands to the floor in front of you and move both of your feet back to a men's pushup.

ardha virabhadrasana

half warrior 1

8. Pull your left leg forward.

kumbhakasana

plank pose

9. Put both legs back and go into a men's pushup.

adho mukha svanasana

DOWN DOG

10. Raise your backside into the air and let you head hang.

YOGIC

BREATH

11. Step your feet forward between your hands, stand and slowly raise your arms up.

urdhva hastasana

upward salute

12. Clasp your hands over your head.

anuvittasana

standing back bend

13. Extend yourself back for a slight back bend.

urdhva hastasana

upward salute

14. Bring your hands down into prayer position, drop them down and raise them up over your head.

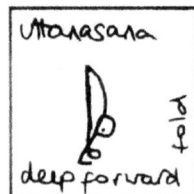

uttanasana

deep forward fold

15. "Swan Dive" forward into a forward bend.

16. Put your hands on your shins and look up and forward.

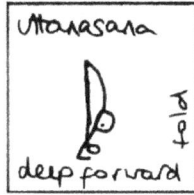

17. Return to a forward bend.

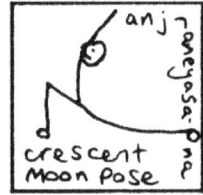

18. Put your hands on the floor, push your right foot back and raise your hands over your head.

19. Return your hands to the floor in front of you and move your left leg back to a men's pushup.

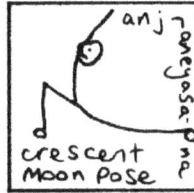

20. Pull your left leg forward and rise into crescent pose with your hands raise up.

21. Put your hands on the floor, bring your back foot forward and rise up and drop your hands down into prayer position.

repeat

Inspiration Practice Schedule

1 Y ✕	2 Y ✕	3 Y ✕	4 Y ✕	5 Y ✕	6 Y ✕
	●	● ♪	● ♪ □	● ♪ □ / M	● ♪ □ / M ☀
7 Y ✕	**8** Y ✕	**9** Y	**10**	**11**	**12**
● ♪ □ / M ☀ ○	● ♪ □ / M ☀ ○	□	1	2	3
13	**14**	**15**	**16**	**17**	**18**
4	5	6	7	8	9
19	**20**	**21**	**22**	**23**	**24**
10	11	12	13	14	15
25	**26**	**27**	**28**	**29**	**30**
16	17	18	19	20	21

To setup your environment, start by laying out your yoga mat and arranging all of the other materials in front of the top of the mat. Then light the three candles with each one representing your Body, Spirit or Mind.

To begin, sit comfortably at the top of your mat and focus yourself entirely on one of your photos. Let your eyes gaze deeply into the photo with the intention of connecting with the feelings you experienced when the photo was taken. Embrace your feelings no matter how intense and let yourself fully experience a full range of emotions. If you find that it is difficult to connect with your emotions, stop the practice and find a photo or memory that you can connect to before beginning again. During the first nine days of the practice, use the same photo. Throughout the last 21 days of the practice you can use different photos that bring out different emotions.

After centering your practice as described above, begin by performing the yoga postures listed in the previous section. The idea behind the yoga postures is that they bring you into union with the Body, Spirit and Mind. Most importantly, these postures enliven the senses and help bring your thoughts away from the center of your attention.

You will begin your practice each time in this same way and then proceed through the first nine days of the practice as shown in the schedule above. Each day you will add a new component to the practice until, after nine days, you have experienced each component separately. Once you have completed the first nine days, you'll repeat the practice in its entirety for twenty-one days.

It is important that you conduct the twenty-one day period sessions consecutively without any breaks in practicing. If you miss a day, don't stop, as it is better to complete the cycle than to leave it incomplete. However, you should pick a period of time to perform your first Inspiration Practice when you anticipate being able to commit to the practice everyday (preferably at the same time every day, wearing the same clothes and in the same location).

Nine Day Orientation

On each day of your orientation you'll <u>add</u> a new component as described on each day's overview below. As such, on each day you'll learn a new dimension of the practice and over the nine-day period become familiar with each component.

Day 1: At the very beginning of every day's practice, begin by centering yourself on an emotion. Pick up one of your *feeling* photos and focus your intention on the image. Let yourself become lost in the emotion that the photo evokes for you. On the first day, you'll simply perform the yoga postures (see above) and experience the sensation of smell. You don't need to be an experienced yogi to perform these movements. As always, consult with your physician before performing any exercise including the yoga postures of the Inspiration Practice. Before beginning the yoga postures, rub two drops of your essential oil of choice into your hands. Rub your hands vigorously together and then clasp your hands over your mouth and nose to smell the wonderful aroma of the oil. Notice as you perform the yoga postures how you catch an occasional whiff of your oil.

Day 2: Before applying your oils, sit in a comfortable position and place your chosen food on your tongue. Savor the flavor of the food and take time to notice the delicate textures of the food. Apply the oils as described in Day 1 and then try another sample of your food. Notice if you detect any differences in flavor before and after the oil application.

Day 3: Before beginning your practice, put on your favorite music. Leave the music on during the practice and listen to the same musical selection on each day of your first Inspiration Practice.

Day 4: After completing the yoga postures, sit comfortably and begin journaling. Pay no mind to structure, grammar or making sense. Simply write down the words, sentences and thoughts that come into your Mind.

Day 5: After journaling, relax with the Energy Ball Meditation from the Moving Energy chapter.

Day 6: Begin your practice by focusing your attention on a flower. Hold the flower in your hand and stare intently into every part of the flower. Let yourself become completely immersed in the flower and look at the flower from every angle. Vary the amount of time you spend focusing on the flower each day.

Day 7: After journaling, go back and circle any words that have meaning to you. Circle any word that is important, insightful or enlightening. When in doubt, circle the word. When you've circled all of your words, copy the words down onto an index card with a thick marker. When you've completed your practice each day, combine your index card words with the cards from previous practices and remove any duplicates.

Day 8: Before beginning your practice, arrange the index card words from your previous practice in front of you. Arrange the words in a way that you find artistically or creatively pleasing.

Day 9: On the final day of the orientation, perform the Inspiration Practice in a state of nothingness. This time perform the practice without first setting an emotion, without smells, absent of flavor and devoid of sound. Perform your last orientation practice in complete silence and notice the difference. As you journal afterwards, become present to the different state of consciousness that is present with and without the 11-dimensions being active in your practice.

After you have completed the nine-day orientation, you are ready to begin the actual Inspiration Practice over the next twenty-one days. On each day, perform the practice in the same manner as you did on day eight. Consistency is key, as you want to prepare yourself to notice the messages conveyed to you rather than the dimensions themselves. Remember that the messages from your Spirit ride dimensions into your awareness. As such, it is important to listen to the message rather than the dimension itself.

Upon completing the 21-day practice, you no longer will need to keep the dimensions of the practice the same. You can then vary the music, oils, and foods (you can even wear different clothes). If you complete the first 30-day Inspiration Practice, you'll find that this is a wonderful Spiritual attunement practice that you can incorporate into your daily life. It doesn't take a long time and can be performed anywhere in the world.

Finding Your Purpose

In performing the Inspiration Practice, you will have established a connection to your Spirit and opened up the communication channels that operate between the Body, Spirit and Mind. In this multi-dimensional experience, the messages from your

Spirit are able to break through the logical constraints typically imposed by the Mind.

Your Inspiration Practice is unique to you and has no influence from anyone else. No one conveyed what you should write about and no topic was introduced for you to focus on. In this, the Mind is clear to run amuck and allow the Body and Spirit to chime in on the conversation. In this communal experience, the true self emerges and your purpose will certainly be contained on the index cards that list the words you found to be important.

On these cards your purpose will emerge. No one can say for sure if your first Inspiration Practice will reveal your purpose, but the practice of bringing the Body, Spirit and Mind into union will reveal your purpose in time. For some people, the words on their cards speak loudly of their purpose. And, for others, the words point them in a direction for further reflection. Either way, the words on your cards are Divinely inspired messages from your Spirit.

The Inspiration Practice is not intended to be a one time exercise to experiment with enlightenment but rather a life long approach to bring one's Body, Spirit and Mind into balanced union and communication. Take the practice and make it your own by creatively drawing the eleven dimensions to the surface and allowing yourself to come into harmony with God. In time, your practice will become as unique as you are. And, in this, you will have contributed to collective consciousness in your own special way.

Bibliography

Special thanks to the Sri Aurobindo Ashram Trust for permission to include the Sri Aurobindo quotes.

Special thanks to Yoga teacher, Justine Aldersey-Williams for her wonderful yoga asana stick figure illustrations (www.YogaWirral.co.uk).

Aurobindo, Sri. *Essays Divine And Human.* Vol. 12. Sri Aurobindo Ashram Trust, 1997.

Aurobindo, Sri. "Letters on Yoga." *Letters on Yoga* (Sri Aurobindo Ashram Trust) 22 (1970): 137.

Aurobindo, Sri. "Savitri -- A Legend and a Symbol." Edited by CWSA. *Savitri* (Sri Aurobindo Ashram Trust) 34 (1997): 648-649.

Bercholz, Samuel, and Sherab Chodzin Kohn. *Entering the Stream.* 1993.

Bercholz, Samuel, and Sherab Chodzin Kohn, . *Entering the Stream.* Boston, MA: Shambhala Publications, Inc., 1993.

Bloom, Ken. "Fermilab's Virtual Ask-a-Scientist." 1 2004.

Brodd, Jefferey. *World Religions.* Winona, MN: Saint Mary's Press, 2003.

Browne, Pat. *Digging Into Popular Culture: Theories and Methodologies in Archeology, Anthropology and Other Fields.* illustrated. Popular Press, 1991.

Chalmers, D. J. *The conscious mind: In search of a fundamental theory.* New York: Oxford University Press, 1996.

Cited, No Author. *Buddhism.* http://www.crystalinks.com/buddhism.html (accessed July 13, 2009).

Cleve Backster, Flora Powers. *Primary Perception: Biocommunication with Plants, Living Foods, and Human Cells.* illustrated. White Rose Millennium Press, 2003.

Csikszentmihalyi, Mihaly. *Flow: The Psychology of Optimal Experience.* New York: Harper and Row, 1990.

Darwin, Charles. *Descent of Man.* 1871.

Davison, Scott. *Prophecy.* 02 18, 2005.
http://plato.stanford.edu/entries/prophecy/ (accessed 02 16, 2009).

Dennett, Daniel Clement. *Darwin's Dangerous Idea: Evolution and the Meanings of Life.* reprint, illustrated. Simon and Schuster, 1996.

Evans, Warren F. *The Divine Law of Cure 1884.* Kessinger Publishing, 2004.

Fisch, Karl. *Did You Know? 2.0.* 6 22, 2007.
http://thefischbowl.blogspot.com/2007/06/did-you-know-20.html (accessed 5 11, 2009).

Forrest, John. *Lord I'm Coming Home: Everyday Aesthetics in Tidewater North Carolina.* Ithaca, NY, 1988.

Freud, Sygmund. *Formulations on the Two Principles of Mental Functioning.* Vol. S.E. XII. G.W. VIII vols. 1911.

Geirland, John. "Go With The Flow." September 1996.

Glen Rein, PhD, Mike Atkinson and Rollin McCraty, PhD. *Science of the Heart, IHM Research Center.*

http://www.heartmath.org/research/science-of-the-heart-emotional-balance.html.

Gough, William C. *Scientific Instincts*. 8 5, 2008.

Hitchens, Christopher. *God is Not Great*. Twelve, 2007.

Hubbard, Barbara Marx. *Conscious Evolution*.

Lefkowitz, Frances. "Master the Mind Body Connection." *Body+Soul*, September 2009: 98-100.

Lewis, Michael, and Jeannette M. Haviland-Jones. *Handbook of Emotions*. Guilford Press, 2004.

Livio, Mario. *The Golden Ratio*. 2002.

Mythbusters Episode 61. 2006.

Rausch, Carol Albright, and Joel Haugen. *Beginning with the End: God, Science, and Wolfhart Pannenberg*. 1997.

Rein, Glen, Ph.D., Mike Atkison, and M.A. McCraty. "The Physiological and Psychological Effects of Compassion and Anger." *Journal of Advancement in Medicine* 8, no. 2 (Summer 1995).

Rein, PhD, Glen, Mike Atkinson, and PhD, Rollin McCraty. "The Physiological and Psychological Effects of Compassion and Anger." *Journal of Advancement in Medicine* 8, no. 2 (1995): 87-105.

Russell, James A. *Core Affect and the Psychological Construction of Emotion*. 2003.

Schultz, Matthew Craig and Sara. *Invisible Galaxies: The Story of Dark Matter.* Summer 2007. http://www.astrosociety.org/education/publications/tnl/72/darkmatter.html#3 (accessed March 19, 2009).

Schwartz, Howard. *Gabriel's Palace.* Oxford University Press US, 1994.

Stock, Byron. *Smart Emotions for Busy Business People: The How to Book that Teaches Five Simple Techniques Proven to Increase Resilience, Personal Productivity and Emotional Intelligence Skills.* ByronStock.com, 2008.

Sunwall, Mark R. *The Suprarational Grounds of Rationalism: Maimonides and The Criteria of Prophecy.* 1996. http://www.meru.org/Advisors/Sunwall/RambamProphecy.html (accessed 02 16, 2009).

Thompson, Jim. *Prophecy Today - A further word from God? Does God-given prophecy continue in today's church, or doesn't it?.* Evangelical Press, 2008.

Umami. http://en.wikipedia.org/wiki/Umami (accessed February 23, 2009).

Walker, Ralph. *11 Dimensions.* June 25, 2008. http://blog.ralphwalker.org/2008/06/11-dimensions.html (accessed July 30, 2008).

Warren, Rick. *The Purpose Driven Life.* Grand Rapids, MI: Zondervan, 2002.

Zimmer, Carl. "Evolving Darwin." *Time Magazine,* February 23, 2009.

Index of Key Points

1

11 Dimensions · *See* eleven
   dimensions

A

afflatus · 315, 317, 318
aging · 104, 106
answers · 4, 11, 12, 42, 96, 141,
   165, 167, 268, 316, 319, 321,
   324, 328, 329
art · 81, 102, 172
Aurobindo · xxiii, 144, 147, 148,
   317, 318
Awareness · 78

B

balloon · 154, 226, 261
Big Bang · 56, 58, 118, 148, 149,
   205, 208
birthday · 334
Buddhism · 39, 46, 138

C

Charles Darwin · 301
child · 42, 64, 74, 76, 82, 95, 105,
   117, 172, 186, 203, 204, 247,
   248, 249, 279
Cleve Backster · 71
collective consciousness · 23, 34,
   61, 123, 125, 147, 159, 160,

163, 164, 207, 209, 210, 212,
   250, 307
common cold · 244, 261, 335
communicating · 59, 63, 68, 69, 78,
   82, 85, 88, 161, 173, 259, 323
Communion · 140
Connecting Bonds · 64
consciousness · xvii, 4, 20, 21, 22,
   23, 24, 25, 26, 29, 30, 31, 34, 43,
   48, 54, 58, 61, 62, 63, 74, 77, 91,
   93, 115, 122, 123, 124, 125,
   126, 129, 141, 144, 145, 146,
   147, 148, 153, 154, 157, 159,
   160, 161, 162, 163, 164, 165,
   166, 167, 180, 187, 206, 207,
   209, 210, 212, 215, 224, 245,
   249, 276, 283, 290, 306, 307,
   308, 320, 324, 327, 329, 334
Core Affect Diagram · 44
crying · 21, 85, 248
Cyclical Universe · 56

D

dancing · 85
Dark Energy · 121, 145, 146, 147,
   148, 150, 151, 153, 154, 160,
   163, 206, 207, 209, 245, 260,
   261, 270, 271, 272, 293, 306,
   307
Dark Matter · 121
Depression · 335
diabetes · 335

Diet · 78

Different Experiences · 78

DNA · 71, 302

dreaming · 85, 293

E

Education · 78

Efficient Frontier · 275, 276, 281, 282, 288, 294, 297

Eleven dimensions · 6, 38

Emotive Dimensions · 44, 45, 76, 225, 282, 283

empathy · 64, 209, 328

Enlightenment · 1, 107, 113, 179, 180

evil · 61, 183, 185, 186, 187, 196, 305, 326

evolution · xiii, xvii, xix, 2, 4, 39, 119, 123, 129, 144, 289, 293, 301, 302, 304, 305, 306, 308, 311, 337

Exercise · 78, 79, 173

F

Father · 1, 67, 202, 203, 204, 205, 209, 211, 315

Flatland · 40

Forgiving · 78, 85, 288

forward ascension · 98, 107, 109, 113, 116, 117, 137, 175, 176, 180, 330, 332, 333, 334

G

Galileo · 140

God · xiv, xv, xvi, xviii, xx, 3, 4, 6, 7, 9, 13, 22, 24, 32, 33, 42, 58, 60, 66, 67, 68, 80, 85, 91, 103, 109, 116, 117, 119, 127, 128, 139, 149, 150, 151, 157, 158, 159, 161, 168, 169, 206, 208, 209, 210, 245, 246, 248, 249, 250, 257, 260, 261, 271, 289, 290, 291, 292, 293, 297, 301, 302, 303, 304, 305, 306, 307, 308, 309, 310, 311, 318, 319, 320, 322, 323, 324, 325, 326, 327, 329, 330, 331, 332, 337, 339

Golden Ratio · See Phi, See Phi

H

happiness · 2, 5, 14, 16, 17, 46, 52, 77, 83, 117, 223, 224, 225, 226, 228, 257, 311, 319, 329, 337

harmony · xvii, xix, 2, 5, 25, 32, 33, 62, 77, 82, 85, 103, 107, 116, 117, 123, 162, 176, 181, 214, 288, 291, 293, 296, 319, 320, 322, 327, 331, 332, 333, 337

Harry Markowitz · 275

heal · 30, 35, 214, 244, 245, 246, 247, 248, 255, 257, 258, 259, 260, 261, 262, 268, 272, 276, 277, 280, 282, 296, 330, 331

health · 81, 94, 106, 109, 118, 268, 270, 272
heart disease · 335
heaven · 127, 135, 138, 329, 332
Helping Others · 78, 288
high blood pressure · 335
Hinduism · 36, 138
HIV/AIDS · 14, 335

I

Ibn al-Haytham · 244
Ideas · 78, 172, 316
integrity · 60, 93, 95, 98, 116, 117, 118, 126, 292, 294

K

Kepler · 101, 140

L

laughing · 85
Leonardo da Vinci · 139
listen · 1, xii, xvi, 4, 53, 62, 65, 73, 74, 76, 80, 81, 119, 141, 158, 164, 167, 210, 213, 214, 216, 248, 249, 287, 288, 311, 312, 317, 318, 319, 322, 323
Loneliness · 335
Loving · 78, 288

M

Marcus Tullius Cicero · 315
Meditation · 78, 79, 288

Michelangelo · 67
Mother · 1, 1, 14, 22, 202, 203, 204, 205, 209, 211
music · 85, 162

N

NASA · 71
Newtonian theory · 140
Nirvana · 85, 91, 126, 127, 167, 332, 333

O

original creations · 146, 154, 158, 159, 160, 162, 163, 209, 260, 261, 306
original ideas · 153, 154, 283

P

Parallel Universe · 56
Phi · 101, 106, 166
Plato · 7, 30, 137, 138, 139, 206
Praying · 78, 288, 290
purpose · ix, xix, 9, 12, 13, 14, 15, 16, 17, 30, 32, 38, 42, 43, 65, 66, 68, 118, 129, 141, 142, 143, 149, 153, 154, 156, 157, 158, 162, 163, 169, 170, 209, 271, 272, 292, 293, 297, 306, 307, 308, 309, 310, 319, 322, 327, 329, 330, 332

Q

questions · 4, 12, 42, 167, 212, 225, 267, 268, 316, 319, 321, 322, 323, 324, 328, 329

S

Sacrament of the Last Supper · 140
Salvador Dali · 140
Self Relatedness · 143
Sensual Dimensions · 46, 50, 52, 62, 64, 76, 160, 225, 244, 248, 256, 258, 280, 283, 286, 324
sex · 202
sharing · xix, 30, 78, 85, 154, 161, 162, 181, 247, 288, 317
singing · 85, 161, 259
Smell · 44, 48, 50, 256, 267
Sound · 30, 256, 258, 267
spiral shaped galaxy · 121
sport · 81
Steady State Universe · 56, 57

String Theory · 58, 140
symbiotic relationship · 142, 245, 306

T

Tai Chi · 81
Taste · 44, 48, 50, 256, 267
Tibetan · 138
Touch · 44, 49, 50, 256, 258, 267
Toxins · 78
twilight · 164, 320, 321

U

unnecessary conclusion · 60
unnecessary memories · 84

V

Vision · 30, 44, 48, 50, 256, 267

Y

yoga · 6, 66, 81, 117, 176, 286, 320

Inspiration Workshops

iD Workshops are being held around the world incorporating the teachings of Inspiration Divine into an experiential workshop. Taught by Kelli Barnett and Darwin Stephenson, Inspiration Workshops guide you through a series of practices that help you connect with your true self and distinguish the language of the Body, Spirit and Mind. For more information, visit the Inspiration Divine website at:

http:// www . inspirationdivine . com

Additional Copies of Inspiration Divine

To order additional copies of Inspiration Divine please visit our website. Discounts are available for students, teachers and book clubs. If you would like to gift a new copy of Inspiration Divine rather than giving away your copy, you can order additional copies for your friends, family and colleagues at the Inspiration Divine gifting page:

http:// store . inspirationdivine . com

Buy 1 Copy Online: http://tinyurl.com/iDBuyNow

Downloadable Workbooks & Book Club Guides

If you would like to fill out the Book Club Guides or "Your Practice" exercises at the end of every chapter outside of the book (or if the previous reader used a pen), you can download individual worksheets from the Inspiration Divine documents link below:

http:// documents . inspirationdivine . com

Workbooks, essential oils and other Inspiration Divine items can be found on our website. The password for the worksheets is: **purposeful**

Connecting

We want to connect with people like you who are ready to change the world so please sign up for our newsletter on our website, e-mail us at connections@inspirationdivine.com or via Twitter at digitaldarwin.

For information about having the author speak to your organization or group, please contact speaking@inspirationdivine.com or call us to discuss our speaking programs at: (415) 843-1012

Your Message

As this one book is passed from person to person, each will have a moment of understanding that helps clarify the beauty of a Spiritual existence. What you have learned and come to understand may help another unlock their own path. Your contribution will make a difference and sharing your insights might be the one key that someone else needs.

Below is an area where each reader can leave their own message for future walkers of the path:

www.ingramcontent.com/pod-product-compliance
Lightning Source LLC
Chambersburg PA
CBHW060237100426
42742CB00011B/1564